Indian-Caribbean Test Cricketers and the Quest for Identity

Frank Birbalsingh

HANSIB

First published in 2014
by Hansib Publications Limited

P.O. Box 226, Hertford, Hertfordshire,
SG14 3WY, United Kingdom
info@hansibpublications.com

www.hansibpublications.com

Copyright © Frank Birbalsingh, 2014

ISBN 978-1-906190-74-3

All rights reserved.
Without limiting the rights under copyright reserved above,
no part of this publication may be reproduced, stored in or
introduced into a retrieval system, or transmitted, in any form
or by any means (electronic, mechanical, photocopying,
recording or otherwise), without the prior written permission
of both the copyright owner and the publisher of this book.

A CIP catalogue record for this book
is available from the British Library

Printed in Great Britain

For Kai

ACKNOWLEDGEMENTS

I am grateful to Rosanne Kanhai, Clem Seecharan and Cecil Gray for permission to quote from their publications and, since it is impossible to recall all those with whom I discussed cricket over the years, I mention only more recent names here: Keith Sandiford, Baldwin Mootoo, Kissoon Lall, Ronald Reid, Moti Makund, Harry Ramkhelawan, Stanley Algoo. Thanks also for computer services from Christine Birbalsingh and Kevin Freeman, and for statistics from Ray Goble. Final thanks to Arif Ali, Kash Ali and Hansib Publications for unstinting support.

CONTENTS

PREFACE 7

INTRODUCTION 11

CHAPTER ONE
Sonny Ramadhin: Investing West Indians with power 27

CHAPTER TWO
Rohan Kanhai: A new dimension in batting 53

CHAPTER THREE
Joe Solomon: What immortal hand or eye? 77

CHAPTER FOUR
Alvin Kallicharran: The curse of apartheid 89

CHAPTER FIVE
1957-1994: Spin bowlers – lepers in West Indian cricket 103

CHAPTER SIX
1994-2013: There is no West Indian anthem 119

CHAPTER SEVEN
Shivnarine Chanderpaul: He kills with a thousand scratches ... 145

CHAPTER EIGHT
Ramnaresh Sarwan: A simple sport can unite West Indians 173

APPENDICES 185

WORKS CITED 235

TEST CAREER STATISTICS 238

1ST CLASS CAREER STATISTICS 240

INDEX 243

PREFACE

Powerful empires generally conquer weaker nations and colonise them, leaving an imprint of their imperial language and culture behind. In former British colonies like Nigeria or India, for example, the British ruled for a period then withdrew; and in Australia or New Zealand, the British again ruled before withdrawing, this time leaving behind their own settlers whose descendants today form the main population. In the Anglophone Caribbean, the region was first de-populated of its Amerindian indigenes by British and other European conquerors, and then re-populated through enforcement mainly by Africans, and also by Indians and smaller groups such as Chinese, Madeirans and others.

The process of imprinting British culture on essentially foreign groups in the Caribbean was profoundly different from that in Nigeria or India where British manners were imprinted, despite resistance, on large and ancient cultures. It was also different from the practice in former colonies like Australia or New Zealand where dominant British customs, including language and culture, were transferred wholesale by large numbers of British settlers. In the Caribbean, there was no ancient culture to resist imprinting because the indigenes were removed or eliminated. Nor were there large numbers of British settlers since Caribbean plantation culture required merely temporary officials, managers, merchants or other businessmen. The struggle for survival of a variety of powerless, imported cultures, without an indigenous base, in a new land is what produces Anglophone Caribbean problems of cultural discontinuity, divisiveness and doubtful nationality.

Whether there is a hidden connection between a society's local conditions and its quality of art or sport may not be entirely clear; but these two, Caribbean language/literature and its sport of cricket, form the main planks of social unity or shared sense of nationality connecting Anglophone Caribbean territories. The thesis in *Indian-Caribbean Test Cricketers and the Quest for Identity* is exactly this: that cricket, if not the strongest link, is as strong as Caribbean or Creole-English language/literature in fostering connections between Anglophone Caribbean territories.

Indian-Caribbean Test Cricketers and the Quest for Identity considers the effectiveness of cricket both in fostering connections, as well as overcoming or reducing problems of discontinuity and divisiveness in the Anglophone Caribbean. For example, Cecil Gray affirms that, in bowling a red-coloured cricket ball, Sonny Ramadhin delivered, "an orb investing us [West Indians] with power". In other words, by helping to achieve West Indian success over other nations in cricket, Ramadhin exhibits the working of a collective West Indian will or nationality. In one instance, according to Gray, West Indians listening to radio commentary on Test matches occurring oceans away, in Australia, could not hold back tears of sorrow when they heard, bleary-eyed, early on Christmas morning, in 1952, that Ramadhin was denied the wicket that would have brought their team victory against Australia.

Consider also another instance in *Indian-Caribbean Test Cricketers and the Quest for Identity*, more than fifty years later, when Indian-Guyanese batsman, Shivnarine Chanderpaul is knocked unconscious by a bouncer from the Australian fast bowler, Brett Lee in a Test match in Jamaica in May 2008. Chanderpaul picks himself up and after a cursory, on-the-spot medical examination, continues batting as if nothing had happened. Why does the largely Jamaican crowd, neither Indian nor Guyanese, leap exultantly to their feet, openly shedding shameless tears of joy and solidarity when, shortly afterwards, he reaches his century?

Since Indian-Caribbean Test cricketers are, by definition, members of the West Indies team, it goes without saying that *Indian-Caribbean Test Cricketers and the Quest for Identity* tells us as much about Indians who play for the West Indies team, as about West Indies Test cricket. While two of eight chapters in the volume – Chapters Five and Six – offer brief career summaries of every Indian cricketer who has represented West Indies, the bulk of *Indian-Caribbean Test Cricketers and the Quest for Identity* consists of a lengthy historical Introduction, and six chronologically arranged, chapter-length analyses of the Test career of each of the main Indian-Caribbean players – Sonny Ramadhin, Rohan Kanhai, Alvin Kallicharran, Joe Solomon,

Shivnarine Chanderpaul and Ramnaresh Sarwan. That among these six most successful Indian-Caribbean Test cricketers Ramadhin is the only Trinidadian illustrates an anomaly typical of a new, frontier-like society, without settled conventions, where currents of untested individualism and improvisation combine to produce top Test cricketers in a ratio of five Indian-Guyanese to one Indian-Trinidadian. It is equally anomalous that Indian-Trinidadian writers in the 1950s proved more internationally successful than Indian-Guyanese writers in almost exactly the same ratio.

INTRODUCTION

In May 2012, in their Third Test against England at Edgbaston, for the first time in their history, West Indies picked a cricket team that included a majority of Indian-Caribbean players, six in all: Adrian Barath, Assad Fudadin, Narsingh Deonarine, Denesh Ramdin, Sunil Narine and Ravi Rampaul. West Indies first entered lists of Test cricket, against England, in June 1928, when their team consisted entirely of (White) Europeans, (Black) Africans, and ('brown') mixed blood Euro/Africans. [Appendix 6] The first Indian member of the team, Sonny Ramadhin, was not selected until 1950. In 1957, Ramadhin was joined by Rohan Kanhai in the First Test against England at Edgbaston, then in the Second Test at Lord's by Kanhai and Nyron Asgarali. In the 1960s, after White West Indian players had virtually disappeared, and the team had settled down to a predominantly Black membership, one, two or three Indian-Caribbeans – rarely four and twice five – appeared up to 1982. But during a long period from February 1982 to March 1994, no Indian-Caribbean player was included in the West Indies team. That is why inclusion of six Indian-Caribbean players in May 2012 is such a red-letter event.

The inconsistent presence of Indian-Caribbean cricketers is a legacy of Caribbean history, society and culture, conceived out of the iniquity of slavery and indenture, and dedicated to the proposition of profit. The legacy breeds submerged feelings of victimisation, insularity, and suspicion of class or ethnic bias in everyday West Indian life and cricket. Issues of ethnicity, for instance, in every nook and cranny of West Indian experience, derive directly out of European settlement of the region, and a mixed racial profile that evolved soon after voyages by Columbus at the end of the fifteenth century. By the nineteenth century the whole region was divided into colonies controlled chiefly by Spain, Britain, France, Holland and Portugal, with Britain establishing English-speaking colonial administrations in many islands, including Jamaica, Barbados and Trinidad (today Trinidad and Tobago), and two mainland territories – British Guiana (today Guyana) and British Honduras (today Belize).

In the beginning, during the sixteenth or seventeenth century, English-speaking colonial populations consisted mainly of European conquerors and indigenous Amerindians, but this changed after the indigenes were either eliminated or forced to take refuge in impenetrable forests, and millions of African slaves brought, in the next two or three centuries, to work on British plantations. This large-scale infusion of Africans into British colonies transformed the population ratio, turning Africans into the largest ethnic group in most British Caribbean colonies, followed by (White) British rulers and mixed Euro/Africans, or brown people, until slavery was fully abolished in 1838.

The emancipation of Africans proved as major a turning point in the history of the English-speaking Caribbean as did their arrival, for in an attempt to compensate for the loss of slave labour, British sugar plantation owners brought other ethnic groups to do the work of the freed Africans; and between 1838 and 1917, under a system of indenture, workers arrived from China and Madeira, but chiefly from India. Of nearly 430,000 indentured Indian workers who went to British Caribbean colonies, the largest numbers – about 240,000 – settled in British Guiana (now Guyana), and about 144,000 in Trinidad where there was an urgent need of agricultural labourers.

Africans retained their status as the majority ethnic group in most British Caribbean colonies, by more than ninety per cent in many cases, for example in Jamaica and Barbados, but not in Guyana and Trinidad where the regular arrival of indentured Indians, between 1838 and 1917, eventually created large enough numbers of Indian-Guyanese and Indian-Trinidadians to rival the dominance of Africans in these two territories. This explains why Indian-Caribbean Test cricketers come only from Guyana and Trinidad, and why the West Indies team remains mostly African: the small numbers of Indian-Caribbeans outside of Guyana and Trinidad, together with Indian-Guyanese and Indian-Trinidadians make up altogether no more than twenty per cent of the population in the whole English-speaking Caribbean. The Indian-

Caribbean majority membership in the West Indies team, in May 2012, thus seems more of a temporary anomaly than a radical departure.

When they first arrived in the Caribbean, their minority status in a population with an already established African majority, imbued Indians with a feeling of being outsiders. The society these Indian immigrants encountered, with Blacks or freed Africans and smaller groups of local Whites and 'browns', was steeped in an emerging Creole culture that included the English language, the Christian religion, and a mixture of customs drawn principally from African and European sources.

For the newly-arrived immigrants, mainly Hindus and a small percentage of Muslims, most of whom spoke Bhojpuri from northeast India, and dressed and ate differently, the prospect of adapting to the new Creole culture was daunting, for the Whites, 'browns' and Blacks had a head start of centuries of indigenisation or Creolisation over them. Since the indenture system provided work for a period and a free return passage to India at the end, some, about one quarter, of the immigrants took advantage of this provision and returned to India, while a majority either re-indentured themselves or remained in the Caribbean where their descendants form today's Indian-Caribbean population.

The option of return to India which lasted only for four or five decades added a "transitory" label that stuck to Indian-Caribbeans, confirming them as culturally marginal, even if it later became obvious that their only practical option was to remain in the Caribbean and become Creolised or indigenised in speech and habits, even religion. In time, feelings of transition, ambiguity, marginalisation or fluidity dogged the original Indian immigrants and became ingrained in Indian-Caribbean culture. These feelings now invited suspicion from the larger Caribbean-wide community, mainly of Blacks who, having endured the agony of slavery for a longer period and in much larger numbers than Indians endured indenture, developed their own feelings as primal victims and true inheritors of the Caribbean political kingdom once the White victimisers had gone. Ensuing suspicion between Indian-Caribbeans and African-Caribbeans then became a distinguishing feature of the DNA of Caribbean experience: even if it is diminishing, it appears in most aspects of political and social relations in Guyana and Trinidad and Tobago, the only two territories in which Indians possess numbers sufficient to threaten Black political legitimacy.

Indian indentured immigrants in other parts of the former British empire, for instance, in Africa and Fiji, were able to form a middle class in a generation or two, while the process took longer in the Caribbean where Indian-Caribbeans remained locked into their original role as plantation peasantry or coolies for nearly four generations, from the 1830s to the 1960s or 1970s. This view of them persisted in popular Caribbean imagination as illustrated by this report on Indian-Trinidadians in 1911, after about seventy years of indenture, by Dr Eric Williams (1911-1981) a Black Trinidadian historian, and the first Chief Minister, Premier and Prime Minister of Trinidad and Tobago:

> There was no question that the Indian occupied the lowest rung of the ladder in Trinidad. Cribb'd, cabin'd, and confin'd in the sugar plantation economy, from which other racial groups had succeeded in large part in escaping, the few who did escape to the Mecca of Port of Spain [the capital city] were concentrated on the outskirts of the town in a sort of ghetto known as 'Coolie-Town' – today St James, a bustling suburb of the capital – which tourists interested in Oriental scenes and ceremonies were advised to visit in order to see 'the Son of India in all his phases of Oriental primitiveness.' [Williams, 21]

Williams led the People's National Movement (PNM) a political party that ruled Trinidad without interruption from 1956 to 1981, supported mainly by African-Trinidadians. By that time, politics had become polarised along ethnic lines so that the PNM represented mainly African-Trinidadians, while the Democratic Labour Party (DLP) was supported mainly by Indian-Trinidadians. [Appendix 9]

In Guyana, ethnic polarisation was inspired by a similar definition of Indian-Guyanese as lowly coolies or plantation labourers who were not as Creolised, urbanised, educated or civilised as White, 'brown' or Black Guyanese who had long adopted British manners of speech, dress, religion and culture as their ultimate model. Edgar Mittelholzer

(1909-1965) a 'brown' Guyanese, and one of the most prolific West Indian novelists, outlines the interplay of race, colour and class in the joint ethnic and feudal, class structure of British Guianese society up to about the period of the Second World War:

> Indeed, sad to relate, it was my own class – people of coloured admixture but of fair or olive complexions – who dispensed any colour snobbery that it was possible to dispense. It was my class which looked down upon the East Indian sugar plantation labourers ('coolies' we called them, whether they were labourers or eventually became doctors or barristers or Civil Servants). [Mittelholzer, 155]

Mittelhozer spells out the hierarchical, feudalistic, social framework that functioned like the medieval king/barons/serfs model in British Caribbean colonies, with the British – Whites – at the apex, his own 'brown' class second, then other indentured immigrant groups like the Portuguese and Chinese who quickly distanced themselves from the plantation, followed by Blacks, and lowest of all, Indians or coolies working in virtual exile in rural plantations.

The truth is that Indians, who themselves came in different skin colours from almost white to black, did not exactly fit into the White/'brown'/Black categories in the Caribbean; but they were excluded willy-nilly because of their plantation experience and differences of speech, religion, dress, and cultural forms such as diet and music. Such was the alienating curse of the plantation that even Indians who, in time, had entered the professions, found it difficult to cleanse themselves of its stain as Mittelholzer confirms. Up to the independence period of the 1960s, only because Indians were numerous enough in Guyana (50 per cent) and Trinidad (40 per cent) to rival Africans for political power did they achieve slightly better status in these two territories whereas, in other English-speaking Caribbean territories where Africans were supremely dominant, Indians continued to be dismissed, in Mittelholzer's terms, as a rustic, coolie minority.

Son of Guyana, a memoir by the African-Guyanese, Arnold Apple leaves little doubt about attitudes to Indians in Guyana, at least up to the 1940s or 1950s:

> The attitudes of negroes (African-Guyanese) in those days made me believe that the place [Guyana] was owned by them and they were superior to all the rest of the nationalities. I had the belief that East Indians were the last class of people... Of course at that time all the low degrading, and dirty work jobs were done by them; [Indian-Guyanese] also the rice and cane fields. [Apple, 9-10]

If Eric Williams's opinion of Indian-Caribbeans has the authority of a professional historian and politician, and Mittelholzer's the sensitivity and insight of a novelist, Apple's view carries the visceral authenticity of the ordinary Guyanese man-in-the-street. In 1961, Apple migrated to England where he worked as a mechanic. In *Son of Guyana*, he pulls no punches: he reveals Guyana as riven by sharp divisions of class and colour and ethnicity while revelling in his countrymen's colonial legacy of gratuitous violence, artful duplicity and sheer amorality.

Arriving as they did in the colonial Caribbean with its unequal and divisive social structures, in the middle of the nineteenth century, and living and working on sugar plantations, in rural districts, Indians were not as exposed to cricket as fully, or as long as Africans who lived mainly in villages or towns from where cricket was regulated and formally administered. [Appendix 4] But isolated as they were, and even if they wished to, Indians could not resist being seduced either by Creolisation or by the magnetic pull of cricket as an increasingly integral aspect of their process of indigenisation.

Cricket may have originated in England in the sixteenth century [Appendix 1] but it was brought to the Caribbean by British soldiers and residents, as early as the eighteenth century. In his diary, for instance, the English plantation owner Thomas Thistlewood records seeing the game in Jamaica in 1778, [Appendix 7] and there are similar records of the game in Barbados. In 1979, for instance, a buckle was found in Scotland carrying the engraving of a slave playing cricket in Barbados around the turn of the nineteenth century, although it is believed freed slaves played cricket in Barbados even earlier, in the middle of the eighteenth century.

English-born historian James Rodway speculates that officers of the British Garrison in Guyana probably played cricket on the Parade

Ground in Georgetown, the capital, before 1856 and suggests 1858 as the year in which the Georgetown Cricket Club (GCC) was first established. It is impossible to over-estimate the importance of the (exclusively White) GCC: "As the only body then in existence [from the 1860s] with the necessary experience and resources, the GCC assumed the mantle for the organisation of cricket. It arranged domestic cricket and ran and financed Intercolonial [regional] Tournaments and International matches." [Camacho, 3]

The first example of a cricket match that Rodway found is between the GCC and [British] officers and men of the 21st Fusiliers on 11th June 1860, and the first rules of the club that he saw were dated in 1864. [Appendix 1] Writing in 1903, he asserts, "Since that time (1864) cricket has spread all over the colony, until every little coolie and Black boy – even – the boviander [mixture of Amerindian and African] is an ardent lover of the game." [Rodway, 241] In Guyana, as elsewhere in the Caribbean, this feudalistic pattern of White dominance in cricket remains and gradually filters down to 'browns' and Blacks, with Indians as the last to enlist.

Within the feudalistic, Anglo-centric yet Creolising structures of an emergent British colonial Caribbean culture, the role of cricket as a civilising influence is acknowledged by many commentators notably C.L.R. James, Keith Sandiford, Hilary Beckles and Clem Seecharan. [Appendix 3] Through its pioneering scholarship and fluent writing, James's *Beyond a Boundary* has acquired revered status as the bible of writing on West Indian cricket. In a brief introduction to his 1966 essay 'Kanhai: A Study in Confidence', reprinted in a volume of his selected writings, *C.L.R. James: At the Rendezvous of Victory,* James acknowledges the ambivalent minority situation of Indian cricketers in the Caribbean: "People felt it [his essay on Kanhai] was more than a mere description on how he [Kanhai] batted; it was significant of something in us as cricketers. They [West Indians] felt it was not only a cricket question, because Kanhai was an East Indian, and East Indians were still somewhat being looked down upon by other people in the Caribbean." [C.L.R. James, *Rendezvous,* 166]

This is a huge claim: that Kanhai's batting, coming from an ostensible, outsider Indian-Caribbean player of socially low rank in the 1960s, expressed a style that is uniquely Caribbean. In the same essay, James also claims that in one innings of a Festival match at

Edgbaston in 1964, when Kanhai scored 170 runs, he had reached regions Bradman never knew. Most importantly, James also says in his essay: "in Kanhai's batting what I have found is a unique pointer of the West Indian quest for identity."

Kanhai's stunning achievement is made possible by peculiar Caribbean conditions explored in Seecharan's *From Ranji to Rohan: Cricket and Indian Identity in Colonial Guyana 1890s-1960s* which reflects the crucial importance of cricket to Creole culture: "Education and cricket would become the premier instruments for establishing one's place in the diverse Creole universe...no ethnic group could really be recognised as belonging to the British West Indies if they failed to manifest competence in cricket." [Seecharan, *From Ranji to Rohan*, 18-19] Citing James, Seecharan notes that even the Chinese, scarcely forming noticeable numbers, either in Trinidad or Guyana, could not resist the call of Creole cricket and, a decade and a half before Sonny Ramadhin, produced Ellis 'Puss' Achong, a mixed African/Chinese, left-arm off-spinner who represented West Indies in six Test matches between 1930 and 1935, and achieved a career total of eight Test wickets.

Seecharan also relates the account of Surgeon-Major D.W.D. Comins, a British official who visited British Guiana in 1891 and reports, with something like wonder, the astonishing passion for cricket of a group of fifteen or sixteen young Indian-Guyanese from the countryside who requested leave from plantation work in order to tend to their personal rice plots, but instead attended cricket matches; and when charged by the estate manager, and given a choice in penalty between paying a fine of three dollars or going to jail for seven days, resolutely chose jail, almost in reverence to cricket as a religious rite. Equally revealing is the formation of the first nationally representative Indian-Guyanese cricket club, the East Indian Cricket Club (EICC), in 1916, two years before the creation of a British Guiana East Indian Association (BGEIA) which was intended to represent Indian-Guyanese interests nationally.

In peculiar Caribbean conditions, cricket provides a nexus that, in combination with education and Creolisation, weakens the grasp of deeply rooted divisiveness. This is certainly true in ethnic relations especially in Guyana and Trinidad and Tobago where ethnic voting patterns and racial rivalry still prevail. It also applies to the cultural fluidity created by the smallness of Caribbean territories and their closeness to the US, the dominant super power which, through the Monroe Doctrine, has taken over a colonial relationship toward the Caribbean formerly exercised by Britain. The most divisive effect of this new Pax Americana is not only its magnetic pull that drains human resources from the Caribbean through brisk immigration, but the irresistible power of American media, communications and cultural influence which, for example, attract Caribbean youth to games such as baseball and basketball rather than cricket.

But the most serious example of divisiveness in the Caribbean is geography itself – mainly islands scattered like pebbles in the Caribbean sea and, especially in earlier times, before air travel, without adequate means of travel or communication between each other. For example, Jamaica, the largest English-speaking Caribbean island, could only take part infrequently (after a long sea voyage) in inter-colonial or regional cricket tournaments with its three partners, Guyana, Barbados and Trinidad and Tobago, which are clustered together, 1400 miles away in the South Eastern Caribbean where these three islands could compete as frequently as they liked with each other. [Appendix 7] Hence the germination of feelings of insularity or disunity that obstruct the growth of pan-Caribbean mechanisms promoting unity.

The West Indies Cricket Board, (WICB) for instance, the governing body of cricket in all territories, and itself a creature of shambolic ineptitude, is defeated before it begins:

> From its inception the West Indies Board of Control was plagued with an incurable disease called 'insularity and parochialism'. It is incurable because the physical geography of the region cannot change; the Caribbean Sea and the Atlantic Ocean separating the entities are not likely to dry up. In this region comprising 6-8 million souls there are ten prime ministers, ten national anthems and ten flags." [Ganteaume, 65]

Vivian Richards supports Ganteaume: "There is too much island nationalism ... What I long to see is one flag ... We are simply too small as islands not to have come together as one unit or force." [Vivian Richards, 88]

Clyde Walcott who was President of the West Indies Cricket Board, tells a story about dining in a restaurant when he was a selector, and receiving a note threatening to put arsenic in his food if a certain cricketer from that island was not selected. Walcott writes: "It highlighted the problem of parochialism in West Indies cricket. Some think the players in their island or territory should be picked first." [Clyde Walcott, 96]

Insularity, parochialism and politics make a potent mix. Suspicion of injustice is rife, for instance, when players from one territory are chosen over those from another because of social, political or personal connections or special pleading. Sir Trevor McDonald explains efforts to secure the appointment of Vivian Richards as captain of the West Indies team in succession to Clive Lloyd in 1985:

> "West Indian politics entered the debate, Antiguans [Richards is from Antigua] and the Prime Minister and Richards's father and Andy Roberts [Antiguan cricket hero] ... have pressed their man's claim to the captaincy." [Trevor McDonald, *Clive Lloyd: The Authorised Biography*, 161]

From its origins in England, where ancient distinctions of class and breeding have persisted for centuries, cricket carried ingrained traditions of divisiveness to all parts of the former empire where they emerged in India, for instance, in religious and caste rivalries, or in apartheid South Africa where White privilege was jealously guarded by inhuman laws, and in the Caribbean where race, class, ethnicity and colour were standard criteria for both cricket club formation and team selection. [Appendix 1] The paradox is that, at the same time, the game serves as one of the most effective solutions to divisiveness in the Caribbean.

In his autobiography, former West Indies cricket captain and selector Garry Sobers admits his disapproval of "island politics" in the selection of West Indies teams, "when they [fellow selectors] picked teams and left out players I knew should be going or picked others because of island politics." [Sobers, 90] In preparing for the New Zealand tour of 1956 Sobers, "was introduced to the interminable inter-island politics that have always blighted West Indian cricket. There were controversies about all sorts of things from the selection of the 19 players to who should be captain." [Sobers, 36] Insularity entered when Roy Marshall, a White Barbadian, heard that Jeff Stollmeyer, a White Trinidadian, was picked as captain for the New Zealand tour, and migrated to England because, "He [Marshall] just didn't get on with Jeff." [Sobers, 36] When Stollmeyer was later injured and Denis Atkinson, a White Barbadian (like Marshall) took over the captaincy, Sobers writes: "Dennis, of course was a Barbadian and Roy undoubtedly would have stayed and played for him." [Sobers, 36]

Not that any of this is new. Strenuous effort went into an attempt to form a political union by means of a Federation of the West Indies, which was established in 1958 and dissolved in 1962; and today a regional mechanism of economic integration CARICOM (the Caribbean Community) still exists. The hope of a Federation of the West Indies was the eventual evolution of a single new nation instead of the disparate group of nondescript statelets that we have today. Yet, underlying all this lay perhaps the most formidable obstacle to unity: the absence of truly native traditions from the Caribbean indigenes – the Amerindians who suffered genocide. It was this act of primal disjunction that spawned a deeply ingrained sense of cultural discontinuity which, combined with other factors such as insularity and ethnicity, makes the Caribbean region a sitting duck for outside (chiefly American) penetration, influence and mischief. Vivian Richards succinctly expresses the inescapable role of the US: "America, as always, will continue to play the role of big father." [Richards, 89]

To this background of divisive and potentially disintegrating impulses cricket itself (not its administration) serves as the best antidote, according to Clive Lloyd, the most successful of all West Indies captains:

> As captain of the West Indies for ten years I can honestly say that cricket is the ethos around which West Indian Society revolves. All our experiments in Caribbean integration either failed or maintained a dubious survivability; but cricket remains the instrument of Caribbean cohesion – the remover of arid insularity and nationalistic prejudice. It is through cricket and its many spin-offs that we owe our Caribbean consideration and dignity abroad. ['Introduction', Michael Manley, *History*, v]

In his Foreword to a later book, *75 Years of West Indies Cricket, 1928-2003* by Ray Goble and Keith A.P. Sandiford, Lloyd offers an even more succinct acknowledgement of cricket's unifying power in the Caribbean: "... a mosaic game that transcends its boundaries to unity and elevates the Caribbean community as no other sport, cultural or political entity has done." [Goble and Sandiford, *75 Years*)

No doubt, Lloyd has in mind the decade or more after 1982 when, beginning with his term as captain, West Indies ruled the world as champions of Test cricket. The pity is that during this long period of universal West Indies supremacy, from February 1982, when Faoud Bacchus represented West Indies in the Third Test against Australia at Adelaide, to March, 1994 when Shivnarine Chanderpaul made his Test début against England on his home ground of Bourda, Guyana, no Indian-Caribbean player shared in this supreme West Indies achievement! Not only that, Vivian Richards, who served as West Indies captain from March 1985 to August 1991 and was elevated to knighthood and iconic status in cricket circles, is reported to have described the West Indies cricket team as, "a sporting team of African descent," [Hubert Devonish, in Beckles/Stoddart, *Liberation Cricket*, 188] completely erasing Indian-Caribbean history, identity or participation in West Indies Test cricket.

Richards's reported Afro-centricity is not as unusual as it sounds despite the multi-ethnic history of the region. Nor is it merely the result of ignorance. It is probably inspired by an inherited fear of threat to African legitimacy. Popular media portray the region as African, the home of calypso, reggae and Bob Marley, and until March 2012, a majority of the West Indies cricket team was consistently African. Among scholars too, the idea of the Caribbean as African is not unknown, if not always expressed. For instance, the late Lloyd Best claims that, "The Caribbean is really African-America, North America is European-America and South America is American-America. America in the American-Indian sense. The Caribbean is essentially an Afro place. That includes Cuba where perhaps half the population or more is White. Culturally they are almost all Afro." [Lloyd Best, Interview, *Trinidad and Tobago Review*, 25.10, 6 October 2003, 18] What Best means is that the Caribbean is Creole. The trouble is that "Creole" is popularly equated with "African" especially in Trinidad where Best grew up, while there are multiple forms of Creole culture in the Caribbean.

Although his phrasing is ambiguous Best has too much scholarly integrity to see the Caribbean as Afro-centric. Perhaps Afro-centricity had its greatest appeal during the 1970s, in the immediate aftermath of the euphoria over independence, when the world of Anglophone Caribbean poetry was divided between two men – Derek Walcott and the poet and historian, Edward Brathwaite – whose re-discovery of African roots (Alex Haley-style) sparked a militant wave of Afro-centricity, perhaps not advocated by Brathwaite himself, but inspired by his work in those eager to devalue Walcott's *oeuvre* and its assertion of the mixed multicultural nature of the Caribbean.

This Introduction ends with an account by Rosanne Kanhai, an Indian-Trinidadian Professor of English, of her experience as a schoolgirl of eleven, when Trinidad and Tobago gained Independence in 1962. As an Indian-Trinidadian child, Rosanne Kanhai offered no threat, but she felt a sense of not belonging among her African-Trinidadian friends, however inoffensively they may have expressed it.

Professor Kanhai's childhood alienation is expressed in a single article and is prompted by euphoria among her African-Trinidadian countrymen and women celebrating a Black (African) freedom and pride that excluded her or her family. Her teachers, "did not choose Indo students for the school choir or as representatives for the regional Independence celebrations in Tacarigua." There was "near worship" of Dr Eric Williams, the African-Trinidadian Prime Minister, and "Independence celebrations overlay a context in which the small number of Indo students [at Bishop Anstey High School, the best Anglican high school in the country] were already in a place of embarrassment. For example, Indo children hid (for fear of ridicule) to eat their brown-paper-wrapped lunches of roti and alloo, or roti and tomato choka."

Kanhai's family who lived in the countryside were Anglicans, and her father who was the only Indian-member of the local Village Council, as well as captain of the village cricket team, voted for the Democratic Labour Party (DLP) which was supported mainly by Indian-Trinidadians. This sometimes exposed her family to incidents of ugly hostility from their Black neighbours. The social context required that her father push his children (including daughters) to achieve academic excellence which was, "intertwined with this developing concept of pride as a Trinidadian." And academic excellence was to be achieved, "within Afro-dominated schools and under an Afro-dominated government."

At school the author and her sister were, "country bookies" who did not, "qualify for entry into any of the recognisable cliques of privileged students." The curriculum focused on African slavery and post-slavery periods with, "a few lines about the Caribs and Arawaks, and a few about Indian Indenture. Home Economics assumed a middle-class, urban home and ... I did not even notice the absence of dishes such as roti or curry chataigne [breadnut] because I was developing a double-consciousness that kept my two worlds (home and school) apart." When the British principal of her school retired, "the new Afro-Trinidadian principal took down the White Jesus in the school chapel and mounted a Black one. I saw that Independence meant that Jesus became Black."

As "country bookies" Kanhai and her sister found board and lodging in a home in the capital city, Port of Spain, where their school was located. Their landlady, an African-Trinidadian woman who idolised the "doctah," [Dr Eric Williams, Prime Minister] loved all her boarders, Indian as well as African, and acted as moral and spiritual mentor to them. Such was her "big heart," Kanhai writes, that, "it brings me almost to tears to remember her." Yet Kanhai and her sister realised, "we were not included in euphoria of Black pride that permeated the boarding house." [Rosanne Kanhai, *Sunday Express*, 'Express Woman', 2 September 2012, 10/11]

The episode captures the sad inevitability of ethnic alienation as a logical product of Caribbean history rather than any eccentric attempt to inflict hurt or harm. It also catches a potential of continuing victimisation between two ethnic groups who, like Siamese twins, are joint victims of British colonialism. The potential exists in many aspects of Caribbean life, not least in cricket, for example, in the predicament of Sonny Ramadhin being described by an English cricketer and journalist, (Trevor Bailey) entirely without malice, as, "an Indian in a team full of White and Black men," as well as in already mentioned remarks by Vivian Richards publicly proclaiming the character of the victorious 1980s West Indies team as African or Black. In a region so atomised by a history of colonial greed, plunder and pillage, there is no absence of victims or shortage of grievance over anything or everything under a resplendent Caribbean sun.

As their titles indicate, out of eight chapters in *Indian-Caribbean Test Cricketers and the Quest for Identity*, six (Chapters One to Four, and Seven and Eight respectively) examine individual careers of the most successful Indian-Caribbean players – Sonny Ramadhin, Rohan Kanhai, Joe Solomon, Alvin Kallicharran, Shivnarine Chanderpaul and Ramnaresh Sarwan. Chapter Five considers players whose Test careers fall somewhere between 1957 and 1994, while Chapter Six examines careers between 1994 and 2012. The Appendices consist of independent book reviews that discuss issues raised in preceding chapters. Statistics for all players are provided only up to December 2013.

So far, a total of thirty-three Indian-Caribbean players have represented West Indies in Test matches, 11.18 per cent of a grand total of the 295 cricketers who have appeared in the West Indies team after Test status was achieved in 1928. Since Indian-Caribbeans form roughly 20 per cent of the population of the English-speaking Caribbean, this percentage hints at the built-in structure of ethnic alienation indicated by Professor Rosanne Kanhai's experience in Trinidad in 1962. An even stronger hint of ethnic alienation derives from the fact that between 1928 and 1994 only fourteen Indian-Caribbean cricketers were picked in Test matches, while from 1994 to 2013 nineteen Indian-Caribbean Test players appeared, eight of them only in the past seven years. The appearance of six Indian-Caribbean players in a West Indies team in 2012 represents a remarkable acceleration in the selection of Indian-Caribbean cricketers on the West Indies team.

CHAPTER 1

Sonny Ramadhin: Investing West Indians with power

For well known reasons of empire, during the second half of the nineteenth century, West Indian cricket teams consisted either of White players only, or a mixture of White, 'brown' and Black. In the first half of the next century the proportion gradually shifted from a White to a Black majority; and by the time Sonny Ramadhin arrived, the first Indian-Caribbean to appear in a Test match (against England at Old Trafford in June 1950), the West Indies team consisted of three Whites: Captain John Goddard, Jeffrey Stollmeyer and Gerry Gomez; two 'brown' or mixed-blood players: Allan Rae and Robert Christiani; five Black players: Weekes, Worrell, Walcott, Hines Johnson and Alfred Valentine, as well as Ramadhin. Not only were these eleven players drawn from different cricket-playing Caribbean territories – Jamaica, Trinidad and Tobago, Barbados and British Guiana (the so-called Big Four) – they were set apart from neighbouring British colonies, considered smaller both in geographical size and cricket development. [Appendix 2] More importantly, in those colonial times, the players themselves were separated from each other by territorial, ethnic, colour and class differences.

In similar divisive Caribbean fashion, Ramadhin was set apart by his birth as an Indian on 1 May 1929, in St Charles village, in a Trinidadian sugar plantation district that marked him with the life style of Indian, indentured, plantation workers. A "White" West Indian commentator reports the first impression that Ramadhin made on journalists when he arrived as a member of the West Indies team in England in 1950: "One remembers their [the English press] querying the fact that an Indian – Ramadhin – was playing for the West Indies." [Figueroa, 2] Figueroa sneers at the English press for being 'uninformed', [Figueroa, 2] but his reaction, that English journalists should have known that Indians are a part of the Caribbean population, expects too much, since there were no Indians in any of the West Indies

Test teams that toured England since 1928, or indeed in any of the three West Indies teams that toured England in 1900, 1906, and 1923, well before they achieved Test status in 1928. [Appendix 8]

Jeffrey Stollmeyer, captain of both Trinidad and West Indies (after 1952), adds: "Everything in those times [1950] was novel to Ramadhin. He had never been on a ship before, never been out of Trinidad, the menu card on the morning breakfast table presented a difficulty, the diet was different, even the double-decker buses in London were a novelty." [Stollmeyer *Everything*, 109] Not that Stollmeyer might not have made slighting remarks about some of his Black team-mates as well, but they at least would not have found the diet different. While there were social and class differences between his White, 'brown' and Black team-mates, Ramadhin was further differentiated from them all by ethnic habits in eating, speech, religion, music and other cultural preferences. The Australian journalist Ray Robinson claims, "There is a story that when Ramadhin went aboard the ship he was unused to knife and fork and was shown how to handle them in his cabin before dining in the saloon." [Robinson *Glad*, 206]

Stollmeyer also writes: "His [Ramadhin's] initial 'S' stands for his nickname 'Sonny.' The initials 'K.T.' often ascribed to him are purely fictional." [Stollmeyer, *Everything*, 107] Soon after his arrival in England, and although he never found out what they stood for, the initials 'K.T.' were added to Ramadhin's name by English journalists who thought they were essential. There is no real malice in Stollmeyer's remarks, but as someone who studied at Queen's Royal College and the Imperial College of Tropical Agriculture, and came from a White, plantation-owning family of the type who could have employed members of Ramadhin's family in agricultural work, they inevitably carry a touch of condescension or paternalism.

Ramadhin was orphaned early, brought up by his grandmother, and educated at the Canadian Mission School in Duncan Village. He began playing cricket for his school team, then with the local Palmiste Club before he was introduced to Clarence Skinner, a Black Barbadian immigrant who had previously represented his native island in regional cricket. Impressed by Ramadhin's uncanny ability to turn the ball both ways, without apparent change of action, Skinner got the young man a job as storekeeper at Trinidad Leaseholds Oil Company where he played cricket for Leaseholds, the Company club.

Ramadhin was chosen to represent Trinidad in two trial matches against Jamaica in January/February 1950. In the first match he took eight wickets and four in the second. Stollmeyer, the Trinidad captain, lavishes praise on a lad who, "under primitive conditions, and without any tuition... had developed a style of bowling which was quite different from anything yet seen in cricket." [Stollmeyer, *Everything*, 108]

In Stollmeyer's view, some people, not the selectors, were sceptical about Ramadhin's lack of experience, young age, twenty, and slightness of build. Besides, Wilfred Ferguson, the Black Trinidad right-arm leg-spinner, who had taken twenty-three wickets against England in 1947/48, was in good form earning nine wickets in the first trial match when Ramadhin got eight. But if Figueroa is right, it was Ramadhin's destruction of the greatly admired Jamaican batsman Ken Rickards, a batting Goliath facing a mere David, that fatefully tilted the scales of selection in his favour: "It is said he [Ramadhin] so comprehensively bowled Ken Rickards when set on 40 in the first innings, [of the first trial match] and on 57 in the second, that all the cognoscenti present were willing to book his passage to England." [Figueroa, 5]

No doubt the choice of Ramadhin and of the equally young and inexperienced left-arm African-Jamaican spin bowler Alfred Valentine who only managed two wickets in the Jamaican trials, was a daring gamble. Indeed, it proved the most fateful decision ever taken by administrators of West Indian cricket! In his sketch of Ramadhin in the official souvenir of the 1950 tour published by Playfair Books Ltd, the editor, English journalist Peter West, senses the gamble: "Sonny Ramadhin, the youngest player in the team by a few days, has made cricketing history by being the first East Indian to represent the West Indies and by being one of only two players selected for a tour after their first tournament."

Ramadhin and Valentine bowled more than one thousand overs each on the 1950 England tour as a whole, more than twice as many as any of their team-mates except Gerry Gomez who tallied six hundred and eighty overs. Ramadhin ended with one hundred and thirty-five wickets at 14.88 runs each for all First Class matches during the tour, and Valentine with one hundred and twenty-three wickets at 17.94 runs each. In the four Tests Ramadhin recorded three hundred and seventy-seven and a half overs with twenty-six wickets for 604 runs and an average of 23.23 runs, while Valentine totalled four hundred and twenty-two overs gaining thirty-three wickets for 674 runs and an average of 20.42. Together Ram and Val, as they came to be called, sent down more than eight hundred Test overs. The total of their Test wickets was almost four times the joint total gained by their fellow West Indies bowlers. Not only did they win the series, they flatly recanted a traditional West Indian belief in fast bowling as authorised by history, if not God: "The English press in 1950 expected [Hines] Johnson, [Prior] Jones and [Lance] Pierre, the West Indies fast bowlers, to 'do the damage.' Yet they collected only 91 wickets in thirty-one first class games, while Ramadhin and Valentine came off with 258." [Figueroa, 144]

Although the tour began with several exhilarating victories by West Indies against English county teams, their swagger was abruptly blunted in the First Test at Old Trafford which they lost by an emphatic margin of 202 runs. Partly the pitch was to blame; balls reared alarmingly or ducked deceptively and only English batsmen, nurtured on such domestic conditions, mustered the wiles to prevail. Still, Valentine came away with eight wickets for 104 runs in the England first innings. Ramadhin did not fare well even if he did beat the bat a few times; he collected two wickets in each innings including that of Bill Edrich, top scorer in the England second innings.

As if oblivious to this abject surrender, Ramadhin snatched five wickets in the second innings of a county match against Northumberland that followed. There could not have been a more fitting prelude to the glory about to descend on the tourists, and particularly on Ramadhin and Valentine, in the Second Test at Lord's, cricket headquarters! Now ensconced in realms of myth and legend, the story is simple enough: of a resounding West Indies victory – their first in England, after nine Test matches, three on each of three tours to England in 1928, 1933, and 1939. At Lord's, in 1950, West Indies won the toss and, thanks to a patient century from opener Allan Rae (106), and stylish half centuries from Worrell (63) and Weekes (52,) gained a first innings lead of 175 runs to which a huge second innings century from Walcott (168 not out), in a partnership of 211 with Gomez (70), allowed their team to set England an impossible target of 601. In the event, England stumbled to a total of 274, and despite a brave century from Washbrook, fell short by 326 runs.

S.C. Griffith believes West Indies won because of three factors: "Ramadhin's magnificent bowling, the approach of their [West Indies] middle order batsmen, and the fact that vital chances were taken." [*The Cricketer* # 6, 8 July 1950] In a prescient analysis of the match Griffith singles out Ramadhin's contribution:

> For one so young in cricket experience, Ramadhin's performance was truly remarkable, and will forever be remembered in cricket history: he maintained a beautiful length and accuracy, and yet spun the ball sufficiently to beat the middle of the bat – even the subtleties of flight were there. No England batsman could be said to have wholly unravelled the 'mystery' of the direction of his spin, and he was allowed to enjoy the delights of an always aggressive close-in field... His figures for the match [11 wickets for 152 runs from 115 overs, 70 of which were maidens] make staggering reading, as, indeed do those of his able lieutenant, Valentine – the latter, accurate though he was, would, however, be the first to admit that he owed something to the batsman's state of mind created by his colleague, Ramadhin." [Griffith, 281-282]

Griffith's comments are spontaneous. He was a former Test wicket-keeper for England, cricket correspondent for the *Sunday Times* and Secretary of the MCC. His comments set the tone for subsequent assessments, notably of Ramadhin's 'mystery,' and his destabilising effect on batsmen from which Valentine may have profited.

Jim Laker is equally outspoken: "I'm sure that Valentine greatly benefited from bowling at the other end to 'Ram' on that [1950] tour. 'Val' then was just another left-arm spinner. He could turn the ball tremendously, but his direction was all awry... But because batsmen became bemused by 'Ram' at the other end they would lash out when facing 'Val' and as often as not get themselves out." [Laker, 123-124] Laker's comments, coming from a right-arm off-spinner who faced Ramadhin when he played against West Indies in the Old Trafford Test in 1950, and four Tests in England's tour of West Indies in 1953-54, also carry the conviction of someone who holds the world record for most wickets in a Test match: nineteen wickets for England in the Fourth Test against Australia, at Old Trafford, in 1956.

Laker claims that few accredited batsmen were able to, "tell when he [Ramadhin] would bowl his leg-break instead of the off-spinner" [Laker, 131] and suggests that Ramadhin's, "great success in England was due to England's inferior light and our lack of sight screens on Test grounds coupled with the dark texture of his [Ramadhin's] hand, and the quickness of his arm action." [Laker, 132] Laker concludes that Ramadhin, "has such great natural gifts and is such a canny bowler that he still earns a world rating." [Laker, 124]

John Arlott agrees about the mechanics of Ramadhin's technique in the Lord's Test: "He [Ramadhin] was bowling chiefly off-breaks but, good as they were solely as off-breaks, they were doubly dangerous by virtue of the fact that he was varying them with a leg-break which neither batsman [Edrich and Washbrook] could detect." [Arlott, *Days*, 53] English uncertainty insinuated suspicion of mystery and magic; you only have to look at the large percentage of maidens bowled by Ramadhin – twenty-seven out of forty-three in the first innings, and forty-three out of seventy-two in the second. Except for Johnny Wardle, a bowler who slogged 33 runs at the end of England's first innings, the England batsmen were transfixed into immobility: "Ramadhin's bowling, until Wardle's arrival, showed 34 overs, 26 maidens, with scoring strokes played to only 9 of the 204 balls he bowled. In fact, those nine strokes were spread over more than two and a half hours – one scoring stroke per eighteen minutes." [Arlott, *Days*, 57]

Despite its defiant spirit, there is no aura of mastery or confidence in Washbrook's century; on the contrary, it gives an impression of practised, artful guesswork. Here is Arlott again:

> I am convinced that he [Washbrook] could not distinguish between Ramadhin's off-break and his leg-break, yet he contrived to play him by delaying his stroke and by skilful estimation of the point of the pitch in relation to either break. He played only those balls which he was forced to play, covering his wicket so that, if the ball was not breaking on to the stumps, he missed it by too great a margin to give an edged catch. [Arlott, *Days*, 64-65]

Sonny Ramadhin made cricket history when he became the first Indian-Caribbean player to represent the West Indies. CENTRAL PRESS/GETTY IMAGES

Arlott agrees with Robert Christiani, Ramadhin's West Indies teammate in the Second Test, who ascribes Washbrook's successful defiance to luck: "He [Washbrook] was lucky, and he did not make an aggressive stroke unless it was a half volley. Also, out of his 114, I would guess that no more than about 10 were scored off Ramadhin." [Birbalsingh, *Guyana*, 131]

Christiani's view of Hutton's batting technique against Ramadhin is similar to Arlott's on Washbrook: "What I noticed about Hutton was that he played each ball on its merit ... He did not anticipate. From the time the ball was delivered his left foot would go forward but there was no decision ... Then, at the last moment, his stroke was made. This was his method, and it worked particularly against Ramadhin." [Birbalsingh, *Guyana*, 131]

There is no hesitation in Arlott's final opinion on Ramadhin: "This [Ramadhin's performance] was great bowling by any standards in the history of the game. Ramadhin was bowling a good length, coming quickly off the pitch – in the last analysis the essential characteristic of the great bowler- he was varying his flight, and no one knew which way he would turn." [Arlott, *Days*, 65]

The Second Test at Lord's in 1950 was a unique event in the annals of West Indian cultural and political history, and the contribution of specific heroes is inescapable. [Appendix 11] If batsmen like Rae and Walcott played important roles, as did Weekes who contributed two scores of 63 (the second, a run-out), or close-in fieldsmen like Goddard and Christiani whose stopping or catching was fearless and acrobatic, the match was ultimately won by Ramadhin and Valentine who captured a grand total of eighteen wickets – Ramadhin went away with five in the first innings and six in the second, and Valentine four in the first, and three in the second innings.

Their bowling excited such universal celebration among West Indians that a "Victory Calypso" was composed in three stanzas and a chorus by Aldwyn Roberts (alias Lord Kitchener) and popularised by Egbert Moore (alias Lord Beginner). Here is the first stanza:

> Cricket, lovely cricket
> At Lord's where I saw it
> Yardley [England's captain] tried his best
> But Goddard [the West Indies captain] won the Test

They gave the crowd plenty fun
Second Test and West Indies won

The chorus, repeated after each stanza, then follows:

With those little pals of mine
Ramadhin and Valentine

The calypso immortalised Ramadhin and Valentine in West Indian popular imagination, and translated them into beloved folk heroes. [Appendix 12]

More heroic deeds were repeated in the Third and Fourth Tests which West Indies again won by wide margins that reinforce the emblematic impact of the Lord's Test as vindication both of West Indian self esteem, and the role of an Indian-Caribbean cricketer in helping to achieve it. For one thing, the first West Indies Test win on English soil symbolised a deeply felt West Indian potential for freedom from colonial domination by Britain; for another Ramadhin's performance transformed the colonial image of Indian-Caribbeans as despised plantation coolies by presenting them as participants in the struggle for a distinct West Indian cultural and political nationality.

Most of all, the Second Test at Lord's, in 1950, is the symbolic West Indian Declaration of Independence, herald of political agitation that would lead to independence by the 1960s. The title of this chapter, for instance, comes from a poem that sees the cricket ball bowled by Ramadhin at Lord's as an orb investing West Indians with (psychological and political) power. For the Lord's Test brought West Indians together despite divisions of race, colour, class and all, into a common enterprise that was internationally recognised as a victory over their imperial overlord, and liberation from colonial subjection. [Appendix 8]

It was no accident either that the declaration of independence occurred side by side with a literary renaissance spearheaded by authors like Edgar Mittelholzer, George Lamming and Samuel Selvon in the same decade. To decipher the precise alchemy of independence or nationality may be elusive, but the facts are that West Indies won a famous cricket victory at Lord's in 1950, that West Indian literature became internationally recognised in the 1950s and 60s, and that the largest British Caribbean colonies – Jamaica, Trinidad and Tobago, Barbados and Guyana – became independent nations in the 1960s. All these were surely crucial steps in the West Indian quest for identity.

The view of Ramadhin as Valentine's more menacing partner has already been mentioned by S.C. (Billy) Griffith and is supported by Trevor Bailey, Cambridge graduate and England all-rounder, who played in the First and Fourth Tests of the 1950 summer series, and is remembered as "Barnacle Bailey" for his dour, defensive batting:

> Although Valentine took ten wickets in the match [the fourth Test at Kennington Oval] for me it was the silent Ramadhin who got us [England]. He was already known in the West Indies at the time, less so in England. He was shy and sensitive, considering he was an Indian in a team full of White and Black men. We had never faced someone like that, bowling from that position, and at that pace, who turned the ball on a good wicket. Valentine had an easier style, bowled quicker and was a big spinner. [Trevor Bailey, 'Those two little pals of mine', WEB, 21 August 2008]

Bailey shows surprising insight into Ramadhin's ethnicity as the only Indian-Caribbean member of the 1950 West Indies team.

Perhaps touring the region with the England team, and later writing a biography of Garfield Sobers, gave Bailey the right perspective into Caribbean history and social relations. His comments meet a need to assess Ramadhin's challenge and triumph if not exactly as someone culturally alien to the West Indies team, as one perceived as different, in terms of his ethnicity and spin bowling prowess, from the previously most successful West Indian bowlers – all African-Caribbean – and all notable for their blistering pace, for example, Learie Constantine, Herman Griffith, George Francis or Manny Martindale.

Had the euphoria of achieving retribution over their imperial overlord not blinded them, West Indies might have realised that England who had already been steam-rollered by the "all-conquering" Australians under Bradman in 1948, were in the process of rebuilding their team after the Second World War. So turbulent was England's period of transition that no England player, for instance, appeared in all four of the 1950 Test matches. They were also handicapped by injuries, selection blunders, and dependence on two amateur captains. According to Trevor Bailey, "Had England been able to open with Len Hutton and Cyril Washbrook with world class Denis Compton, Bill Edrich and Reg Simpson to follow, they would certainly have drawn the series – perhaps even won." [WEB, August 21, 2008] Bailey's speculation contains not a little wishful thinking; but his acknowledgement of England's transitional difficulties is fair.

Pinning faith on the mystical powers of Ram and Val, West Indies confronted Australia in the First Test of a five-match series at Woolloongabba, Brisbane, in November 1951. Their first innings total was 216 on an easy-paced pitch of which their highest individual score was 45 from their captain, John Goddard, who had scarcely shone as a batsman in England the previous year. Still, forty-nine overs from Ram and Val, out of a total of sixty-four and a half, restricted the Australia response to a manageable 226, with Val snatching five wickets and Ram sowing doubt and anxiety among Australian batsmen, but taking only one wicket. After being set 236 for victory, Australia slumped to 149 for five, raising expectations of a West Indies victory, but the home team revived to win by three wickets with Ram being satisfied with five wickets and Val one.

Loss by such a narrow margin, despite several dropped catches suggests a degree of nervousness among the tourists. Their top heavy reliance on Ram and Val who accounted for one hundred and twenty-nine out of one hundred and forty-nine and a half overs in the match also betrayed lack of confidence. Such was Goddard's faith in his spinners, that he simply rubbed the shine off the new ball on the ground, in the second innings, before giving it to Ram and Val! If Australia had erred on the side of caution in the first Test they now completely revised their plan in the second at Sydney, when Hassett and Miller collared the West Indies pair of spin prestidigitators in a record fourth wicket stand of 235 that brought Australia a convincing seven-wicket victory.

Ramadhin's contribution of one wicket for 196 runs, and Val's four for 156 again tell a sorry tale of weak support from fielders and poor tactics from their captain. With two losses already in the five-match Test series, a loss in the Third Test at Adelaide would put the rubber beyond their reach. West Indies fielding improved in the Third Test when both teams managed only low scores in their first innings and, for once, other West Indies wicket-takers – Worrell and Goddard – claimed nine wickets between them. In the second innings, Val roused himself to six wickets for 102 alongside Ramadhin's one for 76, as West Indies produced a series-saving victory by seven wickets.

With a first innings lead of 56 in the Fourth Test at Melbourne, West Indies set Australia the difficult task of making 260 to win in the fourth innings. In spite of a century from Hassett, they needed 38 runs from their last pair – bowlers Doug Ring and Bill Johnston. According to Jim Laker, the tension proved too much for some West Indies fielders: "Just before the winning hit was made, Ramadhin went off the field with tears running down his cheeks. No one went to his appointed place in the field, and John Goddard, the captain, found that about three others were trying to captain the side in the gripping final stages." [Laker, 123] Ramadhin was still a relative youth at the age of twenty-one, at the time, and was considered by some to have a propensity for wilting under pressure. Laker, for instance, reveals that Keith Miller was fond of sledging Ramadhin: "Keith Miller always got after Ramadhin. Keith waged a successful mental war against 'Sonny'." [Laker, 209]

The incident of his tears increased affection for Ramadhin among West Indian supporters straining to catch every word from static-interrupted, short wave radio broadcasts of Australia Test matches, across distant seas in the Caribbean, in the early morning hours of Christmas day, 1951. West Indians were as distraught as their hero, with what they thought was inadequate umpiring when appeals were turned down during the critical Ring/Johnston partnership in the Fourth Test. Still, Ramadhin collected three wickets for 93 runs in the match, and Valentine five for 88.

The following lines from 'Sonny Ramadhin', the poem by Cecil Gray, expresses warm affection for Ramadhin in the Caribbean. The quote focuses on the Fourth Test at Melbourne although it first extols Ramadhin's exploits in England in 1950:

> Here in these islands we [West Indians] screamed joyous shouts
> as every wicket fell. We'd taught our masters [England] how to play their game. The name of Ramadhin

made pride flush our veins. Then we sent you with
your guile to beat Australia. Our little marvel
off to twist the mighty giants by their tails.

At four o'clock one morning, Christmas Day,
you had Doug Ring out. We'd won. The umpire
said no. Oceans away here, like you, we wept.

What you sent down for over after over
was not a ball with stitches in red leather.
It was an orb investing us [West Indians] with power.
[Cecil Gray, 105]

Poetic insight perceives Ramadhin's role in helping to liberate West Indians from colonial servility and inferiority. The pity is that none of this could relieve disappointment in a tour that promised to be a contest between world champions, but turned out to be one with West Indies running away with tails between their legs. Australia won the Fifth and final Test by 202 runs, and finished with a decisive 4:1 margin of victory.

Following this drubbing, West Indies took on New Zealand, in two Tests, in February, 1952, and emerged from purgatory into heaven, romping home with victory by five wickets in the First Test in Christchurch. They settled for a draw in the second at Auckland, where they ran up an invincible first innings total of 546 for six wickets declared, including three centuries. At last, in New Zealand, West Indies found the form that boosted them in England, in 1950. Now the New Zealand batsmen were mesmerised by Ramadhin who snatched nine wickets in the first Test for 125 runs from seventy-four overs, while Valentine inveigled five wickets for 124 runs from fifty-nine overs. Even the mighty Ws who failed so dismally in Australia got into the runs again.

In hindsight, any disputed decision off Ramadhin's bowling in the Melbourne Test is critical. Had an appeal been upheld it would have brought the series level at 2:2, and most probably injected fresh zest into West Indies. In these circumstances, Goddard might not have withdrawn from the final battle in the Fifth Test, and the result could have turned out differently. Laker, a neutral outsider, acknowledges that the two sides were much closer in strength than reflected in the 4:1 capitulation. Laker offers a psychological explanation of the one-sided result in Australia: "Curiously, the West Indies have always shown an inferiority complex towards the Australians." [Laker, 122]

Sandwiched between their transcendent success in England in 1950, and predictable triumph over lowly New Zealand in 1952, the West Indies capitulation to Australia calls for further investigation, like a corpse in a post mortem. Perhaps the most popular reason for failure is the hardness of Australian wickets which negated the effect of Ramadhin's spin. This is plausible since Ramadhin's greatest success was at Brisbane, the softest of the five Test wickets, where he teased out five victims for 90 runs from forty overs in the second innings.

Other reasons are the willingness of Australian batsmen to use their feet compared with crease-bound Englishmen, or faulty tactics such as crowding Ring and Johnston with close-in fieldsmen in the Fourth Test and allowing them to hit lofted boundaries. Also, except for Worrell, the catastrophic failure of the other two Ws – Weekes and Walcott – due to injuries, drastically depleted West Indies' totals. In six Test innings in England, in 1950, Weekes luxuriated in an average of 56.33 runs, while in ten Test innings in Australia his average was 24.50. Walcott similarly averaged 50.83 runs from six Test innings in England and 16.67 from six in Australia.

But the main reason may come from Tony Cozier, the West Indian cricket journalist, who quotes Worrell as saying that Goddard had received much praise for the West Indies victory in 1950 and:

> "apparently annoyed the many players who had made a bevy of good suggestions during the tour. The annoyance was so great that, on our tour to Australia [in 1951-52] the advice was withheld, leaving Goddard a captain without officers and we drifted on the rocks. The reason was simple but, from a West Indian point of view, a catastrophic one, a withdrawal of brains at a time when they were really needed. The West Indies team never really recovered from the splinter groups of this tour until Gerry Alexander began to mould the team in 1958." [WEB November 2005]

Worrell's comments confirm both disarray in the West Indian camp, and a fundamental issue of flawed leadership stemming from the old colonial, White-captains-only policy.

At the end of the Australia tour in 1951/52, Stollmeyer publicly criticised Goddard ostensibly on personal grounds, as implied by Worrell. [Appendix 10] Stollmeyer had long coveted the West Indies captaincy, and in his diary of the West Indies tour of India in 1948/49 frequently makes derogatory remarks about Goddard's captaincy. [Ramchand/Teelucksingh 64] West Indian cricket pays the price for this rivalry which affects the performance of many players, perhaps Ramadhin most of all, because of his youth and inexperience. It is curious how, in the second innings of the Fifth Test after Stollmeyer was captain, he made 104, nearly half the total of the entire side, and his highest score by far out of ten Test innings he played during the series.

After the Australia tour Stollmeyer was appointed as West Indies captain, and Ramadhin next appeared in the first four of five Test matches played against India on their first tour of the Caribbean in 1952/53. One can only imagine Ramadhin's mixed feelings as an opponent to batsmen from India while being surrounded by spectators like himself many of whom, Indian-Trinidadians or Indian-Guyanese, were torn between a largely sentimental or romantic admiration of players from their ancestral homeland, and more grounded identification with their fellow West Indians. After all, there were still a few time-expired indentured Indians living in Guyana and Trinidad, with decreasing hope or desire of claiming their return passage to India.

Ramadhin was in the position of West Indian and South Asian immigrants or their children in contemporary Britain whose sympathies were regarded as suspect unless they took a test, as proposed by the British Conservative politician Norman Tebbit, in April 1990, to prove their loyalty to the England team. Not that anyone would dare to raise such a question about Ramadhin's Caribbean credentials, although the sympathies of Indian-Caribbean spectators did provoke controversy during subsequent visits by Indian and Pakistani cricket teams touring the Caribbean.

As his first home series of Test matches, India's tour of the Caribbean in 1952/53 was disappointing both for Ramadhin, and for West Indian fans who had heard of his legendary feats in England in 1950. He emerged with four wickets in the First Test that ended in a tame draw, in Trinidad, but the Second Test in Barbados was the brightest spot of the tour for Ramadhin. Strangely, it is his batting that first catches the eye. Coming in with the West Indies first innings score at 222 for 8 in the Second Test, Ramadhin defended with surprising stubbornness at one end, while Walcott – the last accredited batsman – pushed the score up to 280 at the other before he was out for 98, and Ramadhin was left with 16 not out – then his highest Test score.

After India replied with 253 to their hosts' first innings total of 296, West Indies added a further 228 in their second knock, setting India a target of 272 to win on a rain-affected wicket; but Ramadhin extracted figures of 24.5 -11-26-5 and sealed victory for West Indies by 142 runs. Although Ramadhin's lacklustre performance in the Third and Fourth Tests earned him only two more wickets, his total of seven wickets in the Second Test ensured that West Indies won the rubber one-nil, with four matches drawn.

In less than one year after their Fourth Test match against India, in March 1953, West Indies took on the second of three consecutive home series, this time facing England in the First Test of a five-match rubber starting in Jamaica, in January 1954. With a score of 168 for two on the first day of the match the home team made a brilliant start since, unlike the jaded post-war English players they had encountered in 1950, they were now confronted by a tougher England force fortified by brilliant young batsmen such as Peter May and Tom Graveney and vigorous, new fast bowlers like Fred Trueman and Brian Statham.

The outcome was by no means certain after England was set a target of 457 runs to get in the final innings, and started the last day on 227 for two, enjoying the benefits of a fast outfield and a wicket still playing well; but Stollmeyer who continued as West Indies captain deployed defensive bowling that made an England victory charge more hazardous and induced a collapse after lunch, ensuring a comfortable West Indies victory by a margin of 140 runs. It seemed like 1950 all over again with Ramadhin capturing six wickets and Valentine three. At an early stage of the first innings when Ramadhin and Valentine were already on the rampage, E.W. Swanton noticed the comparison: "The flower of the England batting had gone for 94 runs and Ramadhin and Valentine were back seemingly where they left off three years ago. They had shared four wickets in 33 overs for 57 runs and that on a wicket more or less like marble." [Swanton, *West Indian Adventure*, 42]

Fantasies of 1950 continued to hover around Ramadhin and Valentine in the Second Test, in Barbados, when they once again took on the bulk of the bowling, sending down 180.5 overs altogether – 90 from Ramadhin and 90.5 from Valentine – with Ramadhin collecting seven wickets and Valentine three. Ramadhin's first innings statistics by themselves are even more impressive; 53-30-50-4. A comparison with results from the England spinner Tony Lock in the same match gives some idea of Ramadhin's accuracy and control: in the first innings Lock bowled forty-one overs for 116 runs and one wicket, and in the second thirty-three overs for 100 runs and no wicket.

The Third Test at Bourda, Georgetown, at the end of February 1954, changed everything, not only because England won by nine wickets, nor because it transformed the direction of the rubber, but because of an ugly incident of bottles and other missiles being thrown on the ground to interrupt play on the fourth day of the match. On the face of it, a section of spectators vented anger over the run-out of fellow Guyanese Cliff McWatt when his partnership with Holt had reached 98, thus falling short of the prized century that the crowd, in anticipation, had started to celebrate with their clapping. (Ramadhin was the incoming batsman and had already reached the crease when the commotion erupted)

There is no question that McWatt was out of his ground. The decision of Indian-Guyanese umpire Badge Menzies was correct, but the crowd was incensed by Menzies' earlier decisions on dismissals of Christiani and Weekes; and Menzies' ethnicity was probably as much of a factor as strained relations between some members of the visiting team and umpires, or an unstable political situation in Guyana (then the colony of British Guiana) following the forcible dismissal of the colony's first popularly elected government by the British governor a few months earlier. Ill feeling had been building after Christiani and Weekes both stood their ground until umpire Menzies raised his finger. McWatt's dismissal, the third in a row, was the last straw.

Since Hutton, the England captain, scented victory after England made 435, and had West Indies struggling at 238 for 8, he refused to take his team off the field. The follow-on was enforced, and a West Indies second innings score of 256 left only 75 runs needed for a victory which England easily scored. Despite the interruption and defeat,

Ramadhin returned his best figures of the series, 67-34-113-6, during England's first innings. It gave him a total of nineteen wickets in the three Tests so far, better than any other West Indies bowler, although it did not prevent the home team from having to settle for a drawn 2:2 rubber.

The high-scoring Fourth Test was drawn in Trinidad and West Indies lost the Fifth Test after Trevor Bailey demolished seven West Indies wickets in the first innings for 34 runs. Coming back to even their account, after being two games down, undoubtedly gave England a moral victory in the Test series, although Ramadhin seemed to recover what form he lost against India, and emerged with final tour figures of twenty-three wickets in five Tests for an average of 24.30. It gives some sense of Ramadhin's value to realise that he earned nearly three times as many wickets as the next best West Indies bowlers – Frank King and Valentine – who each played in only three Tests.

Hopes of a continuing revival in Ramadhin's fortunes were dashed by the Australia tour of West Indies that immediately followed. Although the Australians had been humiliated by England – 3:1, with one drawn match that ended on 3 March only three weeks before the first Test between Australia and West Indies in Jamaica on 26 March 1955 – it offered no hint of the blitzkrieg they were about to unleash. A few Australian totals illustrate their deadly intent: 600 for 9 declared in the second Test in Trinidad; 668 in the Fourth Test in Barbados; and 758 for 8 wickets declared in the Fifth Test in Jamaica. All that Ramadhin could salvage from such wreckage were five wickets in four Tests. Valentine scraped together the same number of wickets in three Tests. But statistics do not explain the unequal forces of history, fragile structure, and improvised, *ad hoc* organisation of West Indian cricket behind this debacle.

After the crushing West Indies defeat by nine wickets in the first Test and narrow escape from further humiliation through a draw in the second, it was decided to drop Ramadhin and Valentine. An Australian visitor captures the absurdity of this decision by West Indies selectors: "News of the omission of Valentine and Ramadhin was received in responsible cricket circles in the same way as the House of Commons listened to Winston Churchill tell of the fall of Singapore." [Pat Landsberg 94-95] After his bad experience in Australia in 1951/52 Ramadhin still commanded respect:

Ramadhin is not a bowler who can be fathomed in a few easy lessons and the general opinion among the Australians was that he was by far the most dangerous bowler, with Valentine of course, whom they had to face. Even in far off Colombo Len Hutton, on his way back to England, [from a 3:1 victory over Australia] was quoted as having said: "Ramadhin is the best bowler I have played against." [Landsberg, 92]

Ramadhin returned the compliment when he later singled out Hutton as the most difficult batsman he had encountered. [Birbalsingh, *Indenture*, 248]

The reason for omitting Ramadhin and Valentine in 1955 was fear that the Bourda wicket would not take spin, but after inspection by Captain Stollmeyer there was near panic in getting hold of Ramadhin to inform him he could play. In any case, Australia won the Third Test by eight wickets.

The fiasco illustrates the shambolic process for choosing selectors themselves who had to satisfy criteria of race, colour and class. There was public protest, for example, against the choice of a White Barbadian – Denis Atkinson – rather than Frank Worrell as captain in the First Test. Worrell was better qualified than Atkinson; but he was Black. Worrell was the only Black person on the selection panel along with three Whites, one of whom was Atkinson. This is not to disparage Atkinson as a player; in the Fourth Test, he and wicket-keeper Depeiza contrived a magnificent world record partnership of 347 runs which, along with Clyde Walcott's astonishing aggregate of 827 runs in the five Tests, were the two most redeeming features of West Indies performance in the series. [Appendix 14] The Fourth Test was drawn thanks to the extravaganza staged by Atkinson and Depeiza, while the Fifth Test in which Ramadhin did not play was lost by an innings.

Three and a half years after the Melbourne Test that brought Ramadhin to tears, Australian journalist Pat Landsbergh admits some justification in West Indian feelings of grievance over the incident: "Memory recedes slowly in cricket and West Indies felt, to some extent with justification, the victory had eluded them in two volcanic overs and that if the fates had not looked with benevolence upon Ring they [West Indies] might well have gone to Sydney [the Fifth Test] at two-all instead of three-one down." [Landsbergh 17] West Indians would probably prefer to believe it was Australian umpiring rather than the fates that looked with benevolence on Ring.

In the next West Indies venture, their first full series of four Tests against New Zealand, from January to March 1956, Ramadhin reaped a veritable harvest of twenty wickets at the excellent rate of 15.80 apiece, while West Indies persisted with Atkinson as captain while Goddard appeared in the team for the first three Tests only. In the First Test in Dunedin, in February, Ramadhin posted one of the most fruitful returns of his career with six wickets for 23 runs from 21.2 overs, together with his highest ever batting score in Tests – 44 runs.

Altogether Ramadhin collected nine wickets in the match in which West Indies prevailed by an innings and 71 runs, and he almost repeated the feat in the second Test at Christchurch where his pickings were five first innings wickets for 46 runs from 26 overs. This, along with a second century from Weekes, earned West Indies another triumph by an innings, and although Ramadhin managed only three wickets in the Third Test, a third century from a seemingly revitalised Weekes helped the team to another handsome win. But New Zealand turned the tables with a victory in the Fourth Test when Ramadhin had to be contented with only two wickets.

The West Indies tour of England in 1957 is pivotal, serving if not as the end, at least the beginning of the end of his career as a bowler. The First Test of the tour at Edgbaston, in May/June 1957, contained both the high drama and potential for continuing controversy worthy of Shakespearean tragedy. The climax of the tragedy comes after Ramadhin, in the best bowling of his entire career, had despatched seven batsmen for 49 runs in England's first innings of 186 runs, and West Indies had replied with 474. Facing a deficit of 288, England had reached 113 for three when, Peter May (England's captain) and Colin Cowdrey put on a partnership of 411 runs that changed the direction of Ramadhin's career. [Appendix 11] England declared at 583 for three, and shortly after had West Indies at 72 for seven when time ran out and the tourists escaped with a draw.

A partisan West Indian view of the match runs as follows:

> They [May and Cowdrey] were university graduates whom we admired and respected; and they were

obviously acting on a pre-arranged plan. England were 113 for three, 175 runs behind, when Cowdrey came to the wicket. Insole at No. 3 had been bowled for the second time in the game by Ram. Enough was enough. The bats were hidden; the pads were brought out. The game was drawn, and one of the cleverest bowlers to confuse English batsmen had been broken. All is fair in love and war; and what's all that lore about certain things not being cricket? [Figueroa, 78/79]

In Figueroa's opinion, smarting from their "utter defeat in 1950," England decided to, "try to take Ramadhin out of the game of cricket." [Figueroa, 77] He is convinced that the lbw rule was manipulated against Ramadhin by May and Cowdrey going forward without playing a stroke and letting the ball hit their pad, and reports that Goddard, West Indies captain, used the same strategy in the second innings of the match and, "refused to play the ball – except with his pads, and to all intents and purposes dared the umpires to give him out." [Figueroa, 78]

If Figueroa's view is regarded as too partisan, consider the following version of events from staff of the English cricket magazine *Cricket Lore*:

May and Cowdrey came forward to almost every ball, whenever possible pushing their front leg outside the line of off-stump and padding the ball away. It has been conservatively estimated that during this long stand Ram had "at least 50 balls that pitched on or outside the off-stump which would have hit the wicket but were padded away ... without attempting a shot." One of England's leading batsmen of the time has observed that, "this was the biggest farce of all time and ... practically sealed the fate of batsmanship and English cricket." [*Cricket Lore*, November 1991, 36]

Ramadhin bowled 588 deliveries in the second innings of the Edgbaston Test, the most ever in a single innings, and his match total of 774 deliveries is the highest in a Test match. When asked about his experience in the Edgbaston Test Ramadhin answers frankly: "I think it just put an end to my cricketing career. But in the first innings I remember bowling 7 for 49, and then in the second innings Colin Cowdrey and Peter May kept me bowling for two and a half days ... After that Test they all began using their pads to keep the ball out." [Birbalsingh, *Indenture*, 245]

The theory of the plan carried out by May and Cowdrey is outlined by W.E. Bowes in his coverage of the Edgbaston Test in *The Cricketer* at the time of the match:

> I am convinced that the England batsmen must play Ramadhin as an off-spin bowler – a good one, admitted – but never, never, as a bowler who with an undetectable action can bowl leg-break and off-break. His leg-break, I am sure, is nothing more than a roll. It will not turn on a good pitch and if Ramadhin needs to turn it he must toss the ball high in the air or give an unmistakable wristy leg-break action which can be seen by a No. 11.
> [*The Cricketer* Vol. XXXVIII. No. 4, 8 June 1957]

Bowes contradicts Ramadhin's already accepted ability to turn the ball both ways without detection largely to justify his ruse of de-clawing or demystifying Ramadhin to give batsmen the confidence to play him with impunity outside the off-stump. He expresses delight when not only May and Cowdrey but other England batsmen like Close and Richardson adopted his strategy and began to middle the ball.

In his autobiography, Sobers sees through the English stratagem: "English batsmen put the bat behind the pad, pushing the pad out as though it was the first line of defence instead of the bat." [Sobers, 113] To be fair, May and Cowdrey's stratagem caused an outcry, and the lbw rule was later changed so that pads could not be used with impunity to block balls that would hit the wicket. For all that, Ramadhin still gained fourteen wickets, the most among his West Indies team-mates, in their five Tests, of which England won three and two were drawn. But his experience at Edgbaston greatly distorted Ramadhin's series figures with his fourteen wickets costing 547 runs for an average of 39.07.

As for the ill-fated series itself, it is strange how closely it repeats the West Indies ordeal in Australia in 1951/52 when disunity and disarray also spelled disaster. Indeed, West Indies may be said to have done better in Australia in "losing' the Fourth Test by only one wicket and the Fifth by 202 runs whereas, in 1957, they lost both the Fourth and Fifth Tests by an innings. The other similarity is that Goddard, captain both in 1951/52 and 1957, had to give way to another captain for the Fifth Test – in 1952 to Stollmeyer, and in 1957 to Clyde Walcott. In *Sixty Years on the Backfoot* Walcott says he took over as captain because Goddard came down with flu' after the first day's play in 1957. [Walcott, *Sixty Years*, 87]

Ramadhin did not play during the Pakistan visit to West Indies for five Tests in 1957/58. He appeared in two Tests during the West Indies tour of India in 1958/59 when he gained two wickets, and also in two Tests against Pakistan when he gained seven. There was one last brief flourish when he surfaced in four Tests against England in the Caribbean, in 1959/60, and accounted for seventeen wickets, including three occasions when he got three wickets each and one when he got four. But the writing was on the wall with the emergence of younger spin bowlers, notably Lance Gibbs. A new captain was appointed too, mixed blood Gerry Alexander, representing a brief inter-regnum between White and Black captains, before Frank Worrell was crowned as captain for the tour to Australia in 1960/61. Ramadhin appeared in only two Tests under Worrell in Australia, claiming his last three Test wickets, while Gibbs extorted nineteen in three Tests.

Something of a pattern of highs and lows may be detected in Ramadhin's bowling career beginning with a high of 26 wickets against England (1950); low of 14 against Australia (1951/52); high of 12 in two Tests against New Zealand (1952); low of 13 wickets against India (1953); high of 23 wickets against England (1954); low of five wickets against Australia (1955); high of 20 wickets against New Zealand (1956); low of 14 against England (1957); low of 2 wickets against India in two Tests (1958); low of 7 wickets against Pakistan in two Tests (1959); high of 17 wickets against England (1959/60); low of 3 wickets in two Tests against Australia (1960).

His best, most consistent results – 80 wickets for an average of 27.15 – were against England, perhaps because he lived in England since 1950 and knew English players best. He thrived against New Zealand – 32 wickets from only 284.4 overs for an average of 15.06, and also gained 9 wickets from Pakistan for an average of 13.44; his least impressive achievement was against Australia – 22 wickets for an average of 55.13. Ramadhin's career total of 158 Test wickets remained the highest by a West Indian bowler until overtaken by Wes Hall in 1966; and it was gleaned from 43 matches at an average of 28.98. Two of his West Indies Test records, however, still hold good fifty years after his last Test; his match analysis of eleven wickets for 52 runs in the unforgettable Lord's Test of 1950, and his seven wickets for 49 runs against England at Edgbaston in 1957.

From June 1950 at Lord's to May 1957 at Edgbaston, Ramadhin's pioneering effort as the first Indian-Caribbean Test cricketer and the first internationally recognised West Indian spin bowler transformed West Indies fortunes on numerous occasions, and left a lasting impact on West Indian cricket. For one thing it opened the way for other Indian-Caribbean cricketers, and led to the phenomenon of six Indian-Caribbean players appearing on the West Indies team, for the first time, in May 2012. Ramadhin also influenced West Indian attitudes/ prejudices against spin bowling by demonstrating its effectiveness, in consistently spearheading West Indies victories. Most of all, as Cecil Gray affirms, in Ramadhin's hands, the cricket ball, like a regal orb, wielded an influence that many West Indian politicians of that era would have died for; it acted as a symbol of psychological self respect and national identity to a people long tormented by the self hatred of colonial subjects.

In purely cricketing terms, Barbadian cricket historian and statistician Keith Sandiford sums up Ramadhin's career:

> Many of Ramadhin's West Indies bowling records have been surpassed by Guyana's Lance Gibbs, but he still ranks as the second most effective spin bowler thus far produced by the West Indies, a region better known for its galaxy of fast bowlers. As the first player of East Indian ancestry to represent West Indies, he became at once (and has ever since remained) an important role model for Indo-Caribbean cricketers. He is also a vital source of inspiration to under privileged youth everywhere. [Sandiford, *Sonny Ramadhin*, 40]

It is true that some of Ramadhin's bowling records have been overtaken, but his pioneering achievement as the first Caribbean spin bowler to make an impact, worldwide, will endure. What will also endure, as a foundational narrative in any future account of Indian-Caribbean Test cricket, is the example of Ramadhin inspiring change in a West Indies team in which he was just "an Indian in a team full of White and Black men" to a more representative one, not only with spin bowlers like Devendra Bishoo and Sunil Narine, but with other Indian-Caribbean players like themselves.

CHAPTER 2

Rohan Kanhai: A new dimension in batting

In his already quoted essay "A Study in Confidence," C.L.R. James suggests that Kanhai's batting may contain aspects of West Indian identity and asserts: "He [Kanhai] discovered, created a new dimension in batting." [James, *Rendezvous*, 169] It is hard to be precise about something as dynamic as national identity. James sees in Kanhai, "a West Indian proving to himself that henceforth he was following no established pattern but would create his own." [James, *Rendezvous*, 169] What James detects, it seems, is a species of Whitmanesque individualism: "That could be Greek Dionysius, the satyric passion for the expression of the natural man, bursting through the restraints of disciplined necessity." [James, *Rendezvous*, 169]

As with Whitman too, the first major English-speaking poet in the Americas, individualism is hard to define (Whitman's persona, for example, boasts of containing multitudes), but it is not surprising that James sees something of Whitman's breathless, New World ambition in Kanhai's batting, and perhaps what he sees is not very different from what the Barbadian novelist George Lamming discerns in Kanhai as the most original batsman of his time; for Whitman was nothing if not original, and whatever else one may fault Kanhai for, whether a disinterest in statistical rigour, or distaste for persevering merely to avoid defeat, there is no shortage of originality, daring or adventure in his quest for identity.

Like Ramadhin, who came from rural Trinidad, Rohan Bholalall Kanhai was born in Port Mourant, a sugar plantation in the county of Berbice, Guyana, where he lived not far from other Guyanese who also became Test cricketers, for example, John Trim, Basil Butcher, Joe Solomon and Ivan Madray. In *Blasting for Runs*, Kanhai is unapologetic for his adventurous style of batting which he ascribes to the calypso: "Put it all down to the calypso spirit in which West Indians love to play their cricket. Or the fact that [like Ramadhin] I've had no coaching whatsoever from the day I was born." [Kanhai, 11] There is some confusion whether he was coached by Clyde Walcott who went to Guyana in 1954 to develop cricket on sugar plantations, and was stationed at Plantation Albion, near to Port Mourant; even if there was no formal coaching, Walcott certainly encouraged Kanhai.

Born on 26 December 1935, Kanhai's first chance to play First Class cricket came in 1954 when a vacancy was created by the illness of a Berbice cricketer who had been selected to play in a match in Georgetown. [Appendix 9] Like Ramadhin again, Kanhai was not accustomed to urban manners or technology: "I had never even seen a first class match before let alone played in one. Names like Walcott and Pairaudeau [then current West Indian players who lived in Georgetown] belonged to the newspapers and radio, not real everyday life on the sugar plantation." [Kanhai, 20] His appearance in the Georgetown match led to trial matches, and selection for Guyana against the touring Australians, in 1955, when he impressed everyone by scoring 51 and 27. The next year he did better with 129 against Jamaica at Bourda, and 195 against Barbados also at Bourda and, irresistibly, he was picked for the West Indies team to tour England in 1957.

Prospects for the tour were not good. John Goddard, the West Indies captain on the victorious 1950 tour, had played no Test cricket between 1952 and 1955, taken part in only a few Test matches in New Zealand in 1956, and was suddenly thrust into the captaincy of West Indies in 1957. At the same time, Stollmeyer, his arch rival, promptly withdrew from First Class cricket. In his book *My Story: The Other Side of the Coin*, Andy Ganteaume reports that Stollmeyer, "always had a burning desire to captain West Indies on tour." [Ganteaume, 50] As it happens, Stollmeyer's relationship with the President of the West Indies Cricket Board, Sir Errol Dos Santos, nicknamed the 'Great White Lord,' was "fractured irreparably," and Dos Santos reinstated Goddard as captain, [Appendix 10] making it look like the fate of West Indian cricket was at the mercy of a few White men and their peccadilloes. No wonder Everton Weekes betrays some vehemence in his Preface to Ganteaume's book: "The atrocities that existed and prevailed way back when West Indies was given Test match status must be properly recorded. The injustices experienced by some players mainly because of social and economic advantages must not be allowed to go unnoticed." [Ganteaume, iv]

How much all this affected Kanhai personally cannot be unrelated to the spectacular failure of the West Indies team of which he was part, in England, in 1957. He was picked as opening batsman and wicket-keeper for the First Test at Edgbaston, which today acquires notoriety as Ramadhin's Waterloo. Gerry Alexander, the first rank wicket-keeper stood down because he could not read Ramadhin and, as we know, England were shot out by Ramadhin for 186 on the first day, after which Kanhai and Pairaudeau opened for West Indies. Pairaudeau was quickly yorked by Trueman, and Walcott and Kanhai took West Indies to 83 for one by the end of the first day with Walcott on 40 and Kanhai 42. The next day, first ball, Kanhai was lbw to a straight half-volley from Statham; he didn't prosper in the second innings either, which brought him exactly one run.

In the Second Test at Lord's West Indies were thrashed by an innings, and Kanhai could muster scores of only 34 and 0. He did a little better in the drawn Third Test with 42 and 28, and reached a tally of 47 in the Fourth Test before England swept the series 3:0, with two matches drawn. Kanhai admits that the innings' defeat in the Fifth Test when West Indies were reduced to shameful totals of 89 and 86 was, "the worst display it's been my misfortune to see in nine years of Test cricket." [Kanhai, 35] Goddard was reported ill with influenza in the Fifth Test in which Walcott took over as captain.

As a member of the 1957 West Indies touring team who didn't play in any Test, Andy Ganteaume reports: "West Indies fielded first [in the Fifth Test] and after the first day Captain Goddard was not seen again on the cricket field. On the following day I heard that he could not play in the rest of the match." [Ganteaume, 55] It seems that disorganisation reigned throughout Kanhai's inauspicious entry into Test cricket. He scrambled to a total of 206 runs in five Tests, and scraped together an average of 22.88. His 1,093 runs for an average of 31.22 in First Class matches slightly redeem him, although he ended the tour without a century in thirty-nine innings. Someone who is often seen as a rival batsman, Garry Sobers, scored 320 Test runs for an average of 32.00, with 66 as his highest score, and outstripped Kanhai with 1644 runs, an average of 43.26, three centuries, and a highest score of 219 in First Class matches.

For the next series, against Pakistan in 1958, Alexander was appointed captain when Kanhai preferred Collie Smith or Worrell.

[Kanhai, 39] Kanhai makes no secret of his admiration for Worrell: "He [Worrell] is without a shadow of a doubt, the greatest skipper and handler of men it has been my good fortune to meet." [Kanhai, 39] Five months after their defeat at Kennington Oval, West Indies started their first home Test against Pakistan whom they resoundingly defeated 3:1. Five Tests passed without a century from Kanhai, although he reached 96 in the first innings of the Second Test and an aggregate of 299 in the series, followed by an average of 37.37 almost doubling his figures in England a few months before. His team-mate Sobers, meanwhile, achieved a [then] world record score of 365 not out in the Third Test, a series aggregate of 824, and an average of 137.3.

If he was not exactly in Sobers's league, in the next West Indies rubber, in India in 1958/59, Kanhai demonstrated batting gifts of his own. In the first innings of the Second Test at Kanpur, Subash Gupte who had toured West Indies in 1953, struck with nine wickets, and reduced West Indies to a total of 222, including Kanhai for a duck. West Indies then set India an impossible target that they failed to reach by 203 runs. Kanhai was Gupte's victim twice in the match. Whether there is any truth in a story that this led to Gupte boasting that Kanhai was his rabbit, Kanhai cut loose in the Third Test at Kolkata, and recorded a score of 256 that included forty-two fours and a partnership of 217 with his fellow Guyanese, Basil Butcher, who chalked up his maiden Test century – 103.

This huge total, the highest in Kanhai's Test career, was both a personal landmark, and the highest individual score in a Test in India until it was eclipsed by V.V.S. Laxman's 281 against Australia in Kolkata in March 2001. The margin of victory too (an innings and 336 runs) was then the second largest in Test cricket. It helped Kanhai achieve his highest series aggregate (538 runs) and a tour average of 67.25.

In a three-match rubber with Pakistan, the home team prevailed in the first Two Tests in Karachi and Dacca where Fazal Mahmood was virtually unplayable on matting wickets. Kanhai recalls: "Nothing, of course, really overcame Fazal and his mat. This combination was the reason why Pakistan never lost a home series." [Kanhai, 48] A turf pitch in Lahore told a different story. West Indies won by an innings and 156 runs following another double century (217) from Kanhai; and the three Pakistan matches altogether yielded 274 runs to Kanhai and an average of 54.80. At last Kanhai's batting seemed to have gained its stride.

Kanhai argues that the absence from Pakistan of Roy Gilchrist who had topped the West Indies bowling averages in India, was: "the major reason for our defeat in Pakistan." [Kanhai, 47] Gilchrist was sent home from India because of bowling beamers after being warned to desist by his captain, Gerry Alexander. Kanhai reveals: "A few of us formed a deputation to plead Gilchrist's cause but the rift was too great to be bridged." [Kanhai, 47] Kanhai's plantation origin enables him to see deeper implications of the incident as expressing a "rift" in the relationship between Alexander and Gilchrist, rather than a simple difference of opinion.

The rift sprang from differences between Alexander's 'brown', middle class Jamaican background along with his training as a veterinary surgeon at Cambridge University, and Gilchrist's origin in the Black, Jamaican working class. No doubt there are fraught relationships between members of other teams based on class/race/religion/speech/ culture or personal matters. Not long ago English cricketers were divided between Gentlemen and Players, essentially class criteria, and India's cricketers also began playing in teams segregated by religion. Apartheid in South Africa was legally institutionalised; another thing altogether. But the Alexander/Gilchrist saga is rooted in the uniquely divisive soil of Caribbean race/class/colour relationships of which both men were historic victims.

Gilchrist perceived real or imagined provocation from his captain and responded in a way that, for the sake of team discipline, no responsible captain could tolerate. In his book, *Hit me for Six*, Gilchrist expresses the class division between him and Alexander as he saw it: "The trouble with the whole outlook between us was that I always had a feeling that Gilly on the plantation could never be on the same level as Gerry from the varsity. While fellows knew me as Roy Gilchrist, or Gilly, everyone seemed to regard Gerry as Mr F.C.M. Alexander, Cambridge University and West Indies." [Gilchrist, 115] Kanhai also comments on the incident: "... he [Gilchrist] was not always the naughty, undisciplined problem boy built up by one or two officials and the Press ... I reckon a few individuals ruined Gilly on that tour ... But underneath was a real nice guy – if he took to you. Somehow you never hear the tales of the fellows he's helped with a few words of advice and encouragement." [Kanhai, 38/39]

In a region where, after Emancipation, offence could be given or taken at the drop of a hat, social relations are a minefield. Andy Ganteaume explains how Goddard gave offence to players in England, in 1957, by his generally distant manner, and setting his field by pointing and calling out to players, for instance, the wicket-keeper: "You behind". [Ganteaume, 55] Whether he realised it or not, Goddard's instructions ran the risk of arousing ancestral memories of a colonial, slave society in which a White master gives orders to his Black slave who lacks either name or identity.

The First Test match in Kanhai's second encounter with England, this time in the Caribbean, ended in a draw after large first innings scores from both sides. Until the Second Test at Queen's Park Oval in Trinidad in January/February 1960, only three Indian-Caribbean players – Ramadhin, Kanhai and Solomon – had represented West Indies. These three were now joined by a fourth Indian-Caribbean player, Trinidadian spin bowler C.K. Singh who had the misfortune, in his début match, to be involved in an incident which caused a bigger disruption than at Bourda in 1954. Police reinforcements and a riot squad with helmets and batons were needed to restore order. As with the previous incident too, the exact cause was never discovered.

All that we know is that after England had hoisted a first innings total of 382, West Indies were blown away by England fast bowlers Trueman and Statham who had reduced their opponents to 98 for 8 when Singh joined Ramadhin. As a batsman Ramadhin's previous highest score against England was 19, yet he now took it into his head to shelter his young partner by trying to keep the strike and going for a run on the last ball of an over. E.W. Swanton remarks: "Could irony and bathos be stretched further?" [Swanton, *West Indies Revisited*, 111] For it was the attempt to steal this run that got Singh run out and triggered the disturbance. Umpire Lee Kow's decision on the run-out was unimpeachable. Singh himself did not wait for a decision but continued his run straight into the pavilion.

There was some advance notice of discontent over the West Indies Cricket Board's decision to ban Gilchrist from playing in the home series against England. A slogan voicing discontent was circulated before England arrived registering historic feelings in Black West Indians of victimisation by a White coloniser who can take many shapes and forms, in this case, the White officialdom of West Indian cricket.

But no hostility was expressed toward the England team, and the England captain Peter May tried to keep his men on the field, as Hutton had done at Bourda, until the situation became too explosive.

After his highly successful visit to India and Pakistan one year earlier, Kanhai's first two innings against England were disappointing. In the First Test in Barbados where Sobers and Worrell piled up huge scores, Kanhai fell victim to Trueman for 40, and in the first innings in the Second Test in Trinidad he again succumbed to Trueman, lbw for 5, and West Indies collapsed to 112. England then added 230 runs for nine wickets in their second innings, leaving West Indies a forbidding target of 500 runs. Yet, as wickets tumbled around him, Kanhai mounted one of his most memorable displays of batsmanship, accumulating 110 runs when facing impossible odds. Maybe he was fighting a lost cause from the start but, at lunch, West Indies were 184 for four and soon afterwards, Butcher fell. In the midst of such peril, Kanhai hit Trueman for 15 runs in one over and reached his century. Then, with his score at 110, he was out, mis-hitting a full toss from Dexter to mid-wicket.

Swanton surmises: "It is typical for a West Indies cricketer to express his defiance in terms of strokes." [Swanton, *West Indies Revisited*, 129] Alexander was still there shortly before tea, but Kanhai did not relish grafting. After spending six and a quarter hours at the crease, he feels he had played: "a subdued, back-to-the-wall innings." [Kanhai, 60] and confesses: "Playing against the grain like that takes some willpower." [Kanhai, 60] His 110 remains the signature innings of his career – bold, brassy, inventive and combative – but one wonders if his brassiness did not make it easier for England to win the Second Test when only one session and a bit of the match remained.

After running himself out for 18 in the first innings of the next Test in Jamaica, Kanhai had passed 50 in the second innings, and needed a runner because of cramp when Peter May, the England captain of Edgbaston 1957 fame, refused to allow it. Since the umpires couldn't make a firm decision Kanhai had to do without a runner, and continued batting in evident pain. Soon afterward, he was bowled by Trueman for 57. It was later found that May's consent for a runner was not required by the rules, and he apologised both to Kanhai and his captain, Alexander, after West Indies had lost the match. It is strange that a man who applied rules about pad play so strictly to frustrate Ramadhin at Edgbaston in 1957, this time applied a non-existent rule to frustrate West Indies fortunes yet again. Immediately afterwards, May had to return home because of illness, and the two remaining Tests were drawn with England winning the rubber one: nil, and Kanhai settling for a series aggregate of 325 and average of 40.62.

The next rubber, in Australia, marks the beginning of the most productive period for Kanhai. Frank Worrell was appointed as West Indies captain for the series, the first Black player to hold this position. The bitter controversy that surrounded Worrell's appointment only goes to prove the intimately intermixed relationship between cricket and social issues of race/colour/class/ethnicity in the Caribbean. Since Kanhai's admiration for Worrell has already been mentioned, it may not be entirely fanciful to see a connection between Worrell's captaincy and Kanhai's increased productivity after 1960/61.

Kanhai did not make a major contribution to the First Test in Brisbane, the first tied Test in history, except that his 54 was the second highest score in the West Indies second innings. He did better in the Second Test with a score of 84 which rescued the West Indies first innings of 181 from a much worse fate. Kanhai's batting in the Third Test also did not lift off. Not until the Fourth Test at Adelaide did he unleash scores of 117 and 115 to become the, "first West Indian to hit a century in both innings [of a Test match] in Australia." [Kanhai, 74] For those concerned about the cavalier/calypso approach to the serious business of Test match batting, Kanhai freely admits: "I've never attached much importance to figures in record books (dull reading I think) but this [his two centuries in Adelaide] is one entry of which I am deeply proud." [Kanhai, 74] It boosted his reputation in Australia enough for Richie Benaud the Australia captain to consider Kanhai as better than Sobers.

Kanhai reached the highest Test aggregate for the series – 503 runs for an average of 50.30, but took second place in the Test averages behind Alexander who recorded 60.50 runs. Kanhai's over all performance, including First Class matches, brought him a record aggregate of 1,093 runs for the season, 359 runs more than Alexander who came second with 734 runs. His highest score, 252 against Victoria at Melbourne, also helped him to the highest average of 64.29 among his team-mates, and he was awarded the Karl Nunes Trophy for the outstanding West Indies of the tour.

Bringing back memories of the Melbourne Test in January 1952 Kanhai comments on, "a suspect umpiring decision" [Kanhai, 75] in the Adelaide Test when the umpire disallowed a confident West Indies appeal for a catch by Sobers off Worrell's bowling. In this case, Kanhai writes: "Now this was never a bump ball and everyone knew it except [umpire] Egar and [the Australian batsman] Mackay." [Kanhai, 75] At that stage of the rubber, with one win each, and a tie and a draw, there was everything to play for in the Fifth Test at Melbourne. Here again Kanhai reports what he calls, "our second bad umpiring decision." [Kanhai, 77] The Australia wicket keeper Wally Grout played on when late cutting a ball from Valentine, and the umpires ruled not out. [Photographs later showed that Grout had played on and was out, but the umpire claimed to be justified in ruling not out because he was unsighted] Sportingly, Grout deliberately skied his next ball and got out.

Kanhai's next series, against India in the Caribbean, was something of an anticlimax. Worrell's inspired generalship and various Indian problems colluded to produce a complete rout in which India lost all five Test matches, mostly by very wide margins. West Indies, under Worrell, were at their peak, while India was totally outclassed. Besides, India lost their captain Nari Contractor after he suffered serious head injury from a ball by Charlie Griffith in the Barbados colony match, and the reins of captaincy were passed to the young, untried Nawab of Pataudi from the Third Test in Barbados. Worse still, India had left behind probably their best bowler, Subash Gupte, who was banned after an incident during India's tour of England a little earlier. Kanhai revelled in these conditions chalking up two centuries, the first (138) in the Second Test in Jamaica, and the second (139) in the Fourth Test in Port of Spain. He was also run-out for 89 in the Barbados Test which pushed him to an aggregate of 495 runs and the best tour average of his Test career – 70.71.

Confidence from his Australian and Indian successes, propelled Kanhai into another five-match rubber, in 1963, his second tour of England and, sadly, the last before Worrell's retirement and premature death at the age of forty-two. Ninety runs and another run-out in the First Test, at Old Trafford was beginning to look like a habit reflecting on Kanhai's temperament, and it leaves him rueful: "The tragedy of Kanhai one paper called it. I prefer the Foolishness of Kanhai, for I felt in my bones that this could have been one of the greatest innings I have ever played." [Kanhai, 97] This sounds plausible: Kanhai's immediately preceding series totals of 503 runs in Australia and 495 runs against India, proclaim a consistency he had never previously attained.

He followed up with 73 in the first innings of the next Test at Lord's, famous for Hall hurling thunderbolts to a one-armed Cowdrey in the final moments of the game. Kanhai's 92 in the Fourth Test at Headingley – yet another missed century – surely betrays signs of profligacy. But the crowning event of both the tour and Kanhai's career was his second innings score in the Fifth Test at the Oval after England had set West Indies a target of 255 to win, and Kanhai's whirlwind innings sealed victory by eight wickets.

Obviously, for Kanhai, neither runs nor statistics count for as much as style; pure glamour, poise and polish. Hunte and Rodriguez had put on 78 for the first wicket when Kanhai entered the fray; 177 runs were needed. Only six weeks before, Trueman, Shackleton and Dexter had bowled West Indies out at Edgbaston for 91. The respite now was that Trueman, the chief enemy, was injured and out of action. Still, England had Statham, Close and Lock in addition to Shackleton and Dexter; the coast was not entirely clear. But we could tell what was coming from Kanhai's first innings when he was caught for 30 off Lock.

Ian Woolridge discerned Kanhai's mood after he had swept Lock for four and squeezed Shackleton over his head: "The indignity of the shot seemed to infuriate him [Kanhai]. Next ball he flung back his head, bent clearly on hitting it clean over the pavilion. Not even Kanhai could hold the rules in such contempt; he swished clean over the ball instead and was bowled for 30." [Woolridge, 146] In this mood, in the second innings, through a mesmerising display of innovation, imagination and sheer gall, in merely 90 minutes, Kanhai somehow contrived 77 exultant runs that included ten fours and one six which he hooked off Lock, as he and Hunte added 113 runs altogether, of which Hunte contributed 36, less than half his partner's portion!

Seldom on a cricket field has devastation induced such awe, wonder and ecstasy! Brian Close, for example, whose naked chest still bore marks of blows he endured from Hall and Griffith in the Second Test not long before, and whose six overs were now being mercilessly pummelled by Kanhai to the tune of 36 runs, could do nothing but stand helplessly by, watching his hapless deliveries contemptuously despatched to the boundary, and simply join in the applause of a crowd that seemed to be swaying hopelessly lost in delight and delirium. J.S. Barker catches the crowd's mood: "Those who had the space to do so indulged in a demonstration which was a cross between gymnastics, acrobatics and a war dance." [Barker, *Summer Spectacular*, 108]

Kanhai had achieved his aim to entertain the crowd, and went out laughing as Woolridge notes after he crashed a four with his falling hook: "Two balls later, trying a still more audacious sweep he [Kanhai] was caught knee-high by Bolus at mid-wicket and went out laughing hugely." [Woolridge, 156] This is what James also noticed in Kanhai's innings of 170 against Trevor Bailey's side at Edgbaston in 1964 which elicited his remarks about regions Bradman never knew: "All through that demanding innings Kanhai grinned with a grin that could be seen a mile away." [James, *Rendezvous*, 170] For Lara also entertainment was a prime aim as he admitted when he retired from Test cricket during the 2007 Cricket World Cup, and rhetorically asked the crowd, to resounding cheers, "Did I entertain you?"

That Kanhai's entertainment had a lasting effect was proved one year after the Oval Test in 1963 when I attended the Fifth Test between Australia and England at the same ground, one day in August, 1964, before the start of play, and was accosted by a young Indian-Guyanese man, a complete stranger, who desperately wanted to show me the exact spot on the outfield where Kanhai's six off Lock had dropped one year before. In the vast outfield of the Oval, who could remember one spot of grass from one year ago! For this young man fact had been translated into belief and, as all true followers of cricket know, when fact becomes legend, print the legend. Kanhai's 77 at the Oval in 1963 is second in popular memory only to his 110 against England, in 1960, in Trinidad. [Appendix 9]

His next five-Test rubber was with Australia in the Caribbean, from March to May 1965, when Kanhai struck a healthy aggregate of 462 runs and an average of 46.20. This time, though, it was under Sobers' captaincy, with both teams competing for the unofficial championship of the cricketing world, a title which West Indies coveted since their abortive visit to Australia 1951. Sobers accomplished his task as Worrell's heir when he won the so-called world championship by inflicting a 2:1 defeat, with two drawn matches, on Australia. The forces Sobers commanded, after all, were the identical to those under Worrell, except for one or two minor changes. After a low-scoring

First Test which West Indies won in Jamaica, Kanhai notched up one score of 53 in the Second Test in Trinidad and another of 89 in the Third, on his home ground in Guyana, betraying again a seeming penchant for scores over fifty but not over 100, only to come through with 129 in the Fourth Test and 121 in the Fifth.

Kanhai seems to have lost form at the beginning of the 1966 West Indies tour to England when he struggled with a score of 0 in the First Test and 25 and 40 in the second. He rallied to register a studied 104 in the Fifth Test at the Oval, and finished with a Test aggregate of 324 and an average of 40.80. The series, which West Indies won comprehensively 3:1 with one draw, was entirely dominated by Sobers who recorded three centuries, an aggregate of 722 runs and an average of 103.14. Such flagrant discrepancies in batting statistics of Kanhai and Sobers should settle the matter of rivalry in the popular imagination; but it continues. Sunil Gavaskar, for instance, no slouch himself in creating batting statistics, declares that Kanhai is a better batsman than Sobers, while the latter is the supreme all round cricketer. Kanhai impressed Gavaskar enough for him (Gavaskar) to name his son 'Rohan'. Many West Indians, apparently, including Kanhai's fellow batsman Kallicharran and the reggae singer Bob Marley also named their sons similarly.

In an interview with Rajan Bala in 'A Flashing Blade, a Canny Mind', Kanhai admits: "My rivalry with Sobie [Sobers] might have been there initially but then Frank Worrell talked to us about how we were both bulwarks of the batting ... Sobie is the greatest all-rounder ever. But I like to think I had a role to play in influencing batsmen like Clive Lloyd and Alvin Kallicharran." [WEB, 2009] In his *Autobiography*, Sobers admits to, "some sort of riffle between Rohan Kanhai and myself. It was supposedly caused by a little jealousy on Rohan's part; it was said he was happy only when he made more runs than me." [Sobers, 77] Sobers claims he never believed the rumour and, agrees that Worrell settled the matter by advising that Kanhai should bat at No. 3 and Sobers at No. 5 or No. 6, so that it would encourage Kanhai to go for a big score every time, since he could not anticipate how many runs Sobers would make later on. According to Sobers, Worrell realised that he [Sobers] was more adaptable and would be capable of defending if the team was short of runs, or attacking if earlier batsmen had scored heavily.

In his essay 'The Caribbean Flavour' Neville Cardus describes Kanhai as a, "West Indian cricketer ... who often seems to have only one object in life – to hit a cricket ball for six into the crowd at square leg, falling on his back after performing the great swinging hit. The impetus of the hit, its sheer animal gusto, brings him down to earth, but it is a triumphant fall." [Cardus, *A Fourth Innings*, 112] Cardus groups Kanhai with great West Indian cricketers like Headley, Constantine, Worrell, Weekes, Walcott, Sobers, Ramadhin and Valentine. How revealing that perhaps the greatest cricket writer of all should see no difference between the first two Indian-Caribbean Test cricketers and their team-mates or predecessors! Cardus may be going too far in seeing Ramadhin and Kanhai as identical to their fellow West Indians but, like James, he perceives Creole elements in them.

Cardus thinks of Constantine as the first exponent of a recognisable, West Indian cricket style, and finds his movements "swift and apparently unpremeditated," whilst he uses his bat as "an exultant announcement of his own and his countrymen's physical abandon and disregard of all bourgeois decorum." [Cardus, 113] Cardus hopes that prowess in Test cricket doesn't "over-rationalise instinct" in West Indian players: "For all their acquired technical sophistications let there be some echo of the calypso to the end." [Cardus, 113] It is the calypso quality of Kanhai's cricket that Cardus means when he calls for cricket to be instinctive rather than over-rationalised; it is not very different from James's own vision of "satyric passion" in Kanhai, and reminiscent of a discredited negritudinist argument that sees European culture as rational and African as more instinctive or natural. The negritudinist contrast is too generalised and sweeping, and inspires the sort of joke by an English journalist who sneers at "calypso-collapso" West Indian cricketers. [Figueroa, 92] Perhaps Cardus is too influenced by Constantine, the ebullient one-day, limited-overs cricketer *par excellence*.

Like Whitman, Kanhai possesses more inspiration and innovation than balance, judgment or restraint. It is impossible to compare Sobers and Kanhai as Test cricketers because no one can compare with Sobers' extraordinary, all-round exploits in batting, fielding, catching, bowling in different styles, and serving as captain. Sobers is again miles ahead of Kanhai in batting statistics. In his Test career Sobers scored 8,032 runs, 26 centuries, and 35 fifties for an average of 57.78, while Kanhai scarcely compares with 6,227 runs, 15 centuries and 25 fifties for an average of 47.53. But as James argues: "Cricket is first and foremost a dramatic spectacle. It belongs with theatre, ballet, opera and the dance." [James, *Boundary*, 192] Kanhai and Sobers are closer as artists. While technique, originality, variety and beauty of stroke play are basic criteria of assessment, runs also matter, and since cricket is both contest and entertainment, the size of a batsman's score can be crucial to victory. Going down with guns blazing may be entertaining, even uplifting; but it is not the same as the joint triumph of entertaining batsmanship and success through scoring runs.

James takes full measure of Kanhai by identifying his batting as the result of a struggle between passion and reason or discipline. The new dimension he also identifies is the Creole aspect of Kanhai's Indian-Caribbean personality, for this is surprisingly new. Kanhai is not Creole like Sobers, a descendant of people (Europeans and Africans) who have been Creolised in a Caribbean environment for centuries. He is a relatively new arrival. While it is no surprise that Sobers's batting should have antecedents, especially in Barbados, in the likes of Challenor, Walcott and Worrell, it would be a surprise for Kanhai's batting to reflect identical Creole elements as Sobers. Kanhai's direct antecedents are more likely the impulsiveness of Constantine, and the romantic poise, gallantry and artistry of his Guyanese countryman, Robert Julian Christiani, a Creole of African/Italian ancestry.

A glance at the Test career results of Constantine and Christiani clinches their similarity: Constantine – 18 matches, 635 runs for an average of 19.24; Christiani – 22 matches, 896 runs for an average of 26.35. In his day, in matches that lacked restraints of Test match competition, Constantine was incomparable. In the well known West Indies county match against Middlesex in 1928, his scores of 86 and 103 and seven wickets in one innings won an imperishable victory for West Indies, while Christiani's statistics in First class matches – 5103 runs for an average of 40.50 – more than double his Test match figures. They were romantic calypso cricketers like Kanhai and direct progenitors of his new dimension of batting.

Kanhai's falling hook which Cardus christens as "triumphant" is an aspect of this new dimension: the unique creation of a smaller man who drops to the ground from the sheer effort of imparting fullest power to his stroke. It is further proof of Kanhai's originality; it inspires gaping incredulity and pure rhapsodic delight in spectators who, if they remember Kanhai for nothing else will never forget this. It is fresh, new and creative enough to merit the caption of genius. As Ian McDonald writes in *Cricket at Bourda*: "I have not yet seen any cricketer, any sportsman, so touched by the Gods with genius as Rohan Kanhai." [Camacho, 89] McDonald also notices Kanhai's ability to invest ordinary, run-of-the-mill strokes with rare appeal, for example, the simple, forward defensive stroke which, in Kanhai's hands, becomes a thing of beauty, in John Keats's phrase, "a joy forever". It is surely genius for an elementary stroke, in Kanhai's hands, to cause cheering crowds to leap to their feet as they might do when another batsman hits a six. The same may be said for Kanhai's majestic cover drive or his square cut, strokes that glory in purely romantic virtues of grace, elegance and style for the sake of itself.

The new dimension of Kanhai's batting is also seen as romanticism by Michael Gibbes who chooses phrases such as the "Peter Pan of West Indian cricket," or "a puckish and daring stroke player," or yet again as "a dynamic, evergreen, turnstile-clicking cavalier of the willow" to capture Kanhai's prime qualities. For Gibbes, Kanhai's "endearing indiscretions," place him in the mould of batsmen like Trumper, Woolley, McCabe and Wilton St Hill: "With Kanhai as with all truly outstanding batsmen of this [romantic] type the rumbustious and aesthetic elements complement, yet somehow overshadow mere statistical and functional value." [Michael Gibbes, *Kanhai/Gibbs*, 15] This is the dilemma in assessing Kanhai: whether his romantic qualities compensate for batting statistics that do not quite fulfil expectations from his rampant early promise.

Trumper played forty-eight Test matches and scored 3163 runs for an average of only 39.04, while Bradman played fifty-two Test matches, and scored 6990 runs for an average of 99.94. Kanhai's 110 in the Second Test against England, in Trinidad, 1960 is like Trumper's 214 not out for Australia in their Third Test against South Africa in 1911. West Indies lost by 256 runs in spite of Kanhai's effort, and Australia lost by 38 runs despite Trumper's exertions. But the highest individual West Indies score after Kanhai's was 47 out of a total of 244, and the highest individual Australia score after Trumper's 214 not out was 54 out of a total of 465. One distinguishing quality of the romantic is to stand out of the line, not to follow fashion, but to take singular satisfaction in courting style, elegance, beauty. The romantic may not come off as often as we may wish, but when he does, there is nothing like it. James's unforgettable portrait of Wilton St Hill in *Beyond a Boundary* offers eloquent confirmation of his subject's essentially romantic qualities, as does Robert Christiani's century in each innings against Middlesex, at Lord's, during the West Indies tour of England in 1950.

A bad knee reduced Kanhai's Test appearances after 1966 although he managed three Tests on the West Indies tour to India in 1966/67 when he played two notable innings of 90 and 77. He seemed to return to full strength during England's tour of West Indies in 1968/69 when he amassed 535 runs. What is notable about this England tour is an uncharacteristic satisfaction in runs rather than style, for instance, in two scores of 153 in the Fourth Test in Trinidad, and 150 in the Fifth Test in Guyana. In his career, as a whole, he registered twenty-eight scores between 50 and 100, fifteen between 100 and 150, three between 150 and 200, and two double centuries. In India's tour of the Caribbean in 1971, Kanhai posted 158 in the first Test in Jamaica and finished with 433 runs and a tour average of 54.12. He had reached a stage of seasoned maturity as a batsman and seniority as a cricketer.

The approach of the end of Kanhai's career coincided with a crisis in leadership of the West Indies team. When Sobers took over as captain in 1965 it was more or less through anointment by the revered Worrell. As heir to the best team in the world, it was no surprise that Sobers luxuriated in victories against Australia in 1965, England in 1966, and India in 1966/67. But West Indies fortunes began to ebb when they lost to Australia in 1968/69, and could only draw with weak New Zealand in 1969. With further losses against England in 1969 and India in 1971, followed by five drawn matches with New Zealand in 1972, a change in captaincy loomed.

But there would be no anointment this time, for West Indian independence in the 1960s had changed social and political conditions from the 1950s when controversy inevitably preceded the appointment of Worrell as the first Black West Indies captain. It was then felt that traditional colonial criteria of race/class and colour by which West Indies Test cricket captains had been chosen from 1928 to 1960 were gone for good. Now, however, seven years after Sobers' anointment, it appeared that the old colonial demons had not disappeared: they

Considered to be the most original batsmen of his time, Rohan Kanhai's style of play was nothing short of daring. He is pictured in April 1966 during a match against the Duke of Norfolk's XI at Arundel. BOB THOMAS/GETTY IMAGES

had simply transmuted themselves into new goblins by adding post-colonial politics to the old formula of race/class/ colour and insidious insularity or parochialism.

According to Sobers: "Between 1969 and 1973 tours of England, I gave up the captaincy. They had to find a new captain for the Aussies 1972-73 trip to the Caribbean." [Sobers, 100] As outgoing captain, after being asked, Sobers first suggested his cousin David Holford as the new captain, although Holford was not a member of the team at the time. He then changed his mind when he thought a relative would not be acceptable: "I offered Clive Lloyd as an alternative choice, but Clive had not even been invited to join the squad for preparation for the series. So if they weren't prepared to pick him, my third choice would be Rohan Kanhai." [Sobers, 100] As in all his comments, Lloyd is outspoken about Kanhai's selection as captain: "When Kanhai was appointed as his [Sobers'] successor, there were several raised eyebrows, for he did not have an exactly saintly reputation in his many years in international cricket." [Lloyd, *Living*, 56] Still, Lloyd acknowledges Kanhai's, "sense of responsibility to the job and his total involvement [that] communicated itself to the rest of the team." [Lloyd, 56]

Kanhai served as captain in three series: against Australia in the Caribbean in early 1973 when West Indies lost two matches and drew three; against England in 1973 when West Indies won two matches and drew one; and against England in the Caribbean when the series was drawn 1:1 with three drawn matches. That makes for a total of thirteen matches of which three were won, three lost and seven drawn under Kanhai's captaincy. Kanhai batted best against Australia gathering 358 runs for an average of 51.14; 223 against England in England for an average of 44.60; and 157 against England in the Caribbean for an average of 26.66. When Clive Lloyd was appointed captain, beginning with a series against India in 1974/75, the circumstances surrounding his appointment raised the spectre of political intervention.

In early 1972 when the New Zealand/West Indies series ended with five draws, Lloyd's standing was not thought good enough for him to be included among West Indian players who were being considered for selection in the coming series with Australia in early 1973. Lloyd felt disillusioned: "I had become disillusioned with Test cricket in any case and I now felt under no obligation to the West Indies. When a contract to play club cricket for South Melbourne in Australia for the 1972/73 season was offered as a replacement for Tony Greig I accepted, even though I knew it would effectively eliminate me from playing at home." [Lloyd, *Living*, 51]

Later Lloyd was asked by the Chair of West Indian selectors to stand by for selection because one player, Sobers, was having surgery and would create a vacancy. Lloyd correctly assesses the implication if he were to spend the 1972/73 season in Australia: "how could they [West Indian selectors] choose me if I wasn't around?" [Lloyd, *Living*, 51] But the question was answered for him: "It was a question which did not bother me much but it did bother the Prime Minister of Guyana, Forbes Burnham, who proceeded to have me return from Australia so that I *would* be around. He wrote to the Prime Minister of Australia, Gough Whitlam, a personal friend, asking him to use his influence to have South Melbourne release me, an unusual step to say the least." [Lloyd, *Living*, 51]

Upon his return to England where he lived, Lloyd was told by the Guyana High Commissioner in London that the Guyana government would pay his passage back to Guyana; but he was apprehensive: "I realised it would be interpreted as political interference in some quarters." [Lloyd *Living*, 51] Lloyd returned to the Caribbean and was named twelfth man for the Second Test against Australia, in Barbados, in March, 1973, feeling sure he would be selected after team member Bernard Julien fell ill. Instead, Keith Boyce, a Barbadian, was chosen to replace Julien. Lloyd was furious: "All I wanted was my plane ticket back to England because, as far as I was concerned, I was finished. I felt I was being victimised for the fact that Forbes Burnham had brought me back home." [Lloyd, *Living*, 53] Lloyd was only comforted when told by Wesley Hall: "Rohan [Kanhai] was nearing the end of his career and would not have long as skipper." [Lloyd *Living*, 53] Lloyd was selected for the Third Test, and then excelled in the Fourth Test against Australia, in April 1973, with a superb innings of 178 at his home ground Bourda. He played under Kanhai until Kanhai retired early in 1974 and he (Lloyd) became captain.

In *Sixty Years on the Backfoot*, according to Clyde Walcott who was a selector in 1974, Kanhai was recommended to be retained as captain for the forthcoming India series in 1974/75, but the recommendation was rejected by the West Indies Cricket Board who appointed Lloyd instead. Lloyd believes Kanhai lost the captaincy when West Indies were one up in the series against England in the Caribbean, and he allowed England to level the rubber winning the final Test by merely 26 runs. He also believes the strain of captaincy was getting to Kanhai and continues: "Nevertheless most people felt he would be retained for the tour to India ... Certainly I thought so." [Lloyd, *Living*, 58]

Considering that West Indies had not won a rubber under Sobers from January 1968 to April 1972, Kanhai's performance as captain from February 1972 to April 1974, when he won one rubber and lost two, looks slightly better than Sobers's. Besides, as already mentioned, the margins by which Kanhai lost two matches were narrow: one by 26 runs, and another by 44 runs. Lloyd's opinion that Kanhai would be retained as captain is probably based on his claim that under Kanhai's regime: "West Indies cricket was revitalised with our emphatic triumph over England by two wins and a draw in the three Test series." [Lloyd, *Living*, 55] [Lloyd is referring to West Indies winning 2:1 against England in 1973, not to Kanhai's three rubbers as captain.]

So outside intervention seems probable in overturning the selectors' decision to retain Kanhai, and since Burnham's aim in going to such lengths to get Lloyd back from Australia to the Caribbean was to see him appointed as West Indies captain, it would not be surprising if he is responsible for the outside intervention. Only someone with prestige and influence could overrule the decision of selectors appointed by the West Indies Cricket Board. It says something about West Indies cricket if Lloyd was installed as captain through political interference; and it would not be that unusual if, as mentioned in the Introduction, political meddling was also active in the installation of his successor Vivian Richards.

Even though they do not offer documentary proof, many commentators mention Burnham's hand in Kanhai's loss of the captaincy, for example: "As an East Indian from Guyana even the Guyanese President [Forbes Burnham] wanted the West Indies captaincy taken from him [Kanhai] for no reason other than race." [W.E.B. Lloyd Jodah, 'First Bollywood Action Hero') Also, in a conference attended by Ramadhin and Solomon, Kanhai's older brother Richard implies collusion through silence, by other members of the West Indies team in relieving Kanhai of the captaincy: "When Rohan

Kanhai was about to be appointed captain of the West Indies team, there was a lot of opposition ... A lot was done during his career as captain to get him out, and his former colleagues, great West Indian cricketers, kept quiet when manipulation took place to push him out of the captaincy." [Birbalsingh, *Indenture*, 248]

In the face of such shenanigans it seems difficult to understand exactly how Kanhai was appointed captain in the first place. Sobers, who knew him as a team-mate since 1957, only thought of him as third in line for the captaincy after Holford and Lloyd, both younger players with much less international experience. Unless Kanhai disqualifies himself through incompetence in leadership or technical know how, or perhaps some unknown moral or cultural failure (Lloyd does hint at Kanhai's not exactly saintly reputation), his seniority and experience should have placed him first in line to succeed Sobers.

In assessing the relative merits of Sobers and Kanhai as captain, Lloyd does not see much difference, saying only that Sobers was aggressive and Kanhai defensive in approach. As a Guyanese politician, Burnham owed his own position to an electorate sharply polarised between Indians and Africans, with the Indians programmed to win elections because they are a majority. It was fertile soil for both Indo- and Afro-centricity. Burnham's political survival depended on blatant rigging to neutralise this natural Indian-Guyanese advantage.

Through regularly rigged elections, Burnham's party remained in total power from 1968 to 1992. Burnham's support for Lloyd is not based on parochialism or some misguided form of Guyanese patriotism since both Lloyd and Kanhai are Guyanese; his determined advocacy of Lloyd can best be attributed to racial or ethnic loyalty. Yet it is interesting that after his retirement in 1974, Kanhai and Lloyd appeared in the inaugural Cricket World Cup match at Lord's in 1975, although Kanhai was only included as a last minute replacement for Sobers who was ill. In the match, with Lloyd as captain, West Indies beat Australia by 17 runs, and Kanhai and Lloyd shared in a sublime partnership if 149 with Kanhai playing a sage, sheet-anchor role compiling 55, while Lloyd, with regal magnificence, flayed the Australian bowling to the tune of 102 runs. Success from such solidarity and team spirit illustrates the argument for cricket's potential, in the midst of turmoil that separates people and societies, to assuage divisions and heal conflict.

Obvious parallels exist between Rohan Kanhai's career as an Indian-Caribbean Test cricketer and Rosanne Kanhai's experience in Trinidad in 1962. The main connection is that both Kanhais, one in Guyana and the other in Trinidad, were up against a dominant Afro-centricity that, for understandable historical reasons, at least during the 1950s, 60s and 70s, was entrenched in every facet of life whether in politics, education, sport, or anything to do with the administrative infrastructure of their respective countries. Not that this structure was legislated; it was gradually institutionalised and relatively benign. But a potential for injustice or mischief lurked beneath its surface; and suspicion was always rife.

One reason why Burnham's improperly elected régimes prospered was because of patronage from the US for geo-political, Cold War reasons, but also because of unstinting support he received, largely by tacit approval of his rigged elections, from English-speaking Caribbean governments that were all overwhelmingly African. In this context, the rise of an Indian-Caribbean Test cricketer like Rohan Kanhai from a sugar plantation to the captaincy of the West Indies team, for however brief a term, reflects cricket's success in soothing if not healing divisions or conflicts of Caribbean history.

In *Living for Cricket*, Lloyd confidently asserts that Kanhai is the best batsman produced by Guyana, and selects his best West Indies Eleven, awarding Kanhai pride of place as the No. 3 in his batting line up. Lloyd regards Kanhai as, "An individual with enormous natural ability and an almost flawless technique, he was at home against all types of bowling and would be dominated by none ... Apart from Vivian Richards, there has been no other batsman as exciting to watch in my time, if I say he should have got many more centuries than he did, it was undoubtedly due to the chances he would take with his aggressive approach." [Clive Lloyd, *Living*, 127/8]

Lloyd is going on entertainment value rather than runs, but he is also generous knowing that he has a higher career aggregate of Test runs; 7515 to Kanhai's 6227. By the same criterion of entertainment, Lloyd selects Kanhai's two most impressive innings: one was a First Class match between Guyana and Barbados, in Barbados, in 1964, when Kanhai, "cut loose and he just tore those two great fast b*owlers* [Hall and Griffith] apart with every describable shot – and some that were not;" [Lloyd, *Living*, 128] the other innings was in a World Series match in Perth, Australia when Denis Lillee was, "scattering everyone else with his hostility." [Lloyd, *Living*, 128] Like James, who felt Kanhai exceeded Bradman against Trevor Bailey's side at Edgbaston in 1964, Lloyd sees Kanhai at his best in games other than a conventional Test match.

Lloyd is persuasive partly because he has observed Kanhai as a member of the same team, partly because he was Kanhai's rival for the West Indies captaincy, and because, like C.L.R. James, he recognises that it is not a conventional Test match with all its restraints and responsibilities that best displays Kanhai's batting genius. Lloyd seems to support both James and Cardus who said that Kanhai thrived in matches without these restraints when the satyric passion for expression of the natural man could appear with less inhibition. This too is the conclusion of Michael Gibbes who sees Kanhai as a romantic like Trumper for whom statistics and functional value take second place to uninhibited natural exuberance. It is also why James thought Kanhai created a new dimension in batting in his quest of identity.

CHAPTER 3

Joe Solomon: What immortal hand or eye?

At first, although it seems demeaning to argue that Joe Solomon's run-out of two batsmen in a Test match constitutes his chief claim to fame, mere passage of time suggests that his run-out of Alan Davidson and Ian Meckiff, in the second innings of the First Test against Australia at 'the Gabba' in Brisbane, Australia, in December 1960, is now sanctified as one of the most enduring wonders of West Indian cricket. Meckiff's run-out in particular brought lasting fame to Joseph Stanislaus Solomon, a right-handed, middle order batsman, brilliant fieldsman and leg-spinner who was born on 26 August 1930, a few years before Kanhai, in Port Mourant, Guyana. The reason for Solomon's exceptional fame is that his two run-outs were critical events of the first tied Test in the history of cricket; the result of a cricket match, between two teams, lasting thirty hours, during which each team accumulated an identical number of runs – 737. It would no doubt tax the wiles of a mathematical genius to calculate odds on such an unlikely outcome.

In an article in the British newspaper *The Guardian* Frank Keating enthuses on the game as, "probably the most dramatic international cricket match ever played." [*The Guardian*, Wednesday, December 8, 2010] West Indies had set Australia a target of 233 runs to win in the final innings of the match, and Australia had reached 226 runs for seven wickets, when Solomon first ran out Davidson for 80. Finally, Australia needed two more runs to win with one ball remaining when Solomon, positioned at square leg, sideways of the wicket, with only one stump in sight, etched his name forever in the honour roll of cricket, by scoring a bull's eye while Meckiff was still some way out of his crease. Referring to Solomon's exploit, in redolent hyperbole, Ian McDonald claims it, "will never be forgotten as long as cricket is played, and perhaps, after cricket has disappeared from the face of the earth, tales will still be told to wide-eyed children of a hero who saved his people – the David of his day – by aiming straight and throwing true at a time of greatest danger. [McDonald, in Camacho, 90]

The legendary event occurred on the last day of the First Test of the West Indies series against Australia. West Indies had batted first and made 453 to which Solomon, coming in at No. 6, contributed 65. Australia replied with 505, a lead of 52. West Indies then responded with 284 in their second innings. At one stage, thanks mainly to superb fast bowling from Wesley Hall who shattered the stumps of five top Australian batsmen, the hosts were reduced to 92 for six, and stared in horror at impending defeat; but captain Richie Benaud and the redoubtable all-rounder Alan Davidson mounted an heroic rearguard action with a plucky partnership of 134 that brought them to 226. Then, in one of those desperate ventures when a batsman risks everything on fielders being flummoxed by his outrageous daring, Davidson attempted to steal the quick single to mid-wicket that sealed his fate from Solomon, and opened the curtain on the drama to follow.

The sequence of action in the drama of the final over – eight balls under Australian rules – began at 5.56 pm. The bowler was again Hall, and six runs were needed for victory with Benaud and wicket-keeper Wally Grout batting, and the latter on strike.

First ball: Grout is hit on the thigh and Benaud dashes through to scrounge another vital run; five runs to win from seven balls. Second ball: Benaud hooks and gloves Hall's bouncer to wicket-keeper Alexander and is out for 52; the score stands at 228 for eight, and five more runs to win. Third ball: incoming batsman Ian Meckiff plays to mid-off. No run. Five runs to win from five balls. Fourth ball passes Meckiff on the leg-side and Grout calls Meckiff for a bye. Wicket-keeper Alexander throws the ball to the bowler's end in a frantic attempt to run Meckiff out, but misses. Four runs to get from four balls and two wickets left. The fifth ball is a bouncer fended off to square leg where Kanhai stands ready to catch it but Hall comes bounding in, forces Kanhai out of his way, lunges in a vain grab at the ball and drops the catch. In the midst of a field of over-wrought tension, the batsmen quietly run one. Three runs to win from three balls. Sixth ball: Meckiff swings blindly to the mid-wicket boundary but, with truly unbelievable speed and accuracy, Hunte collects the ball smoothly and, somehow, contrives the most magnificent return, directly into the gloves of Alexander who runs out Grout. The score is now 232 for nine with one wicket to fall, one run to win, and two balls left. Seventh ball: Hall bowls to Lindsay Kline who pushes the ball toward mid-wicket/square leg where Solomon is on patrol. Kline and Meckiff make one desperate, daredevil dash for the solitary run that will bring them victory. But Solomon, standing twelve metres away from the wicket, accesses divine intervention to throw down the single stump he can see from sideways of the wicket, and Meckiff is run-out. It is the first tie in almost one hundred years of Test cricket, and it has so far been repeated only once – at Chennai, between Australia and India, in September 1986.

One wonders if such a unique result could have been achieved without the cool head of Worrell, at the beginning of his role as newly-appointed captain and grand master, in the mounting excitement and mind-numbing tension that drove Hall to extend his follow-through on his fifth ball and run down Kanhai waiting expectantly for a catch. Hall had been warned by Worrell not to bowl any bouncers in the last over, although, as it turned out, his bouncer did get Benaud out. According to Sobers, when Worrell later admonished Hall for disobeying instructions and Hall pleaded "But I got him, [Benaud]" Worrell countered: "That's not the point. I told you not to bowl a bouncer. What would have happened if it had taken a top edge and gone for six!" [Sobers, 122] Worrell knew his men, and tried his best to calm Hall down when the score was at 232 for nine. Apart from warning Hall that he would never be able to return to his home in Barbados if he bowled a no ball, he explained a stratagem he was about to use to sow seeds of doubt in the batsmen: "If I move Solomon two steps to his right and then two back to his left, the field will remain the same but the batsman will not know what I have done." [Sobers, 123]

Sobers admits he could not have hit the wicket in conditions that Solomon did. [Sobers, 122] The uncanny co-ordination necessary for such deadly accuracy is one thing; but under such tense, heart-stopping conditions, it conjures up a vision of awe-struck wonder and supernatural provenance envisaged by the English poet William Blake, when he marvels at the 'fearful symmetry' of The Tyger in his poem of the same title: "What immortal hand or eye/ Dare frame thy fearful symmetry?" Like Blake's Tyger Solomon's feat defies comprehension, and implies mystery or genius. Yet, in trying to account for his exploit to Frank Keating, there is neither awareness of the superhuman, nor admission of inner doubt or uncertainty; Solomon, makes it sound perfectly run-of-the-mill: "The secret is balance, to be four-square steady as I took aim. You see, I was an East Indian country boy from Berbice, in the sticks, and before we could walk we'd be pitching marbles; later we'd steal ripe mangoes by downing them with sharp flat stones, not aiming at the fruit, of course, but at their stalks." [Frank Keating, *The Guardian*, Wednesday, December 8, 2010] The rustic plantation origin of mid-twentieth century Indian-Caribbean Test cricketers has its compensations after all!

Since Solomon's social origin is shared with that of Kanhai and Butcher, his career invites comparison with theirs. Not for him the flashing, quicksilver blade of Kanhai's romantic escapades, nor the rhythmic, rocking and punchy on-drives of Basil Butcher. Unsuspectingly durable, Solomon lacked the flair, fluency, variety and range of stroke-play of his more celebrated Port Mourant countrymen, although his most assertive stroke, the square cut, was executed with as much power and ferocity as Kanhai. For the rest, Solomon served more as trusted retainer, a good and faithful servant, one who does the job he is asked to do without fuss or flourish. In the tied Test, for instance, here is another version of Solomon's own business-like, matter-of-fact explanation of his unforgettable feat: "Kline, a left-hander played the last ball from Wes Hall out to square leg. Since only one run was needed, I moved in with the bowler, because I knew the batsman wouldn't make a big hit. I gathered the ball, threw with the same action, and he was out by a yard." [Birbalsingh, *Indenture*, 246] Admittedly, Solomon is recalling an event that occurred nearly thirty years before, but talk about modesty or understatement; there is not the slightest hint of inner turmoil or convulsion; he simply did what he had to do.

Another account of Solomon's feat is given by Peter Lashley a Barbados batsman and member of the First Test team in 1960: "I was fielding close to Solomon. I was at square leg and he was at mid-wicket. It [the ball] was coming to my right hand, which was not my throwing hand. [As each moment passed by it seemed that] I was the likely person to pick the ball up, but he'd just knocked the stumps down to run-out Davidson, and he said 'Move! Move! Move!' So I stopped, which was unusual for me. He [Solomon] swooped and picked the ball up and hit the stumps again. Had I picked up the ball there would have been no tied Test." [WEB Joe Solomon] Lashley's account does not necessarily contradict the report of other commentators (including Solomon himself and Richie Benaud) who confirm that Solomon was fielding at square leg. Fielding positions are flexible, and it is possible that Solomon was close enough to square leg but had to run some distance to displace Lashley and gather the ball. Nor should we quibble about Solomon's claim that Kline was run out by a yard. Not that the exact distance matters, but thirty years make a difference and allow scope for poetic licence.

In his book *A Tale of Two Tests* Richie Benaud gives some insight into Australian tactics. At tea on the final day, Australia needed 123 runs to win in about even time. With Davidson and Benaud still not out, Australia could have avoided risks and played for a draw, but when asked by Sir Donald Bradman at the tea break what he intended to do, Benaud confided that he was going for a win which met with the Don's enthusiastic approval. The Australian strategy, and it all but succeeded, was to make West Indies crack from pressure. The chief obstacle, Benaud knew, was Worrell, the rock of Gibraltar: "They'll crack, if only we can get the pressure on them. Pressure and more and more pressure and they must crack ... they've done it so often before. But although this was the same team as they'd had before, they had a leader this time... a great player in his own right, a shrewd tactician and a man who had the respect and liking of his side... and of the opposition, too. A great cricketer this Worrell." [Benaud, 33] It takes an Australian foe to see the difference between Worrell and the West Indies captains who preceded him.

Although it is rarely mentioned, Solomon's 65 in the tied Test was the second highest score in the first innings, and his 47 was one of only three scores above 40 in his team's second innings; and although we scarcely notice these two scores, in the daze of Sobers' dazzling first innings 132, and Worrell's resilient top score of 65 in the tight and fast-deteriorating conditions of the West Indies second innings, we dare not imagine what might have happened without Solomon's batting, let alone his fielding, in what may very well be the most dramatic match in international cricket.

After the tied Test, it is characteristic that Solomon should appear in all four of the remaining Tests of the rubber without attracting much attention. He opened the innings in the Second Test in Melbourne which was easily won by Australia, Solomon's own contribution being scores of 0 and 4. In the Second Test there was an incident when Solomon's cap fell on his wicket and he was given out hit wicket although the crowd loudly booed the bowler Richie Benaud and his team for appealing. Solomon returned to his position at No. 7 in the Third Test at Sydney, with little better results – 14 and 1. At least West Indies won the game through superb bowling from Gibbs and Sobers who claimed nine wickets between them. Solomon's batting results in the Fourth (drawn) Test at Adelaide were again modest – 22 and 16, and while his scores improved to 45 and 36 in the final Test, in Melbourne, Australia still won the match and rubber 2:1 with one match drawn and one tied.

The view that Solomon's approach to the game is guided by care, caution and calculation is somewhat belied by the glory that seems to garland his entry into Test cricket in India in 1958. In his début match, in the Second Test at Kanpur in December 1958, he immediately signalled attention with scores of 45 and 86, although his run-out in the second innings sabotaged what looked like unaccustomed kudos from a certain début century. In the Third Test at Kolkata when Kanhai excelled with 256 and Butcher with his maiden hundred, Solomon was left stranded not out on 69 when the innings was closed at 614 for five wickets declared. The next Test, once more high-scoring, also did not leave much scope for Solomon at No. 7. But he made sure of his maiden century – 100 not out – in the Fifth Test at Delhi, and concluded his first rubber with a total of 351 runs and an impressive average of 117.00. Not exactly figures extolling caution or care!

A crucial aspect of the India tour was Solomon's relationship with his captain Gerry Alexander. In his début Test appearance at Kanpur when the West Indies were on the ropes in the first innings with their score at 88 for six and all their top batsmen gone, Solomon joined Alexander in a defiant stand that showered 100 face-saving runs on a wilting team that restored them to relative safety with a modest total of 222. In the Third Test when it was not necessary for Alexander to bat because of the huge total already acquired by Kanhai and company, he could not fail to notice Solomon's stout-hearted resilience again with his 69 not out. If Alexander had any further doubt, Solomon's 100 not out in the final Test convinced him that Solomon concealed an iron fist in his velvet glove. Not often does an unassuming exterior form a mere mask that conceals such resolute will.

The Pakistan rubber that followed in the Caribbean was dominated by the home team which won by a margin of two matches to one. Although Solomon was run-out for 66 in the First Test and enjoyed another middling innings of 56 in the Third, he managed a total of only 144 runs and a modest average of 28.80, results that seemed to reverse his prosperity in India. In England's Caribbean series in 1959/60, he was picked in two matches – the Second Test in Trinidad when he was asked to open, and the Third Test in Jamaica. In neither case did he shine, finishing the tour with a derisive total of 50 runs and an uncharacteristic average of 16.66. His career also coincided with the instability of various changes in the team, like replacing Ramadhin with Gibbs, or finding a satisfactory opening partner for Hunte. More importantly, it was a critical period in the history of West Indian cricket when fierce public controversy raged over Alexander's own position as a captain who, in stark and unforgiving historical terms, was seen to represent an oppressive colonial elite in the dying throes of their decline. Here is another example of class trumping race since Alexander, who was mixed blood (European/African) rather than White, owed his appointment less to colour than his high class credentials of social, educational and professional status.

Although Solomon's success in India had attracted attention, the tied Test elevated him to the level of a force to be reckoned with. Alexander had taken note of his resoluteness in India. Now, after Alexander showed rare magnanimity in remaining in the team as wicket-keeper, under the new captain Frank Worrell, in Australia, we do not know whether he and Worrell discussed Solomon. What we know is that Worrell not only retained Solomon as a member of his Test team in Australia, but for India's visit to the Caribbean in 1962, and the West Indies tour of England in 1963, in other words, for the rest of his tenure as West Indies captain. Once Worrell retired after 1963, Solomon was retained for the first four Tests, under Sobers, against the visiting Australians in 1964/65, and picked for the tour to England in 1966, again under Sobers, although he was omitted from every Test that summer, signalling the end of his Test career.

In the 1962 India series, as already mentioned, the contest proved too one-sided, and ended with a 5:0 West Indies triumph partly due to injury of the India captain Nari Contractor, and partly to the absence of India's specialist spinner Subash Gupte. Solomon played in four

Joe Solomon leads the West Indies team from the field after he had taken 8 wickets against a Duke of Norfolk's XI in 1963.   CENTRAL PRESS/GETTY IMAGES

Tests and compiled 148 runs for an average of 29.60. His bright spots were a score of 43 in the First Test and one of 96 the highest West Indies score in the Third. Unusually, Worrell also gave Solomon a long bowling stint in the Third Test with respectable, if innocuous figures of 29-17-33-0. His five Tests in England in 1963 reflected similar batting results – 204 runs for an average of 25.50, his two bright spots being 56 in the Lord's Test, the second highest score after Kanhai's 73 in the first innings of the match, and 62 in the Fourth Test at Headingley, Leeds. Solomon's final series of four Tests against Australia in the Caribbean, in 1965, yielded one high score of 76 in the first Test in Jamaica and a total of 179 in the rubber for an average of 29.83.

Guyanese historian, Winston McGowan suggests additional reasons for paying tribute to Solomon as the, "only Guyanese or West Indian batsman to begin his First Class career with three successive centuries – 114 not out against Jamaica and 108 against Barbados at Bourda in October 1956, and 121 against the Pakistan tourists in March,

1958." Further reasons are the fact that Solomon has the second highest average for batsmen representing Guyana in First Class cricket – 68.03 per innings; and, along with Kanhai, Butcher and Madray, transformed the Guyana team from its usual complement of chiefly Demerara- or Georgetown-based players to a more representative Guyanese one. In addition, it was largely Berbice-based players – Solomon, Kanhai, Butcher, Fredericks along with Georgetonian Gibbs – who, in the 1950s and 60s, made a more recognisably substantial Guyanese contribution to the West Indies team than before. [*Stabroek News*, 'History this Week', #33/2009, 10 September 2009]

These statistics fortify Solomon's achievement as a cricketer, but as he hints in talking to Keating, his career, particularly his expertise in throwing a cricket ball, may also owe something to his candid self-portrait as, "an East Indian country boy from Berbice," which politely refers to the divisive effect of acknowledged ethnic, class or regional issues in West Indian cricket. Like Ramadhin and Kanhai, Solomon began life as a "rustic coolie" in an era shortly before the Second World War, and the claim of his fielding being influenced by his outdoor upbringing is more than plausible. As corroborated by McGowan, Solomon also implies that as a Berbician he could not expect his cricketing skill to be recognised by the ruling cricketing authorities in the capital city of Guyana, Georgetown, in what was regarded as the premier county of Demerara.

In colonial British Guiana, after all, Georgetown was the headquarters of all national institutions, whether in law, government, business, health, education or whatever else, including the residence of the British governor, representative of the British monarch. As McGowan persuasively argues, the advent on the national scene of Berbician cricketers like Kanhai, Solomon, Butcher, Madray, with the exception of Butcher, all Indian denizens of a remote plantation like Port Mourant, revolutionised the game's administration, in Guyana, in the 1950s. The efforts of individual Port Mourant cricketers like Baijnauth who had previously represented Guyana, and John Trim who played briefly for both Guyana and West Indies in the 1940s no doubt served as a prelude, but it was the joint performance chiefly of Kanhai, Butcher and Solomon, in the 1950s, that kicked over the traces, and gave Guyana greater representation on the West Indies team than ever before.

That an African-Guyanese like Butcher (also Trim before him) together with fellow Indian-Guyanese cricketers from Port Mourant both suffered discrimination or neglect at the hands of Georgetown-Guyanese cricket authorities is another illustration of how class can sometimes be more important than race in the Caribbean. For example, it did not stop Port Mourant Indian-Guyanese from discriminating against Butcher, an African-Guyanese, on grounds of race. Despite being captain of the local cricket club at one time, Butcher failed to attract full support from the majority of the plantation who were Indian-Guyanese. For it complicates the picture of ethnic bias in a region where race, class, colour, religion and other factors intermingle and sometimes cross to produce fluid, contradictory or prejudiced attitudes that are morally repugnant yet socially acceptable. Butcher's experience illustrates Indian-Guyanese prejudice against African-Guyanese, and his case is taken up at some length by Clem Seecharan in *From Ranji to Rohan*.

Although Solomon's batting lacks the cavalier, calypso qualities seen in Kanhai, both batsmen seem to excel against India more than other Test teams. Solomon scored a total of 499 runs from eight matches against India for an average of 62.37, which contrasts with 429 runs in nine matches against Australia for an average of 47.66, and 254 from seven matches against England at an average of 36.28 per match. Meanwhile, in eighteen matches against India, Kanhai totalled 1693 runs for an average of 94.05 per match, while from twenty matches against Australia he collected 1695 runs at an average of 84.75, and from thirty-three matches with England he gathered 2347 runs at 71.12 per match. It is curious that except for his 96 against Pakistan in February 1958, it took Kanhai thirteen matches before realising his first big score (256) against India in December 1958. Solomon also started his career in India with 351 runs including the only Test century to his name and an average of 117.00 which he never again came close to achieving. India was not a consistently weak team during this period; they beat West Indies in 1971. Nor can speculation of mysterious psychic reconnection with their ancestral culture be credited since Everton Weekes, for example, an African-Caribbean batsman, was nicknamed the "coolie bully" for scoring more heavily against India than other Test playing countries.

In a career of twenty-seven Tests, Solomon bowled 117 overs and claimed four wickets for 268 runs at an average of 67. He also amassed

1326 runs for an average of 34.00 including one century, and nine 50s. In addition, he held thirteen catches. Of all this, the nine 50s are perhaps the most revealing, since they tell the tale of a middle-of-the road cricketer, not much given to exhibition, but possessed of hidden or unsuspected resources, notably uncanny vigilance in the field, and sturdy reliability in a crisis when he can come through with a sorely needed, match-saving contribution of 40, 50 or 60 runs or, as we have seen, perform some rare and unforgettable wonder in the field. This, no doubt, is miles apart from the quixotic gallantry of Kanhai's 110 in Trinidad, in 1960, in a losing cause, or his rampaging, scorched earth 77 at Kennington Oval in 1963; but it is the hallmark of a man cherished by two captains, Gerry Alexander and Frank Worrell, for honourable, yeoman service to West Indian cricket.

Ian McDonald who lived in Guyana throughout Solomon's cricket career and observed local reaction to him, catches the flavour of his contribution as, "a strong, wise and responsible batsman who, time and time again, rescued Guyana and the West Indies when danger or disaster threatened." [Camacho, 90] Solomon is a unique cricketer for whom it is difficult to find exact parallels in cricket history. He is not among the established, great all-rounders like Richard Hadlee of New Zealand, Kapil Dev of India, Wally Hammond of England, or his own team-mate Garry Sobers, who were all flamboyant match-winners with either bat or ball. Solomon shunned flamboyance; yet in his own way, in two fleeting moments of one blessed Test match, on 14 December 1960, at the Gabba, the East Indian country boy from Berbice summoned up such fearful symmetry of immortal hand/eye co-ordination that it revealed him, without any doubt whatsoever, as one of the most flamboyant cricketers of all time.

CHAPTER 4

Alvin Kallicharran:
The curse of apartheid

As Ramadhin, Kanhai and Solomon dominated Indian-Caribbean cricket in the 1950s and 1960s, so did Kallicharran excel as the leading Indian-Caribbean batsman of the 1970s, except that his path seemed to be strewn with problems of political controversy that somehow never troubled his predecessors. Kallicharran was born on 21 March 1949 and, like Kanhai and Solomon, came from Port Mourant, Guyana. He batted left-handed, and bowled right-arm off-breaks. He entered the Test arena in April 1972, and because of turmoil over South African apartheid in the cricketing world, found his Test career abruptly terminated in 1981. By then he had amassed 4399 runs from sixty-six Test matches, at an average of 44.93 including a highest score of 187.

In his début match, in the Fourth Test against New Zealand, at his home ground of Bourda, Guyana, Kallicharran's auspicious century enabled Captain Garry Sobers to declare the West Indies innings closed at 365 for seven, in hopes of securing a positive decision in a series that, till then, had produced three draws. Through a stubborn opening stand of 387, however, the New Zealanders were able to grind out another draw. In addition, the Bourda crowd caused another match interruption over the run-out of local hero Clive Lloyd. It reveals something of Kallicharran's temperament that he weathered the interruption of his maiden Test innings to come through with a century. Batting next at No. 3 in the Fifth and final Test on what later became his favourite ground, Queen's Park Oval, Trinidad, Kallicharran obliged with a second century that left him with an average of 109.50 in his first two Tests. The certainty of timing and confident stroke-making, in one so young, seemed to herald high promise.

Kallicharran's entry into Test cricket coincided with a period of transition from the regime of Sobers to one with Kanhai as West Indies captain which began with the First Test of the Australia tour to the Caribbean, in Jamaica, in February 1973. Kallicharran made 50 and 7 not out in this drawn match. In another draw, in the Second Test, Kallicharran managed only 14; but in the Third Test at Queen's Park Oval in Trinidad, his scores of 53 and 91 gave West Indies real hope of reaching a target of 334 in the fourth innings of the match. They were well placed with 268 for four at lunch on the last day when, inexplicably, they seemed to run out of steam, losing the game by 44 runs.

The series did not live up either to the high (and probably unrealistic expectations) of Kallicharran as promised in his opening matches against New Zealand, or of Kanhai with his new captain's broom promising a cleaner sweep. In the event, Australia romped home with a series victory of 2: nil and three drawn matches, while Kallicharran had to content himself with a less-than-expected tour aggregate of 294 for an average of 32.50.

Kallicharran's first tour abroad – a three-match rubber in England – began with the First Test at Kennington Oval in England in July 1973 when he chalked up two scores of 80, and his team won easily by 158 runs. Lloyd and Kallicharran (left-handers both) mounted the biggest stand in the match – 208 for the fourth wicket in the first innings – which led to a total of 415 that proved decisive. West Indies bowlers, Boyce and Sobers restricted England to a first innings total of 257 and spearheaded victory by 158 runs.

The next Test at Edgbaston was drawn, Kallicharran doing no better than 34 and 4 in the midst of a rather frosty atmosphere caused when umpire Arthur Fagg turned down an appeal for a catch by West Indies players. Fagg threatened to withdraw, but good relations were quickly restored. The Third Test at Lord's was one-sided with West Indies winning by an innings and 226 runs, and Kallicharran contributing 14 runs. It was a moderately successful first tour for Kallicharran with a Test aggregate of 212 runs and an average of 42.40; he did better in First Class appearances notching up three centuries and an average of 64.78.

In the First Test at Queen's Park Oval, again with England, in February 1974, dampness in the pitch encouraged Captain Kanhai to put England in to bat. After they were dismissed for 131, Kallicharran seemed to take charge of the West Indies reply with a century, leading to a total of 392. England responded with a defiant opening stand of 209 in their second innings, but by the last day, with only 132 needed to win, West Indies got safely home by seven wickets.

With lightning-quick reflexes, nimble feet and supple wrists, Alvin Kallicharran was the leading Indian-Caribbean batsman of the 1970s. He is pictured hooking Geoff Arnold for 4 while Alan Knott looks on during the 1st Test against England at the Oval in July 1973. PATRICK EAGAR/PATRICK EAGAR COLLECTION VIA GETTY IMAGES

One still-talked-about incident from this match occurred at the end of the first day's play when Kallicharran was 142 not out. Kallicharran's batting partner Julien pushed the last ball of the day to Tony Greig fielding at silly point, and immediately headed for the pavilion, as did some of the England fielders, while their wicket-keeper pulled up the stumps. Kallicharran too, who had walked out of his crease in backing up to Julien's stroke, continued toward the pavilion without returning to the crease to ground his bat. Greig instinctively threw down the bowler's wicket and appealed for a run-out that umpire Douglas Sang Hue upheld. The crowd was incensed at what seemed like lack of sportsmanship, and their anger grew so threatening that urgent discussions were held overnight, and the run-out appeal withdrawn.

Kallicharran was reinstated the next morning and finished his innings at 158. Sobers, who played in the match, disagrees with the turn of events: "Tony [Greig] allowed Alvin to come out and bat the next day and he went on to complete 150. In fact he scored 158 out of a total of 392 and set up our victory. Alvin was a good player but I still do not think he should have batted again. It was his own fault and the decision should not have been reversed. I wasn't captain so there was nothing I could do about it." [Sobers, 114]

Kallicharran prospered in the Second Test in Jamaica as well, this time with 93 in a match in which England were made to fight hard for a draw. In the Third Test West Indies ran up a total of 596 for eight wickets declared to which Kallicharran's contribution was a superb 119 – his fourth Test century – compiled in a record-breaking partnership with Lawrence Rowe. The Fourth Test at Bourda, Guyana, was virtually rained off, but England's fighting spirit was already evident from the Second and Third Tests, and although they were one down at the start of the Fifth Test at Queen's Park Oval, Trinidad, they were able to convert it into a remarkable victory by 26 runs to square the series. The value of Kallicharran's batting was underlined in this final Test where he got a pair, and his failure spelt defeat for West Indies.

This match in which Kallicharran made a pair in April 1974 was the last with Kanhai as captain. In November the same year Kallicharran ventured on his first sojourn to his ancestral homeland with Lloyd as new captain. In the First Test at Bangalore the wet pitch caused a late start, and Kallicharran and Greenidge put on 139 helping West Indies to reach a total of 289. Kallicharran made 124 flawless runs in spite of the ball lifting and turning. India were not far behind with 260 in their first innings, but when set a target of nearly four hundred in their second innings, surrendered meekly with a paltry 118 that ceded victory by 267 runs. In extenuation India might claim they were without the services of their captain Pataudi and wicket-keeper Engineer who were both injured. A West Indies victory by an innings and 17 runs in the next Test in Delhi was just as commanding, as West Indies batsmen benefited from a couple of lucky umpiring decisions and punished the Indian spinners.

Tables turned in December 1974, in the Third Test at Kolkata where India won by 85 runs, partly due to the overconfidence of West Indies batsmen and their willingness to take chances. Kallicharran made 0 in the first innings and, with his score of 57 – the highest in the second innings – led his team's vain chase of a second innings target of 310. The Fourth Test pitch in Chennai favoured spinners and India again won, this time, by 100 runs. West Indies were set a final target of 254 and, at 65 for four, seemed well on their way, but after Kallicharran was run-out for 51 by a direct throw from point, there was little further resistance from West Indies.

With the rubber tied at two all, the Fifth Test at Mumbai was extended to six days of which West Indies used up the first two plus seventy-five minutes of the third in establishing an unassailable total of 604 for six wickets in their first innings. Lloyd indulged himself with a double century and the match was briefly interrupted when a young spectator who ran on the field to congratulate him, suffered undue police violence. Kallicharran made 98 in the first innings, although he was dropped at 23. He followed up with 34 not out in the second innings, as West Indies won the match by 201 runs and prevailed in the rubber 3:2. Kallicharran's first Indian sojourn enhanced his career with a tour aggregate of 454 runs for an average of 55.60.

In the brief two-Test tour of Pakistan that followed, West Indies replied to Pakistan's 199 with 214 in the First Test, at Lahore, in February 1975. Kallicharran's brilliant 92 not out dominated the West Indies first innings while his 44 in the second innings confirmed an inevitable draw after Pakistan's second innings score of 373 for 7 declared. Kallicharran was just as impressive in the first innings of the Second Test at Karachi in March. In reply to Pakistan's 406, West

Indies came up with 493, including 115 not out from Kallicharran, who hit sixteen fours in his sixth century and, as a mark of controlled aggression, took 20 runs off one over from Asif Masood; but due to heroic batting from Sadiq Mohammad, Pakistan earned another honourable draw. Kallicharran's tour aggregate of 251 runs in Pakistan netted him 125.50, his highest average for a tour so far.

Kallicharran celebrated his first tour of Australia – six Tests – with a century in the second innings of the First Test in November 1975. Australia established a hefty first innings lead of 152 before Kallicharran (101) and Rowe (107) engineered a face-saving partnership of 198 in their second innings, but in vain, as it turned out, since the West Indies score slipped from 248 for five to 275 for seven after they had gone, and victory eventually went to Australia by eight wickets. West Indies retaliated in the Second Test at Perth, in December, running up a total of 585 (Kallicharran 57) before dismissing Australia for 329 and 169 and winning by an innings and 87 runs. Australia came back to win the Third Test by eight wickets at Melbourne, in late December, when Kallicharran could manage scores only of 20 and 32, and West Indies fast bowlers failed to transfer their success from the hard surface of Perth to a slower Melbourne wicket.

At Sydney, in January 1976, Australia won another victory in the Fourth Test. In the West Indies second innings, for instance, only one batsman got to 50 while none of the others reached 20. Kallicharran contributed 9 and 7, and Thomson won the match virtually one-handed for Australia with a bag of nine wickets. By the Fifth Test at Adelaide, in January, the fight had become totally one-sided. In replying with 274 to an Australia first innings total of 418, only Kallicharran (76) and Boyce (95 not out) achieved scores above 30, precipitating an Australia victory by 190 runs. In the Sixth Test at Melbourne in January/February Kallicharran had scores of 4 and 44 as West Indies capitulated once again. Out of six Tests in this Australian rubber, which Australia won 5:1, Kallicharran emerged with 421 runs and an average of 38.30.

So far, a mere record of Kallicharran's batting statistics establish his crucial value to his team. In a paean to Kallicharran in *Cricket at Bourda*, Ian McDonald puts his finger on an important aspect of Kallicharran's batting – his seeming physical frailty in the face of menacing and genuinely super-fast bowling. The vision of fiery Australia pace men, Lillee and Thomson thundering down at a slightly built, crouching figure, twenty-two yards away, in those days unprotected by a helmet, is indeed fearful to contemplate. The appeal of a dramatic, physical contest like cricket, no doubt, is like the bullfight, where physical danger tests the matador's courage, just as the fast bowler tests the batsman's skill either to avoid injury or score runs, preferably both. McDonald senses the drama of the challenge: "How, one thought, could that schoolboy [Kallicharran] survive, much less overcome, the thundering front-line bowlers charging up to him?" [Camacho, 91]

To overcome fear produces joy in McDonald's view: "What joy to have seen a Snow, a Lillee or an Imran Khan furiously deliver a groin-destroying ball and to have watched Kallicharran meet it with a swift and dapper bat with all the time and timing in the world." [Camacho, 91] Nowadays, one of the most accessible films of Kallicharran's batting captures his performance in the inaugural World Cup final, in 1975, when he hooks Lillee repeatedly and effortlessly. He leaves the clear impression of a small figure who, like Brian Lara, is endowed with lightning-quick reflexes, nimble feet, and supple wrists that enable him to wait for the precise moment, before suddenly swinging into a flurry of action as he flashes, lunges and/or swivels and despatches the ball to some distant corner of the boundary.

For the first time, Kallicharran encountered India in four Tests, in the Caribbean, in March/April 1976. In the First Test in Barbados, in March, West Indies won by an innings and 97 runs, with the aid of 93 from Kallicharran. Exploiting damp conditions in the next match in Trinidad, at the end of March, India took the initiative with their spinners and came close to a surprising victory. Kallicharran's scores were 17 and 12. In the Third Test, again in Trinidad, in April, when Kallicharran made 0 and 103 not out, India won a notable victory with 406 for four wickets in their second innings to become only the second team, at that time, to make over 400 in their final innings to win a Test match. (The Australians, with 404 for three in the fourth innings, had beaten England at Headingley, Leeds in 1948) Kallicharran made 12 in the Fourth Test in Jamaica in a match won by West Indies in circumstances that will be considered more fully in Chapter Five.

Kallicharran's second visit to England for five Tests in June and July, 1976, yielded one score of 97 and nothing above 34 in five other scores, giving him a tour aggregate of 206 runs and an average of

40.10. The first two Tests were drawn. In the First at Trent Bridge, Nottingham, despite a partnership of 303 between Kallicharran and Richards in which Richards revelled in an aggressive double century and Kallicharran added 97 in the first innings, West Indies were unable to dismiss England twice; and at Lord's where the first day's play of the Second Test was rained off, West Indies ran out of time chasing a target of 322 on the last day. Kallicharran made 0 and 34 in the second Test, and 0 and 20 in the Third Test at Old Trafford, which West Indies won by 425 runs, but a shoulder injury prevented him from playing in the final two Tests.

Kallicharran's highest score in five matches of his next home series (against Pakistan) from February to April 1977, was 72 in the Third Test at Bourda. The First Test in Barbados in March was drawn (Kallicharran 17 and 9) while West Indies won the Second in Trinidad by six wickets (Kallicharran 37 and 11 not out). Slow batting may have contributed to another example of unruly behaviour and a brief stoppage of play in the Third Test after Kallicharran expressed displeasure at an lbw decision against him. In the Fourth Test, again at Queen's Park Oval, Trinidad, in early April, West Indies faced a target of 489 runs. While Kallicharran top scored with 45, his team fell short by 266 runs. Nevertheless West Indies came back to win the Fifth Test at Sabina Park, Jamaica, later in April by 140 runs (Kallicharran 34 and 22). They also won the rubber 2:1 with two draws.

Kallicharran's next series, at home to Australia, from March to May 1978, changed his career completely. In the first match at Queen's Park Oval in Trinidad, West Indies inflicted a stinging defeat on Australia by an innings and 106 runs scoring 405 in their only innings, and bowling Australia out for 90 and 209. Kallicharran top scored with 127, his seventh century, and shared in a partnership of 170 with Lloyd. West Indies success was repeated in the Second Test in Barbados by nine wickets (Kallicharran 8). The Australia team was not at full strength. Many of their players like Marsh and the Chappell brothers who had last appeared against West Indies in 1975/76, had now joined World Series Cricket.

World Series Cricket (WSC) was an arrangement of international cricket matches created by the Australian media magnate Kerry Packer, in an attempt to break the monopoly of the Australian Broadcasting Commission over TV cricket coverage in Australia. Packer wanted

nine. Although 6.2 overs of play remained, the umpires argued that there was no provision for continuing the match into a sixth day. But problems had started from the beginning of this unhappy match when the Australians had successfully requested that umpire Douglas Sang Hue be changed. Ironically, it was the replacement umpire who upheld an appeal for a catch from Vanburn Holder and created dissatisfaction in the crowd enough to foment another crowd disturbance.

Kallicharran next led West Indies on a six-Test tour of India between December 1978 and February 1979. The First Test at Mumbai in December 1978 was drawn after West Indies replied to the India first innings total of 424 with 493 to which Kallicharran made the largest contribution — 187. The innings contained two difficult chances at 47 and 53, but was otherwise fluent and graceful, and included twenty-five fours. Rain caused some delay, although the indecisive result was more due to lack of penetration in the bowling of either side. In the Second Test at Bangalore India replied to West Indies' first innings score of 437 (Kallicharran 71) with 371, and West Indies had reached 200 for eight on the fourth day; but play was abandoned on the final day because of unrelated civil unrest caused by the arrest of former Prime Minister Indira Gandhi.

In an exciting drawn Third Test in Kolkata, in December/January, India set West Indies a target of 335 runs and although they were in dire straits shortly before the end, the tourists escaped by holding out until they had reached 197 for 9 wickets, and bad light stopped play. Kallicharran was again in fairly fine fettle with scores of 55 and 46. With a further score of 98 he also dominated the West Indies first innings in the Fourth Test at Chennai in January 1979. India replied with 225 followed by a West Indies collapse of 151 in their second innings that left 125 to win. Although India were struggling at 31 for three at the end of the third day, they reached their target and won by three wickets on the fourth day with an entire day to spare.

The Fifth Test in Delhi was seriously affected by rain and ended in a draw, after West Indies replied to India's 566 for 8 wickets declared with 172 in their first innings and 179 for three in the second. Kallicharran managed only 7 in the first innings and was left not out at the end with 45. Since the Sixth Test was also drawn, due to rain, India took the rubber one: nil with five draws. Kallicharran accumulated 538 runs over the six matches, the most in a series for him, and his

exclusive rights to cricket for his own TV station, Channel Nine, ar WSC matches continued over a two year period from 1977 to 197 until the Australian Broadcasting Commission granted Packer Channel Nine exclusive rights. During this time, Australian as well a several other international cricketers (including West Indians) signe WSC contracts with Packer in the hope of increasing their earning: Kallicharran had also signed but it was discovered that he also had a agreement with a radio station to play for Queensland, and his Packe contract was rescinded.

Meanwhile, West Indian selectors omitted the names of three o their players who had signed Packer contracts – Desmond Haynes Richard Austin and Deryck Murray – from their list of players for the Third Test at Bourda, Guyana in March 1978. The selectors argued that they needed to blood new players for the visit of Sri Lanka later in 1978. But Captain Clive Lloyd himself resigned to join WSC, and new Test players were drafted in the West Indies team, for example, Sylvester Clarke, Alvin Greenidge, David Murray, Norbert Phillip, Sewdat Shivnarine, and Alvadon Williams, in order to continue the Test series with Australia. In one fell swoop, totally out of the blue Kallicharran was appointed as the new West Indies captain.

The Third Test at Bourda continued in March/April 1978 with a opening score of 205 by the new West Indies team under Kallicharrar and a reply of 286 from Australia, to which West Indies added 43$ including centuries from two new players Gomes and Williams; but was not enough to prevent an Australia victory by three wickets. Kallicharran's offerings of 0 and 22 made it look as if he w overwhelmed by circumstances, he bounced back with 92 and 27 the Fourth Test at Queen's Park Oval, Trinidad, and helped to secu victory by 198 runs.

With the tally for the tour now standing at 3:1 in favour of W Indies at the end of the Fourth Test, Australia tried strenuously to ma it 3:2 in the Fifth Test, in Jamaica, in April. They secured a lead of, on first innings, and hurried to a score of 305 for three in their secc innings, setting West Indies a target of 369 to get on the last day. despite a captain's innings of 126 from Kallicharran, the moment shifted inexorably toward the tourists. The hosts found themsel fighting to stave off defeat which they succeeded in doing, narro' when the umpires decided to abandon the match as a draw at 25$

highest series average – 59.77 – except for his extraordinary two centuries in two matches at the very start of his career.

By December, after Packer had made his point and the 1979 WSC had run its course, Packer recruits from all over the world returned to their national teams, and a renewed West Indies prepared to take on a Three-Test series- tour of Australia. As thanks for filling the breach created by Packer, the captaincy was unceremoniously removed from Kallicharran, and temporarily transferred to Deryck Murray, while Lloyd was convalescing from a knee operation. Of the nine Test matches in which he served as captain Kallicharran had won one, lost two and drawn six. With both the Australia and West Indies teams returning to their full, pre-Packer strength, West Indies quickly established dominance by drawing the First Test against Australia at Brisbane in December 1979, and winning the Second and Third early in the new year. In five innings Kallicharran produced 202 runs, including 106 in the Third Test at Adelaide for an average of 50.50.

The three Tests in New Zealand that followed marked a downward spiral in Kallicharran's productivity. All he gathered from three Tests in New Zealand was 146 runs and an average of 24.3. In the summer of 1980 five Tests against England brought Kallicharran 102 runs for an average of 17.00; and as for the tour of Pakistan later the same year, Kallicharran's four Tests yielded 80 runs and average of 16. This precipitate decline had a reason. The career of a brilliant Test cricketer, at the age of thirty-one, could not come to such a lamentable and premature end without explanation.

In this case, the reason is that Kallicharran as well as other West Indian cricketers, had joined in a so-called "rebel tour" to South Africa in 1982, at a time when that country was regarded as a pariah state because of its racist, apartheid policy. Cricketers were banned by the International Cricket Conference as well as their national cricket organisations from participation in South African cricket. [Appendix 15] The charge levelled by apartheid apologists, namely that their enemies had introduced politics into cricket or sport, was completely false since it was apartheid that had first introduced politics and racial discrimination not only into sport in South Africa, but into every aspect of the lives of their Black citizens, including employment, housing and education. Such naked racism was beyond the pale.

The ban against participation in South African cricket was a reaction to the 'D'Oliveira Affair' in 1968 when South Africa refused to admit England's cricket team for its regular Test match series because it included Basil D'Oliveira, a South African-born cricketer, classified as 'coloured' in his homeland, but living in Britain. South African cricket teams had also been banned from taking part in international tournaments by the International Cricket Conference. [Appendix 16] In defiance of the international ban against cricket with apartheid South Africa, some privately formed English teams visited South Africa, and despite bitter controversy in the region, some West Indian teams, although not the official West Indies team, had also joined in these banned visits in 1982/83 and 1983/84. Hence the term 'rebel tours'.

West Indies cricketers such as Kallicharran, Lawrence Rowe, Sylvester Clarke, Richard Austin, Colin Croft and others who had joined 'rebel tours' were consequently banned from playing in the West Indies team. Kallicharran continued to play First Class cricket for the English county Warwickshire until 1990, and he also participated in domestic South African cricket for Orange Free State and Transvaal in South Africa. But the curse of apartheid had brought his Test career to an untimely end, as it did for other West Indies players. The mysterious downward spiral of Kallicharran's Test appearances from 1980 onward may be attributed to his mental turmoil over the decision to join 'rebel' West Indian tours to South Africa.

Kerry Packer had exposed the fact that international cricketers were grossly underpaid up to the 1970s. So money and the incentive that they could generate positive change were used to entice international cricketers to play in South Africa. The real culprits, meanwhile, were Western nations like Britain, the US and France that revelled in lucrative trade agreements with the South African regime while, hypocritically, denouncing the system of apartheid which, at its heart, was nothing but bare-faced economic exploitation of Black South Africans on grounds of race and colour. That Kallicharran had to pay too high a price is indisputable. His case becomes even murkier when, as an Indian-Caribbean cricketer, ethnic issues will inevitably be dragged into it.

Kallicharran was undoubtedly one of the foremost batsmen to come from the Caribbean. In his hypothetical best West Indies XI, for which he picked Kanhai at No. 3, Clive Lloyd chooses Kallicharran as No. 5. Lloyd confesses that there is great similarity between Kallicharran,

Lawrence Rowe and Seymour Nurse and he chooses Kallicharran, "because of his consistency over the years. Kallicharran is one of the best players of spin bowling I have seen, and one only needs to glance at his scores at Queen's Park Oval in Trinidad, a traditional spinner's paradise, to be convinced of this. This is not to say he was inadequate against pace and, at his best, is the complete player. If there is one deficiency it is that he has very rarely advanced to big scores." [Clive Lloyd, *Living*, 129] In a career of 66 Test matches, Kallicharran's highest Test scores are his 158 against England in Trinidad in February 1974, and 187 against India in Mumbai in December 1978. This is a peculiarity Kallicharran shares with Kanhai who, in 79 Test matches, apart from double centuries against India and Pakistan early in his career, registers only three scores over 150, and only at the very end of his career.

Of the three leading Indian-Caribbean batsmen during the mid-twentieth century Kanhai is the most celebrated chiefly for his adventurous and entertaining style. Solomon matches neither Kanhai's array of strokes nor their glamour. Kallicharran may not be as glamorous as Kanhai either, but he is fearless and attacking, quick on his feet, creative with his wrists, and inventive. It is probably because he is attacking that he does not have more scores like his 187 and 158. His rate of converting fifties to hundreds is almost as low as Kanhai's: twelve hundreds out of twenty-one fifties (57.14 per cent) for Kalilicharran, and fifteen hundreds out of twenty-eight fifties (53.57 per cent) for Kanhai.

His mastery of spin, as corroborated by Lloyd, is evident from his success in a lifetime of battles against India's most wily spinners – Bedi, Prasanna, Venkataraghavan and Chandrasekhar. Like Kanhai and Solomon, Kallicharran's batting against India also stands out: 1229 runs in 14 Tests at 87.78 per Test; 1325 runs against Australia in 19 Tests at 69.22 runs per Test; 917 runs against England in 16 Tests at 57.31 runs per Test; 589 runs against Pakistan in 11 Tests at 53.54 runs per Test; and 365 runs against New Zealand in 5 Tests at 73 runs per Test. His entire career, most memorably, his savaging of Lillee in the 1975 World Cup Final, proves that he was equally adept against the fastest bowlers in the world.

But the sad fact is that after Kallicharran participated in two so-called "rebel tours" to South Africa, along with other West Indian players such as Lawrence Rowe, Colin Croft, Bernard Julien and others, his international Test cricket career abruptly ended. The ban could have been lifted from "rebel" players who apologised, but Kallicharran did not apologise because he thought he had done nothing wrong. Like the South African Cricket Union which invited him, he believed that continued cricket contact with South Africa during apartheid would have a positive effect in Black townships and on race relations in South Africa as a whole. It no longer matters whether this was true or not. The pity is that the Test career of one of the most brilliant West Indian batsmen of his time was brought to a premature end that leaves him feeling victimised, even today, long after the curse of apartheid has been lifted.

CHAPTER 5

1957-1994: Spin bowlers – lepers in West Indian cricket

In December 2008, in an article entitled 'West Indian Cricket: The Plight of Spin Bowlers in the Caribbean', D. Victor argues that although spin bowlers then dominated regional cricket competition in the Caribbean, they were not popular in the West Indies team. He claims that not since the end of Lance Gibbs's Test career in 1973, has a West Indies specialist spin bowler collected more than one hundred Test wickets, and concludes: "Spin bowlers are really lepers in the West Indian cricket colony." [WEB, 16 December 2008] It is true that Victor is thinking of West Indian spin bowlers in general. There were good spinners, for example, Elquemedo Willett or Roger Harper, but in the climate of class and ethnic bias already outlined in this volume, the apparently deliberate neglect of spinners raises suspicions of their ethnicity being partly responsible for their exclusion. While Victor thinks mostly of cricketers from the 1980s onward, his comments may apply, less rigorously perhaps, to the 1970s or before.

Although this chapter mostly considers spin bowlers, it opens with a right-hand opening batsman Nyron Sultan Asgarali (1920-2006), a Trinidadian stroke player who scored heavily in club cricket, but less so in regional or inter-colonial matches. Asgarali properly belongs more to the era of the 1950s and 1960s with Ramadhin, Kanhai and Solomon. He first appeared alongside Ramadhin and Kanhai in two Test matches, in England, in 1957. At the time, West Indies were in process of replacing the great Ws with younger players and, since Asgarali was already thirty-seven years old, he was regarded as temporary, chosen because of his experience of English conditions in Lancashire League cricket. He can also claim two or three impressive innings in regional matches: two against British Guiana at Queen's Park Oval, in February 1952, with scores of 18, 103, 128 and 83, followed by 141 once more against British Guiana, at Bourda, in October 1953, and 124 against Jamaica at Sabina Park in February, 1955.

Nyron Asgarali (sub) makes a dynamic catch to dismiss England's Peter Richardson during the Test at Edgbaston in June 1957. CENTRAL PRESS/HULTON ARCHIVE/GETTY IMAGES

Asgarali was not picked for the drawn First Test at Edgbaston in 1957, and opened the batting for West Indies in the Second Test at Lord's. He was lbw to Fred Trueman for 0 in the first innings, while he managed 26 runs in the second innings of a match which England, as if to celebrate their changed fortune after 'de-clawing' Ramadhin in the First Test, won by an innings and 36 runs. Because West Indies endured two more heavy Test defeats on the tour, Asgarali was not picked again until the Fifth Test at Kennington Oval where he mustered 29 and 7 in another losing cause. This time, his team surrendered to the Surrey spin twins, Laker and Lock, who appropriated sixteen wickets between them at minimal cost. Today, Asgarali is remembered more for his First Class appearances, for instance, in the regional games already mentioned, and in twenty-one matches against English counties, during the 1957 tour, when he amassed 1,011 runs for an average of almost 30 runs.

Andy Ganteaume hints at social or ethnic and class reasons for Asgarali's relegation to a secondary role in Test cricket. Ganteaume claims: "Nyron Asgarali was in my opinion, one of the best batsmen

Trinidad and Tobago has produced but he was not given the opportunities he deserved early enough." [Ganteaume, 113] Between his début in 1941, and in 1948, when England again toured the West Indies, Asgarali never played in both preliminary matches before the Test matches.

In one preliminary match, in 1941, he was run-out for 33 after answering a bad call from Gomez, and was abruptly dropped. He was dropped again after another run-out for 42 in a later match; but although he made two hundreds in the Trinidad and Tobago trial matches for the England tour in 1948, he was not selected for the two matches preceding the Test at Queen's Park Oval: "Instead, Denis Atkinson of Barbados who had not very long before become resident in Trinidad and was one of the [White] Establishment, was preferred." [Ganteaume, 113] On his 1957 tour of England Asgarali's 1011 runs in First Class matches distinguishes him from fellow batsmen like Pairaudeau and Ganteaume himself who failed to reach the 1000 mark.

Ganteaume writes with the authority of a player who shared rooms with Asgarali on their joint 1957 tour to England. He also became a selector later on, and developed a keen sense of the ingrained injustice of the outdated, race/colour-based, feudalistic system of cricket organisation that flourished in the West Indies up to the 1960s. It was the structure of Caribbean history and society that stifled his friend's promise as one of the earliest Indian-Caribbean cricketers with pretensions to authentic Test rank.

Ivan Samuel Madray, a right-arm leg-spinner from Guyana also appeared in two Tests – against Pakistan – the Second Test at Queen's Park Oval, and the Fourth Test at Bourda, in 1958. With a total of three runs in three innings as a batsman, and bowling figures of 35-6-108-0, Madray did not flourish as a Test player. He claims he was out of form and, in an interview with Clem Seecharan [Seecharan, *Indo-West Indian Cricket*, 91-135] blames social or ethnic factors for his misfortune: "Everybody knew that in spite of my lack of form in 1958 I was still the best leg-spinner in the West Indies. [Willie] Rodgriguez was given my place because he was a local White, like Alexander, like Gomez, like Goddard ... If I were a light-skin man I would have been selected [for the tour to India in 1958-59]" The best evidence of Madray's prowess as a leg-spinner, at First Class level, was the Guyana match against Australia in April 1955, when he captured three Australia wickets, including those of Neil Harvey and Peter Burge, for 122 runs from twenty-three overs.

Charran Kamkaran Singh, an Indian-Trinidadian left-arm spin bowler, was born in 1935. In the second regional game of England's tour of the West Indies in 1959/60, in reply to a Trinidad total of 301 runs for nine declared, MCC barely scraped through to 171 for nine declared, largely due to Singh's commandeering of five of their wickets for 57 runs in thirty-four overs; but this splendid form eluded Singh in England's first innings of 382 runs, in the Second Test, when he had to be satisfied with only one wicket for 59 runs from twenty-three overs, while his senior spin partner, Ramadhin, secured three wickets for 69 runs from thirty-five overs. England went on to win the Test, and Singh did a little better in the second innings with two wickets for 28 runs from eight overs.

The Fourth Test of the same series was Singh's second and last. Due to illness of their captain, Peter May, England was led by Colin Cowdrey at a juncture in the series when their one win and two draws meant that they could secure the rubber merely with two more draws. This probably explains the defensive, time-wasting tactics on the English side, and aggressive, short pitched bowling from West Indies in the final two Tests. Singh sent down twelve overs for no wicket in the first innings of the Test, and 41.2 overs in the second for two wickets and 49 runs, which gives him a Test cricket career total of five wickets for 166 runs at an average of 33.20. What he is remembered for, even today, is his run-out for 0 during the West Indies first innings of the Second Test.

In reply to England's first innings total of 382, West Indies had declined to 45 for 5 by lunch in the Second Test, when most of their top batsmen were back in the pavilion. Nor did disaster relent after lunch when three more West Indies batsmen were dismissed. With the score at 98, Singh (the eighth batsman) was run-out, and shortly before tea, bottles and debris from the crowd rained down on one part of the ground, provoking another disturbance with police being called in.

As in the Bourda crowd disturbance, the protestors probably expressed underlying political resentment of a cricket team representing their colonial oppressor: England. In addition, the "culprit" who precipitated McWatt's run-out and previous "errors" was Badge Menzies who, as an Indian-Guyanese, could also be seen as a collaborator with British colonial overlords, just as umpire Lee Kow (Chinese) in Charran Singh's incident, could be seen as a collaborator on ethnic grounds by Trinidadian protestors. Shortly before the Test match, a group had protested against the exclusion of Roy Gilchrist from the West Indies team.

In an Afro-centric view, although Indian (or other) indentured workers as well as African slaves were victims of British colonialism, descendants of African slaves assume primacy (because of their arrival in the Caribbean prior to all indentured workers, and the greater victimisation endured by slaves). This view inspires both Richards's reference to the West Indies team as African, and relegation of someone like mixed-race Alexander to the guilty role of a colonial collaborator.

In his article 'The Drama of Cricket', Ikael Tafari analyses another crowd disturbance in the Second Test against England in Jamaica, in February 1968, when England made 376 in their first innings and, to the growing resentment of the crowd, the home team were dismissed for 143. Forced to follow on, West Indies were doing better in their second innings, with Sobers scoring a century, but they were still short of runs to make England bat again, and when they had reached 204 for five Butcher was given out, caught low behind by the wicket-keeper. Resentment, by then, was at fever pitch and exploded in another riot, and police being called in.

The umpire who gave Butcher out was Douglas Sang Hue, a Chinese Jamaican and, according to Tafari: "The majority of Black Jamaicans, suffering under the daily pressures of near hand-to-mouth survival, would have been at least hoping for the satisfaction of seeing these White men [the England cricket team] – symbols of their oppression – defeated by their local heroes" and "here was a 'Chineeman' siding with 'the enemy' and 'teefing out' the Guyanese Black man Butcher." [p.56] [Appendix 14]

Tafari sees cricket as, "not only an art or collective ritual, but a drama of racial consciousness" [p.85] that presumably excludes Caribbean people not of African origin, for example, Indians and other indentured groups. And when we remember that indentured Indians first arrived as temporary workers in the Caribbean, and never fully shook off their transitory "bird of passage" label in the view of many of their fellow Caribbean citizens, it strengthens feelings for their exclusion. This anomalous 'no man's land', culturally and spiritually inhabited by Indian-Caribbeans, is brought out by Rosanne Kanhai in the Introduction to this book.

As Tafari claims, cricket is, "a gladiatorial drama of consciousness depicting the primordial struggle between Prospero and Caliban – between coloniser and colonised." [p.64] The problem is that it does not recognise the more mixed and complex fate of West Indians who are also colonised by Prospero, but not acknowledged as children of Caliban. This is a dilemma that faces not only Indian-Caribbeans, but Caribbean people as a whole, including Whites and Browns; for despite differences in the colonising process, as this account of Indian-Caribbean cricketers attempts to demonstrate, *all* West Indians are, by definition, irreversibly children of Caliban.

A more substantial Test cricketer is another Trinidadian, the left-arm wrist spinner Inshan Ali (1949-1995), who appeared in twelve Tests between 1971 and 1977, picking up thirty-four wickets at the expensive cost of 47.67 runs each; he also held seven catches. But Inshan too excelled chiefly in First Class matches in which he compiled a career total of 328 wickets at 28.93 runs apiece, one of his best performances being at Queen's Park Oval, in February 1961, against Barbados, when he captured seven wickets for 38 runs from thirty-two overs in the first innings, and sent down forty-five overs for 80 runs and one wicket in the second. He also claims a record twenty-seven wickets in the Shell Shield regional competition in 1974.

His Test début, against India at Kensington Oval, Barbados, in April 1971, brought him no wicket for 60 runs in the first innings, and one for 65 in the second. In March/April the next year, Inshan appeared in three Test matches (all drawn) during New Zealand's tour of West Indies, when he was rewarded with eleven wickets, including a haul of five for 59 (his career best) in the New Zealand first innings of the six-day, Fifth Test match at Queen's Park Oval. This meant that in reply to a West Indies total of 368, New Zealand could only muster 162 in their first innings; but after being set a target of 401 runs for victory, and despite fifty-one overs from Inshan, at the parsimonious rate of 1.94 per over, they were able to eke out another dismal draw in a series with five drawn Tests.

In three matches against Australia in 1973, Inshan collected ten wickets at exorbitant cost – 47.30 each. And after his one wicket in the First Test of the West Indies tour of Australia in 1975/76, he was replaced in the remaining five matches by an ageing Lance Gibbs. It was this abject West Indies surrender to Australia, by one match to five in the rubber, that convinced captain Clive Lloyd, after observing the rampage of Australian fast bowlers like Denis Lillee, Jeff Thompson, Gary Gilmour and Max Walker, to abandon spin and build a similar West Indian task force of super fast bowlers. Hence the emergence of a West Indian express battalion of Colin Croft, Joel Garner, Malcolm Marshall, Andy Roberts, Michael Holding, Sylvester Clarke, Courtney Walsh, Curtly Ambrose, Patrick Patterson, Ian Bishop, Winston Benjamin and Kenny Benjamin.

Although admitting its success in ushering in the most successful period ever in West Indian cricket, from 1976 to the early 1990s, the new fast bowling creed also discouraged the development of Inshan and other spinners such as Jumadeen, Imtiaz Ali, Ranjie Nanan, Rajendra Dhanraj, Elquemedo Willet, Derick Parry most of whom happen to be Indian-Caribbean. Ganteaume, for instance, mentions a young Indian wrist spinner, Ganesh Mahabir, who made the Trinidad team and impressed both the former, respected Jamaica and West Indies opening batsman, Allan Rae, and Tony Cozier. Ganteaume, a selector, thought Mahabir was "positively Test material" [Ganteaume, 10] and writes: "Unluckily for him, [Mahabir] he arrived when West Indies had four great fast bowlers who had to be in the team." [Ganteaume, 10] In the beginning, there was speculation that Inshan had the makings of another mystery spinner like Ramadhin, and Lloyd had high hopes of him in Australia in 1975/76. Whether it was Inshan's all-round cricket that disappointed Lloyd or simply Australia's commanding use of pace that turned the West Indies captain against spin remains a mystery.

It would be hard to prove conclusively that spin was frowned upon because it was a specialism of bowlers most of whom were Indian. Keith Sandiford points out that Jack Noreiga, an African-Trinidadian, "who achieved the distinction of being the only West Indian to capture nine wickets in one Test innings, also found himself discarded after only four Tests." [Goble and Sandiford, 102/103] But the issue of ethnicity both in cricket and West Indian affairs is generally more insidious than explicit. Even if it is true that successful Black spinners like Derick Parry and Roger Harper also had to yield to the emphasis on pace, we cannot know how many Indian spinners were discouraged from achieving success by what Sandiford admits was: "the West Indian determination to abandon spin and place all of their eggs in a fast bowling basket." [Goble and Sandiford, 79]

In Noriega's case he was a surprise pick at the age of almost thirty-five when he played in four Tests against India, and claimed nine wickets in the first innings of the Second Test at Queen's Park Oval in Trinidad, March 1971, a match that India won nevertheless. Since Captain Sobers himself could serve as a spinner, and younger bowlers like Inshan Ali and Jumadeen could also be summoned, it is not so surprising that the selectors neglected to pick Noreiga after the Fifth Test against India in 1971.

Raphick Jumadeen, another Trinidadian was, like Charran Singh, an orthodox, left-arm spin bowler who made his début in the Fifth Test against New Zealand at Queen's Park Oval, in 1972, when Inshan had his career best Test figures of five for 59. Jumadeen emerged with match figures of 64-31-64-1, and in a career lasting from 1972 to 1979, appeared in twelve Tests including two World Series matches against Australia, and picked up twenty-nine Test wickets at an average of 39.34 runs each. However, the times were against spin, and apart from one full home series of four Tests against India in 1975-1976, Jumadeen saw cricket action only in fits and starts. He was picked, for example, for the West Indies tour of England in 1976, but selected to play in only the Second Test at Lord's, a tight match, in which his respectable figures of 28-8-64-1 helped to produce a climactic, last day's play when West Indies wanted 323 runs in about five hours for victory and, in the end, relented from the challenge.

In the Second Test against India at Queen's Park Oval in March 1976, Jumadeen shouldered the lion's share of the bowling by sending down forty-two overs for 79 runs and one wicket when India reached 402 for five declared; and in the Third Test of the series, on the same ground in early April, for all the unusualness of seeing him join forces with fellow spinners Imtiaz Ali and Albert Padmore, their combination proved fruitless when India needed 269 in six hours on a wearing wicket for victory on the last day. India won by six wickets despite Jumadeen's own contribution of forty-one overs for 70 runs and two wickets. The inevitable conclusion from statistics is that, despite its accuracy and economy, Jumadeen's bowling was geared primarily to containment and probably fits a conventional view of lacking penetration. This supports Clive Lloyd's apparently supercilious jibe that spinners bowl but do not take wickets.

Like Inshan, Jumadeen is remembered for his participation in a Test match (the Fourth against India at Sabina Park, Jamaica, in late April 1976) when the game was abruptly curtailed. Everything started smoothly when India batted first and confidently declared their first innings closed at 306 for six. West Indies replied with 391, and the match seemed well poised with Lloyd relying on his fast men – Michael Holding, Vanburn Holder and Bernard Julien – and India putting their hopes on spinners Chandrashekar and Venkataraghavan. Because of West Indies reliance on pace, two Indian batsmen, Gaekwad (80) and Patel (14), retired hurt, and Bedi, the India captain, and Chandrasekhar – both spinners – did not bat for fear of being injured. Viswanath, Gaekwad and Patel did not bat in the second innings, either, because of injuries sustained in the first, and Bedi and Chandrasekar refrained from batting, again, because of fear of injury. India's second innings total closed at 97 and West Indies won by ten wickets.

In a historically divisive Caribbean context, it was inevitable that the reliance on pace would be seen, at least in some quarters, as a strategy of ethnic alienation. The argument that pace brought success is not enough. No Indian-Caribbean Test batsmen either appeared between 1982 and 1994. And there were examples like the Fourth Test in Jamaica against India in 1976 that showed how dangerous fast bowling could be. Vivian Richards identifies the West Indies 1:5 loss to Australia in 1976 and: "the kind of savagery we faced on the Australia tour" as sparks for the West Indian emphasis on fast bowling: "The Australians taught us and we took notice of them. We decided that, if we really were going to survive in this game, something similar [to the fast attack of Lillee, Thomson, Walker, Gilmour] would have to be done." [Richards, 73/74]

Richards notes: "the Indians' historic protest against our bowling" in the Fourth Test against India at Sabina Park, Kingston, Jamaica in April, 1976, but argues: "Holding was not bowling in an evil manner but the wicket was not good. There was a ridge which certainly caused tremendous problems for the Indian batsmen." [Richards, 79/80] This is the point: if the pitch was unsafe, it was the responsibility of umpires to take action. On the same Sabina Park pitch, in January 1998, at the start of the First Test between England and West Indies, after 61 balls and a no ball were bowled, the England physio came on the field six times to attend to his batsmen, and the two captains – Mike Atherton and Brian Lara – agreed with the umpires that the pitch posed a danger to batsmen and the match should be abandoned. In 1976, India's batsmen were endangered. In 1998, it was England's batsmen. Perhaps lessons were learnt from 1976.

Surely cricket ceases to be sport when it produces injuries and fears such as those in the Fourth India/West Indies Test in Jamaica in 1976! Comments from Deryck Murray who kept wicket to many of the fast-bowlers of the seventies and eighties, and in the Jamaican Test under discussion, carry some weight: "It was never our intention to intimidate teams, because we had to face fast bowling ourselves... Intimidation is something that the umpires are there to control... That is not to say they [fast bowlers] shouldn't shake up batsmen with bouncers. It is a thin line. But I don't think we overstepped the line most of the time." [Birbalsingh, *Guyana*, 166]

At the same time, fast bowlers like Michael Holding, Andy Roberts, Robert Croft, Patrick Patterson, Joel Garner, Malcolm Marshall, Courtney Walsh, and Curtly Ambrose were not harnessed in pairs like Larwood and Voce of bodyline fame, but in pairs of pairs that allowed opposing batsmen no respite. From the summer of 1980 when they beat England in England, to April 1995 when they lost to Australia in Jamaica, West Indies won nineteen consecutive Test series and drew eight. In the same period they triumphed in fifty-nine Tests out of one hundred and fifteen, and lost only fifteen. Never before had West Indian fortunes risen to such dizzying heights! But except for brief appearances from Bacchus and Kallicharran until 1982, the dizzying heights were reached without the participation of a single Indian-Caribbean player.

The obituary notice of Douglas Jardine, captain of England during the England/Australia series of 1932/33, explains his bodyline theory which left a legacy of bitter feelings behind: "The method involved fast bowling directed to rise shoulder or rib high, pitched on or outside the leg stump, with some fieldsmen placed on the leg side, three close up round about batsman's left trouser pocket." [*The Guardian*, June 20, 1958] England won the 1932/33 series 4:1 and Jardine's plan succeeded; Bradman's average was reduced from the 90s to the 50s. Was success worth the legacy of feelings that rankled for nearly forty years, at least until England's tour of Australia in 1970/71, when John

Snow, the England fast bowler, hit the Australian spinner Jenner on the head, provoking crowd disturbances that forced Illingworth, England's captain, to take his men off the field? For the record, England regained the Ashes in the match.

The four Tests between West Indies and India in 1976 were quite different from the England/Australia series in 1932/33. Not only was there no theory like bodyline, but West Indies won two matches and India one, while one was drawn which India might have won but for time lost due to rain. So the results are closer than they look. Lax observance of rules about intimidatory fast bowling by the umpires and an uneven bounce at one end of the pitch were also factors, rather than nefarious West Indian planning, or stereotypical notions denigrating the manliness of the Indians. India's nineteen-year-old Vengsarkar, for instance, played the West Indian fast bowlers with ease, and made 39 and 21. Nor did all the wickets fall to fast bowlers in the India second innings when Jumadeen, the sole West Indian spinner, accounted for two wickets.

Of Indian-Caribbean batsmen who appear in the same period, Leonard Baichan was a left-handed batsman and right-arm medium pace bowler who was born in Rosehall, Berbice, Guyana on 12th May, 1946, and played in three Test matches, two as opening batsman against Pakistan. He made a début century (105) the ninth West Indian to do so, in the First Test match in Lahore in February 1975, and 36 and 0 not out in the second match in Karachi. He also played in the Sixth Test against Australia in 1976, batting fearlessly at No. 3 against Lillee and Thomson, and making scores of 3 and 20. Baichan's career figures are three Tests, 184 runs, for an average of 46 and highest score of 105. He was cautious and focused while batting, and if his career seems to stop abruptly, it is because the opening batsmen slots for West Indies were already taken by two stalwarts – Fredericks and Greenidge.

Imtiaz Ali, like Charran Singh, Inshan Ali, and Jumadeen, was another spinner from Trinidad. He was born on 28 July 1954 and was picked as a right-arm leg-break, googly bowler who appeared in one Test match – the Third Test against India in 1976 at Queen's Park Oval Trinidad. He was one of three West Indian spinners in the match and together they claimed five of the twelve India wickets to fall, while the Indian spinners accounted for all sixteen of the West Indies wickets.

In February 1982, Faoud Bacchus played his last Test for the West Indies against Australia in Adelaide. His appearance marked the last time an Indian-Caribbean player would represent the team until March 1994. BOB THOMAS/GETTY IMAGES

Lloyd, the West Indies captain, no doubt felt confident in setting India 406 runs to get in the fourth innings, a target achieved only once before at that time in Test cricket; but his spinners could not break through, and India won with six wickets to spare. It would not be surprising if the experience helped to set Lloyd's mind even more firmly against spin.

Sewdat Shivnarine, a lower order batsman, was born in Albion, Berbice, Guyana on 13th. May, 1952, and took part in eight Test matches beginning with the Third Test against Australia at Bourda, in Guyana, in 1978. Regular West Indian players had left to join World Series Cricket, and fresh players were recruited to fill their vacancies and continue the series against Australia. Shivnarine made an impressive start with innings of 53 and 63 in his début, demonstrating strength as an off side player. He had another good innings of 53 in the final Test in Jamaica before going to India for a Five-Test rubber, where he again impressed with an innings of 62 in the Second Test at Bangalore, and scores of 48 and 36 in the Third Test at Kolkata in December 1978. But he rather faded out by the end of the tour and could not find a place in the team once the regular players returned from World Series Cricket.

Because of the vacancy created by outgoing World Series cricketers, Sheikh Faoud Ahumul Fasiel Bacchus who was born on 31 January 1954, in Campbellville, Guyana, was also drafted into the Fourth Test against India at Queen's Park Oval, in April 1978, when he opened his account with inauspicious scores of 9 and 7. Bacchus also appeared in the Fifth Test against India in Jamaica, the next West Indies tour to India, and showed his true colours in the Second Test at Bangalore with an innings of 96, followed by a string of low scores and, finally, in the Sixth Test at Kanpur, his *piece de résistance*, a magnificent innings of 250 which stands out from the rest of his not exactly imposing achievements like a lonely eminence.

Once the regular players returned to the West Indies team, however, Bacchus was not needed until the West Indies tour to England in 1980. In the First Test at Trent Bridge, in June, he had scores of 30 and 19, plus consecutive noughts in two separate Tests, 61 in the Fourth Test, and 11 in the Fifth. On his next tour, as an opener, he produced yet another 0, in the First Test against Pakistan in Lahore, and 45 and 17 in the Second Test in Faisalabad. Altogether, in Pakistan, he compiled a total of 119 runs for an average of 19.83, and was not selected when England toured the Caribbean in early 1981. His final appearances were in two Tests on the West Indies tour of Australia in 1981/82, and his second appearance in the Third Test at Adelaide, in February, 1982, was the last time an Indian-Caribbean cricketer was seen in West Indies colours until twelve years later, in the Second Test against England, in March, 1994.

Ranjie Nanan, a right-arm, off-break bowler and right-hand batsman, was born on 29 May 1953 in Preysal, Trinidad, but like Imtiaz Ali, was selected for only one Test – the Second Test against Pakistan at Faisalabad in December 1980. Nanan contributed four wickets, took two catches and made 16 runs in a record tenth wicket stand with Sylvester Clarke; an all-round contribution that, in all likelihood, was indispensable to a West Indies victory by 156 runs. Between 1972 and 1990 he also took, "more wickets in the regional (Shell Shield) competition than any other player. In 88 first class matches, he recorded 2,533 runs (av: 21.46), 351 wickets (av: 22.81) and 61 catches. Nanan certainly deserved more than one Test cap." [Goble and Sandiford, 103] Nanan's case is a clear travesty, heavy with implication that he was not omitted purely for cricketing reasons.

But the issue of the special efficacy of fast bowling cannot be laid to rest without acknowledging its true origins in the history of Atlantic slavery, and its special resonance for descendants of enslaved Africans. [Appendix 15] From Herman Griffith, Constantine and Martindale to Holding, Marshall, Ambrose and Walsh, West Indies fast bowlers – all African – have always had an atavistic appeal in the Caribbean. Tafari writes: "In terms of Caribbean history, he [the fast bowler] is an archetype of the rebellious field slave trying with all his might to defeat, if not destroy the [White] master." [p.53] Hence the note of celebration when Vivian Richards asserts West Indies world supremacy in cricket, and attributes it to a team of African descent. But this is no excuse for neglecting spin.

The argument that fast bowling in the 1980s and 1990s was an exclusive panacea for previous West Indies failure may be nothing more than a fig leaf. In the bodyline series of 1932/33, although England's armoury consisted of express speedsters like Larwood and Voce, the celebrated England spinner Hedley Verity appeared in four out of the five bodyline Tests, and despite the presence of Australian fast bowlers like T.W. Wall and L.E. Nagel on the other side, Australian spinners W.J. O'Reilly, Clarrie Grimmett and H. Ironmomger were almost always there. O'Reilly played in all five bodyline Tests.

It is probable that West Indies' success in the 1980s and 90s had as much to do with team discipline and unity as the express deliveries of Holding and Marshall. Deryck Murray makes this case:

> By the time Lloyd came in, around the mid-1970s, players were being exposed to English county cricket and becoming more disciplined and professional, so there was little need to impose discipline: it was already self imposed ... Lloyd had the loyalty of players who had rallied around him during the Packer years. The team almost dictated its own strategies and tactics. Lloyd was simply the focal point around which we functioned as a unit. [Birbalsingh, *Guyana*, 164]

Worrell had similar loyalty and discipline, but although he relied on the speed of Hall and Griffith, Gibbs was never very far away. And although Australian fast bowlers like Glenn McGrath, Brett Lee and Jason Gillespie could be fearsome they were often accompanied by Shane Warne.

Fast bowling is not inherently preferable to spin. True aficionados of the game relish both. The sight of Michael Holding's long, graceful run up, gathering steam through co-ordination of rhythm, balance and breathing before he delivers a ball that drops in line with leg stump and swings to take off stump, is no more dramatic than Shane Warne's so-called "ball of the century" at Old Trafford on 4 June 1993, a huge leg-break that dropped slightly wide of leg stump, turned to hit off stump, and leave Gatting, vaunted master of spin, stewing in suspicion and doubt and looking, for all the world, like a man who has just found that he has terminal cancer. Holding and Warne are supreme artists testing relative skills in a contest, not a war. George Orwell said sport was war without the fighting and, like other sports, cricket can summon feelings of war almost from the bottom of fear and terror to the top of triumph and ecstasy, but without the fighting, damage and destruction of war.

CHAPTER 6

1994-2013: There is no West Indian anthem

As in Chapter Five where the deeds of less well known players during the 1950s, 60s and 70s are considered, Chapter Six discusses the doings of players of less Test experience than Chanderpaul and Sarwan between 1994 and 2013. The more rapid induction of Indian-Caribbean cricketers into the Test team, in this later period, confirms both past neglect of these players and present acceptance of them. Six Indian-Caribbean members in one West Indies team would have been unthinkable between 1950 and 1994. The period between 1950 (the year of Ramadhin's Test cricket entry) and 1994, produced no more than fourteen Indian-Caribbean Test cricketers, one every three or four years: Sonny Ramadhin, Rohan Kanhai, Joe Solomon, Alvin Kallicharran, Nyron Asgarali, Ivan Madray, Charran Singh, Inshan Ali, Raphick Jumadeen, Leonard Baichan, Imtiaz Ali, Sewdat Shivnarine, Faoud Bacchus, and Ranjie Nanan.

The later period from 1994 to 2013, introduced many more Indian-Caribbean players to Test cricket making it seem one per year: Rajindra Dhanraj, Dinanath Ramnarine, Daren Ganga, Suruj Ragoonath, Mahendra Nagamootoo, Dave Mohammed, Narsingh Deonarine, Ryan Ramdass, Denesh Ramdin, Sewnarine Chattergoon, Amit Jaggernauth, Adrian Barath, Ravi Rampaul, Devendra Bishoo, Assad Fudadin, Sunil Narine and Veerasammy Permaul, along with Chanderpaul and Sarwan. (This makes a total of 33 Indian-Caribbean Test cricketers since it does not include Rabindra "Robin" Singh who was born in Trinidad in 1963 and played in one Test match for India against Zimbabwe in 1998.)

The difference in numbers between these two groups of cricketers is not caused by some mysterious loss of interest in cricket which, as James Rodway wrote, had taken root, among plantation Indians in Guyana, before the end of the nineteenth century. The difference is consistent with the history of Indians who, as late arrivals in the region, lived, up to about 1950, as a socially marginalised community, if not directly on Caribbean plantations, in adjacent areas, both in Guyana and Trinidad. Indians were marginalised because of their newness and ethnicity. Coming from an Asian culture with ancient divisions of region, language, caste and colour, they undoubtedly brought a legacy of divisiveness with them too, but the sheer will to survive in a new environment demanded mixing and adaptation.

Rosanne Kanhai's account of leaving her home in the countryside to find lodgings and attend school in the city of Port of Spain is all too true of Indian-Caribbean experience, and may be connected, for instance, with a story "Pooran, Pooran" by the Indian-Trinidadian novelist, Ismith Khan, for a similar atmosphere surrounding Indian-Trinidadian childhood experience and the impact of education on it. [Birbalsingh *Jahaji*, 1-14] That was in the 1950s and 60s; but the essence of more formative Indian-Caribbean experience, probably in the 1930s and 40s, is captured by another Indian-Trinidadian novelist Samuel Selvon:

> "You remember the old days Poya? You remember when it only had barracks for the people to live in? You remember when it didn't have no school? You remember when we used to work for a shilling a day and cut more cane than any blasted machine? And you remember that big strike in nineteen ... when we march from San Fernando to Port of Spain? "[Selvon, 87]

Selvon admirably captures the emotional warmth of ethnic solidarity in a group that is both socially marginalised and economically exploited, but he also recognises forces of political resistance, education, modernisation and Creolisation.

In addition to Indian-Caribbean rusticity, the mid-twentieth century period still carried distinct marks from feudal structures and social habits, provincial or insular attitudes and ethnic bias which did not all, suddenly, at the stroke of independence in the 1960s, disappear into oblivion. After the 1960s, the stranglehold of these structures, habits and attitudes gradually began to give way to the impact of modernisation by means of new trends in education, wider opportunities of travel, electronic means of communication, the

In November 1994, Rajindra Dhanraj became the first leg-spinner to play for the West Indies since 1977. He is pictured in the 5th Test against England at Trent Bridge in August 1995.   DAVID MUNDEN/POPPERFOTO/GETTY IMAGES

almighty internet, and population movement, both within the Caribbean region and outside. Hence the evolution of large West Indian diasporas worldwide, especially in North America. The increased presence of Indian-Caribbean cricketers in the West Indies team since 1994 is part and parcel of these post-independence changes in Caribbean society.

Rajindra Dhanraj, the first of the contemporary players, was born on 6 February 1969 in Barrackpore, Trinidad. A right-handed leg-break, googly bowler, and right-handed batsman, he appeared in four Tests, the first against India, at Mumbai, in November 1994 (seven months after Chanderpaul re-started Indian-Caribbean participation in Test cricket) when he took two wickets for 93 runs; the second against New Zealand at Wellington, in February 1995, when he secured his biggest bag of four wickets for 146 runs. The third was against England at Trent Bridge, Nottingham in August, 1995, when he was savaged for 191 runs without any wickets; and the fourth against New Zealand

After his premature retirement in 2002, Dinanath Ramnarine moved to a career of advocacy for the welfare of West Indian cricketers. His efforts have led to players' issues being taken more seriously than before. DAVID MUNDEN/POPPERFOTO/GETTY IMAGES

in Antigua, in April, 1996, when he collected two wickets for 165 runs. Dhanraj was the first leg-spinner to play for West Indies since David Holford in 1977; but although the art of the right-arm leg-spinner is known to be costly, Dhanraj's total of eight wickets for an average of 74.37 is clearly prohibitive, and may partly explain his infrequent Test appearance and short-lived Test career. No doubt Dhanraj and Ramnarine who follows him lend credence to the stereotype of spin bowling as traditional among Indian-Caribbeans.

Dinanath Ramnarine was born in Trinidad on 4 June 1975 and became better established than Dhanraj as a right-arm leg-spinner, playing in a total of twelve Tests, from 1998 to 2002, and securing forty-five wickets for an average of 30.73. In the first innings of the First Test against England at Bourda, Guyana, in February, 1998, when England were bowled out for 170, Ramnarine's figures were 17-8-26-3, and in the second innings 11-5-23-0, suggesting a useful contribution to a West Indies victory by 242 runs. In his second match in the same series, in Antigua, Ramnarine increased his intake to four wickets for 29 runs from seventeen overs in England's first innings of 127, and two for 70 runs from forty-six overs in a match that England won by an innings and 52 runs. Like Dhanraj, Ramnarine did not appear regularly, but after being picked for one Test against New Zealand in Hamilton, New Zealand, in December 1999, when he took three wickets, he appeared in all five matches of the rubber with South Africa in March/April 2001.

His best performance was in the Third Test of the South Africa series at Kensington Oval, Barbados, beginning on 29th March, when he returned figures of six for 164 runs, and West Indies achieved a draw through dubious tactics of gamesmanship. Ramnarine took one wicket for 86 runs in South Africa's first innings of 454 runs to which West Indies replied with 387. In the South Africa second innings of 197 he enjoyed his only five-wicket haul and the best figures of his career – five wickets for 78 runs from 31.5 overs. West Indies needed 265 runs for victory, but in their second innings, instead of victory, they suddenly faced defeat with their score at 82 runs for seven wickets, with the only batsmen left – two bowlers, Walsh and Cuffy. At this strategic moment, Ramnarine and Dillon – the two not out batsmen – chose to engage in blatant time-wasting tactics such as Ramnarine calling for physiotherapy services on the field, and Dillon changing his boots, which helped them to use up twenty-five minutes to play out the last five overs of the match, and achieve a draw. Umpire Bucknor issued a warning, and Shaun Pollock the South Africa captain later disclosed receiving apologies from senior West Indies players, although none of this alters the result of the match.

Ramnarine took two more wickets in the Fourth Test against South Africa in Antigua, and four in the final Test of the South Africa tour in Jamaica, before joining the West Indies tour of Sri Lanka later the same year, in November 2001. His best figures in Sri Lanka were in the Second Test, at Kandy, in late November, when he scuppered seven wickets for 147 runs. His final Test was against Pakistan in Sharjah, in February 2002, after which Ramnarine's dissatisfaction with the administration of West Indies cricket led him to take premature retirement, and move to a career of advocacy for the welfare of West Indian cricketers.

In 2001, Ramnarine became President of the West Indian Players' Association (WIPA) which was formed in 1973 with Rohan Kanhai as President and Deryck Murray as General Secretary. WIPA was run by the West Indies captain and active players. In its early days, the Association did not carry the image of a professional, pro-active body representing the interests of West Indian cricketers that it now enjoys, with its own office, staff, and availability of experts to provide professional advice on legal, labour or other problems. Since 2003, for instance, there have been strikes by players and disputes about issues such as match fees and contracts; and there is no doubt that much of this is the result of changes spearheaded by Ramnarine who, it is fair to admit, is also regarded as obstructionist in some quarters.

Acrimonious relations between WIPA and the West Indies Cricket Board (WICB) led to an invitation for Ramnarine to join the WICB which he did in 2007, although the collaboration did not last. Whether he has been obstructionist or not, Ramnarine's efforts have led to players' issues being taken more seriously than before. This is the view in "The militant Man of the People," an article by journalist Garth Wattley: "Arguably no single player or administrator has influenced the direction of the game in the Caribbean as much as Ramnarine has done in that time. [Ramnarine's Presidency from 2001 to 2012 when he resigned] He leaves the WIPA ship a stronger vessel, even if one that steers through rough waters." [WEB March, 31, 2012]

Daren Ganga, a right-handed opening batsman, was born in Barrackpore, Trinidad, on 4 January 1979, and appeared in 48 Tests, scoring 2160 runs, including three centuries. His record is one of being omitted and recalled several times, leaving an impression that he never fulfilled his ambition in Tests, whereas he had great success both as a player and captain for Trinidad and Tobago. His Test career began with three matches against South Africa, in South Africa, in December, 1998/January, 1999 when he first batted at No. 6 in the Third and Fourth Tests, and opened in the Fifth when he scored 0 and 9. In three Tests he produced 75 runs from six innings. He was nevertheless thrown in the deep end against mighty Australia in November 2000, again as an opener, when his eight innings yielded 107 runs including two noughts. His first fifty-plus score came in a Test against Zimbabwe in July 2001 when he made 89. Three Tests against Sri Lanka beginning in November 2001 were also unproductive, but scores of 34 and 65 appeared against Pakistan in January and February 2002, and 40 and 63 against Bangladesh in December 2002.

A breakthrough for Ganga came in April 2003 when he took two centuries off Australia. The first – 113 – occurred in the second innings of the Bourda Test – his eighteenth Test match, and the second (117) followed in the next Test in Trinidad, although the remaining two Tests in the series produced scores of no more than 26, 6, 6, and 8. For the next few years Ganga maintained fitful Test appearances producing the occasional fifty-plus knock, for example 73 against Zimbabwe in November 2003, and 60 against South Africa, one month later. In March 2006, he barely missed a third century with 95 against New Zealand at Auckland. But the best was yet to come in the Third Test against India at St Lucia in June 2006 when Ganga exceeded everything that went before: scores of 135 and 66 that ensured a rubber aggregate of 344 and an average of 49.14. He followed up with two 80s against Pakistan, at Multan and Karachi, in November 2006.

Perhaps Ganga's off-and-on career is not as unusual as it looks. What makes Ganga stand out is his capacity for leadership which comes out most strongly in the summer of 2007 when he was vice-captain on the West Indies team to England, and was vaulted into the captaincy, in the Third and Fourth Tests, after Captain Sarwan was injured in the Second Test at Headingley. Ganga offers this explanation of his uneven career:

Daren Ganga had great success both as a player and captain for Trinidad and Tobago but more of an on-and-off career with the West Indies. What makes him stand out is his capacity for leadership. RAJESH JANTILAL/AFP/GETTY IMAGES

My entry into international cricket was premature. I had just played three of four First Class matches, and I was on my first tour with West Indies to South Africa in 1998. Initially I was told by Brian [Lara] and the selectors that it was a learning tour for me and that I would be playing most of the practice matches to help my development. I ended up playing in three of the five [Test] matches of that dreaded tour. The experience made me stronger. It built my character as a cricketer. But as a batsman it scarred me very early in my career. I have had to learn my game at the international level. I always wanted to hone my skills at the First Class level, where you can try and make mistakes and get away with it. In international cricket you make one mistake and you're out. That is my one regret as a batsman." [WEB, 27 September 2011]

Ganga speaks as a Trinidadian rather than an Indian-Caribbean cricketer although he is inescapably both:

When you play for your country, the country you were born in and brought up in, and you sing your national anthem, it brings a different individual spirit to you. Saying you are West Indian, yes, there is a certain amount of patriotism, but there is no West Indian anthem, there is not that sort of closeness. Yes, historically we have achieved great things and when you travel across the world you hear people talking about our legacy. But to be close to it, feel it and interact directly with it on a daily basis, no it is not present. [WEB, 27 September 2011]

Since cricket is the principal, most enduring measure of West Indian nationality and identity, these views from a prominent Test cricketer merit consideration. This chapter of *Indian-Caribbean Test Cricketers and the Quest for Identity* takes its title from Ganga's observation reminding us of the built in, problematic nature of West Indian nationality.

Suruj Ragoonath was born in Charlieville, Trinidad on 22 March 1968, and had his Test début on 5 March 1999 when he was a couple

Mahendra Nagamootoo cites his West Indies cricketing lineage as nephew to both Rohan Kanhai and Alvin Kallicharran. DAVID MUNDEN/POPPERFOTO/GETTY IMAGES

of weeks short of thirty-one. He was an aggressive right-hand opening batsman but probably a little late in starting his Test career. He was run-out for 9 in his first Test innings and made 2 in the second innings. He was lbw cheaply to the same bowler in the next Test as well and was not picked again.

Mahendra Veeren Nagamootoo who claims both Kanhai and Kallicharran as uncles, was born at Whim in Berbice, Guyana, on 9 October 1975, and became a right-arm leg-break, googly bowler, left-handed batsman and all-rounder. He played in five Test matches between 2000 and 2002, and took twelve wickets for 637 runs – an average of 53.08. He also made 185 runs for an average of 26.42 and took two catches. In his first Test, the Fifth in West Indies tour of England in 2000, at Kennington Oval, he had scores of 18 and 13 as well as three wickets. In the Fifth Test against Australia at Sydney, in January, 2001, in the Australia first innings of 452, he claimed three wickets for 119 runs from thirty-five overs, and achieved a top score of 68 in the West Indies second innings of 352, when runs were desperately needed to make Australia bat again. In the end, given 174 to make, Australia won by six wickets, but Nagamootoo will be remembered for bowling Steve Waugh for 103 with a leg break that dropped in the rough, Shane Warne style, a foot outside leg stump, and turned behind the batsman to hit his back leg and wicket.

After his 68 too, Nagamootoo is supposed to have said that batting comes more naturally to him than the bowling for which he was picked. His third appearance was in the First Test against India at his home ground of Bourda. The match was rain-affected and ended in a draw leaving Nagamootoo with 15 not out and one wicket to his credit. In his final Test against New Zealand in Grenada, in 2002, Nagamootoo made 32 in the first innings, and took two wickets for 75 runs from forty-two overs in New Zealand's second innings.

Another spinner Dave Mohammed was born on 8 October 1979 in Princes Town, Trinidad, and played in five Test matches. Although he was picked as a specialist left-arm, chinaman bowler who collected 13 wickets at an average of 51.38, he was also a left-handed batsman who scored 225 runs for a batting average of 32.14, and may well be considered an all-rounder. In his first Test match against South Africa, in Cape Town, in January 2004, he secured three wickets at the expensive price of 140 runs in a drawn match, and in his second match

Dave Mohammed celebrates the wicket of Jacques Rudolph during the Third Test against South Africa in Cape Town in January 2004. TOUCHLINE/GETTY IMAGES

against England at Old Trafford, Manchester, in August 2004, he bowled without reward and England won by seven wickets.

Mohammed's third match was the First Test against India in Antigua in June 2006 when he ended a threatening 54-run partnership between stalwarts V.V.S. Laxman and Yuvraj Singh by clean bowling the left-handed Yuvraj with a chinaman. Not only did Mohammed collect four wickets in the match, albeit at the exorbitant price of 186 runs, but he ensured a draw for West Indies through an aggressive innings of 52 that occupied him until only nineteen balls were left in the match. His fourth match was the First Test against Pakistan in November 2006 at Lahore which Pakistan won by nine wickets. In Mohammed's last Test match, the Second Test against Pakistan at Multan, also in November 2006, his three wickets for 101 runs in the Pakistan second innings again helped to ensure a draw.

Narsingh Deonarine, a left-handed batsman and right-arm off-break bowler, was born on 16 August 1983 in Albion, Guyana and so far has played eighteen Test matches, scored 725 runs with 82 as his highest score, and an average of 29.89. He has also taken 24 wickets at 29.70 apiece. He was first drafted into Test cricket for the South Africa tour of the Caribbean in March /April 2005 during the absence of Lara and six other members of the team over a contract dispute. Chanderpaul took over as captain and Deonarine made his début in the First Test of the tour at Bourda which ended in a draw. Deonarine made 15 not out and, in the South Africa second innings, had a long bowling spell of thirty overs and settled for one wicket for 35 runs. Deonarine next played in the Fourth Test of the South Africa tour in Antigua when he bowled eighteen overs for 69 runs and took no wicket.

On the West Indies tour to Sri Lanka in July 2005, Deonarine played in the First Test in Colombo, a match in which he made 12, and the hosts won by six wickets. In the Second Test in Kandy, he managed scores of 40 and 29. He did even better in the single match he played in Perth, the Third Test against Australia, four years later, in December 2009, when West Indies were given a target of 359 and made 323 in the second innings. Deonarine and Nash put on a dogged partnership of 128 for the fourth wicket, and Deonarine made his highest score, 82, which was also top score in the innings.

On the South Africa tour of the Caribbean in June 2010, Deonarine appeared in all three Tests but performed best in the Third Test in Barbados when he chipped in with 46 out of a first innings total of 231. In the second of two Tests that Australia played in Trinidad, during their tour of the Caribbean in April 2012, Deonarine also had one of his better matches: he scored 55 in the West Indies first innings of 257, and bowled twenty overs from which he claimed two wickets at a moderate cost of 32 runs. His best performance, however, was on the tour of the Caribbean by New Zealand in July and August 2012. In the first innings of the First Test, in Antigua in July, Deonarine recorded his second highest score, 79, and in the first innings of the Second Test in Jamaica, he bowled twelve overs and took two wickets for 43 runs, while in the second innings he excelled himself with four wickets for 37 runs from twenty-two overs.

Ryan Rakesh Ramdass, a right-hand batsman and right-arm off-break bowler, was born on 3 July 1983 in Ogle, Guyana, and played as an opening batsman in only one Test match – the Second Test against Sri Lanka in Kandy in July 2005. Ramdass was run-out for 3 in the

Right-arm off-break bowler and left-handed batsman, Narsingh Deonarine made his West Indies Test début in 2005 against South Africa at his home ground of Bourda in Guyana. ROB JEFFERIES/GETTY IMAGES

first innings and made 23 in the second innings of a match which West Indies lost by 240 runs. He is better known as a regional First Class cricketer.

Denesh Ramdin, wicket-keeper and right-hand batsman, was born on 13th March, 1985, in Couva, Trinidad, and had his début in the first Test against Sri Lanka in July, 2005, at Colombo, where he scored 56 and 11. In his fourth match, in the Second Test against Australia at Hobart, in November, 2005, Australia had a first innings lead of 257 runs, and held West Indies to ransom at 140 for six in their second innings, facing certain defeat, probably by a huge margin. With their top six batsmen already out, Ramdin (71) and Dwayne Bravo (113) joined forces in a stand of 182 runs that won West Indians a modicum of self-respect, since it forced Australia to bat again and score 78 runs to win.

Ramdin's batting prowess and generally competitive spirit emerge from another innings against India, in the Fourth Test, in Jamaica, during June, 2006, when a visiting Indian journalist wrote: "He [Ramdin] almost pulled off a miraculous victory ... On a pitch where only two other batsmen reached fifty, Ramdin showed remarkable skill against the Indian spinners. His persistent sweeping drove Harbajan Singh out of rhythm and a languorous six off Kumble had India wincing for a while." [WEB, Kanishkaa Balachandran, 6 July 2006] Faced with a fourth innings target of 219, West Indies were in terminal decline at 144 runs for seven wickets, when Ramdin strode in and hit a lightning 50 from a mere 68 balls, bringing victory almost in sight until, at 62 not out, he suddenly ran out of partners, and ceded victory to India by 49 runs.

Altogether, in 56 matches, Ramdin scored 2235 runs, including twelve fifties and four centuries. He also took 156 catches and made 5 stumpings. It wasn't always smooth sailing, however, as there were periods when his batting consistency lagged, and his position was under scrutiny by the selectors. Reaching 166, his highest score, in the Second Test against England, in Barbados, in March 2009, for instance, was a long-awaited event, and the first time that Ramdin celebrated his achievement by holding up a previously written note to the crowd. He repeated his feat in the Edgbaston match, in England, in June 2012, when he again scored a century (107 not out) although this time the note made negative remarks about Vivian Richards for which Ramdin received a fine from the match referee. His third hundred was against

In 2005, Denesh Ramdin became the second Indian-Caribbean player to keep wicket for the West Indies. The first was Rohan Kanhai. MARTY MELVILLE/AFP/GETTY IMAGES

Adrian Barath made an eye-catching début against Australia in November 2009 with a first appearance Test century. PUNIT PARANJPE/AFP/GETTY IMAGES

Bangladesh at Dhaka in November 2012. Ramdin will certainly be remembered for his originality in expressing his feelings through written notes held up to cricket fans.

Sewnarine Chattergoon, a left-handed opening batsman and leg-break bowler, was born on 3 April 1981 in Fyrish, Guyana, and had a short career of four Tests beginning with the First Test against Sri Lanka in Trinidad in April 2008 when he made 46 and 11. He next played in the Third Test against Australia, in Barbados, the same year, making 6 and 13. In December 2008 he toured New Zealand and appeared in two Tests producing scores of 13, 13 and 25 that altogether give him a career total of 127 runs with an average of 18.14. As an opening batsman, Chattergoon was admired for his solid defensive technique. He was also a very good slip fielder.

Another cricketer is Amit Jaggernauth, a right-arm, off-break bowler, who was born on 16 November 1983, in Trinidad, and played in only one Test against Australia in Jamaica, in May 2008. He scored no runs and took one wicket for 96 runs. Jaggernauth had a more active career in domestic cricket and made his début in first class cricket since 2002, but the selectors concentrated on fast bowlers at the time.

Adrian Barath, a right-hand batsman and right-arm off-break bowler, was born on 14 April 1990 in Chaguanas, Trinidad, and has so far appeared in fifteen Tests matches after an eye-catching début against Australia in November 2009, when he had the rare distinction of compiling a first appearance Test century. Barath was mentored by Lara who noticed him at a young age, which might explain why he is the youngest West Indian player since Sarwan to make his début in First Class cricket. Barath is also the youngest ever West Indian player to score a Test century, a record he snatched from the illustrious George Headley. In fifteen Tests he has amassed 657 runs for an average of 23.46, and his début 104 so far remains his only century, although he also has four fifty-plus plus scores. The first is exactly 50 in the First Test against Sri Lanka at Galle, in November, 2010, when he put on 110 runs in partnership with Gayle, while his 64 in the First Test against India in Jamaica, in June 2011, was the top score out of a West Indies total of 173 in a match that India won by 63 runs. Barath also made 62 out of 463 in the First Test against India at Kolkata in November 2011, and another 62 in the Third Test of the same series in Mumbai where he shared in an opening stand of 137 with Brathwaite.

Ravindranath (Ravi) Rampaul, a right-arm fast medium bowler and left-hand batsman, was born on 15 October 1984 in Preysal, Trinidad, and has so far appeared in eighteen Test matches. Rampaul is truly a rare bird – the first and only Indian-Caribbean Test cricketer who bowls close to 90 miles per hour. One of his most successful exploits was in the First Test against Pakistan at Providence, Guyana, in May 2011, when he claimed three wickets for 27 runs from seventeen overs in the first innings and, more importantly, four for 48 from twenty-one overs in the second innings. The result was that Pakistan was bundled out for 178 runs, and lost a close-run match by merely 40 runs. Between this Test in Providence and the second on the same tour in St Kitts, Rampaul accounted for eleven Pakistan wickets.

Devendra Bishoo, a right-arm leg-spinner and left-hand batsman was born on 6 November 1985 in New Amsterdam, Guyana. He has so far played in eleven Tests and taken forty wickets for an average of 39.55. In the First Test against India, in Jamaica, in June 2011, India made 246 and Bishoo bowled eleven overs grabbing three wickets for 75 runs. In the second India innings of 252, Bishoo commandeered four wickets for 65 runs from twenty-four and a half overs, an excellent return for a leg-spinner, although India won the match.

In the Second Test against Bangladesh in October 2011 Bishoo again had a good haul of three wickets for 62 runs from twenty-three overs in the Bangladesh first innings and, in their second innings, when they faced the impossible task of acquiring 508 runs for victory, Bishoo registered the best bowling figures of his career: 25-6-90-5 – his only five-wicket haul to date, and one that clinched West Indies victory. Bishoo's figures for the match – eight wickets for 152 runs – were the best ever from a West Indian bowler in a match outside of the Caribbean, since Lance Gibbs's nine wickets for 143 runs, in India in 1974/75. Later in 2011, Bishoo won the 'Emerging Player of the Year' award from the ICC.

Assad Fudadin, a left-handed batsman and right-arm, medium-fast bowler, was born in Guyana on 1 August 1985, and has so far played three Test matches and scored 122 runs for an average of 30.50. Batting at No. 3 in his first Test at Edgbaston, in June 2012, the historic Test with six Indian-Caribbean players, he contributed 28 to a West Indies first innings of 426, but the rain-affected match ended in a draw. In two other matches against New Zealand in Antigua and Jamaica, in

Ravi Rampaul is the first and, so far, only Indian-Caribbean West Indies fast bowler.
DANIEL BEREHULAK/GETTY IMAGES

In 2011, Devendra Bishoo won the 'Emerging Player of the Year' award from the International Cricket Conference (ICC). JEWEL SAMAD/AFP/GETTY IMAGES

In his first Test appearance, at Edgbaston against England in June 2012, Assad Fudadin helped make history by being one of six Indian-Caribbean players in the West Indies team. He is pictured surviving an appeal from wicketkeeper Matt Prior and Andrew Strauss. STU FORSTER/GETTY IMAGES

July and August, the same year, Fudadin added scores of 55, 7 not out, 5 and 27.

Sunil Philip Narine, a right-arm, off-break bowler and left-handed batsman, was born in May 1988, in Trinidad. Primarily a bowler, he made his début in the Edgbaston match in June 2012 when he bowled fifteen overs for 70 runs and no wicket. He also played in two matches against New Zealand in Antigua and Jamaica in July and August, and two in Pakistan in November 2012. In the first innings of the First Test against New Zealand, in Antigua, in July, Narine had his first five-wicket haul: 43-9-132-5, and in the second innings he had 42-13-91-3, giving him notable match figures of eight wickets for 223 runs. In the second New Zealand match in Jamaica, he claimed another four wickets. In the second innings of this match his figures read 12-1-19-3.

Sunil Narine made his West Indies Test début against England at Edgbaston in June 2012.

Veerasammy Permaul is one of a small handful of Indian-Caribbean cricketers whose spin bowling has become a permanent feature of the West Indies repertoire.
MICHAEL BRADLEY/AFP/GETTY IMAGES

So far, in six Tests, he has gained twenty-one wickets for 851 runs and an average of 40.52, his best performance being in the first innings of the Third Test against New Zealand at Hamilton in December 2013, when he scooped six wickets for 91 runs.

Veerasammy Permaul is a slow, left-arm, orthodox spin bowler who was born in Albion, Guyana, on August 1989. He had his début in the First Test of the West Indies tour to Pakistan, in Dhaka in November, 2012, when he took one wicket in the first innings and three in the second, giving him a match analysis of four wickets for 107 runs. In the Second Test at Khulna he claimed four wickets. In a career so far of four Tests, he has taken twelve wickets for 452 runs and an average of 37.66. Along with Bishoo and Narine, Permaul fulfils the legacy of Sonny Ramadhin who, more than sixty years ago, to acclaim from cricketing nations the world over, established spin bowling as a permanent feature of the West Indies repertoire.

CHAPTER 7

Shivnarine Chanderpaul: He kills with a thousand scratches

Born in Unity, Guyana on 18 August 1974, Shivnarine Chanderpaul has an auspicious antecedent in Sir Garfield Sobers who, as a slender, willowy teenager from Barbados, was drafted into Test cricket in March, 1954, more for his spin bowling than his left-handed batting. Chanderpaul too, as a teenager, was granted his début, exactly forty years later, in the Second Test against England in March, 1994, as much for spin bowling (leg-breaks) as for his left-handed batting. But four half-centuries, one each in Chanderpaul's first four Tests, prove that if the selectors had picked him for the wrong reasons, they had listened to the right omens; for, on his début at St John's, Antigua, when he made 62 and shared a partnership of 126 with Jimmy Adams, Chanderpaul revealed the unostentatious, business-like manner and safety-first stroke play that, for much of the latter half of his career, often transformed him into the very bed rock on which West Indies fortunes rested.

Chanderpaul's 50 in the Third Test in England's 1994 series in Trinidad, was marred by two chances at 4 and 29. But his 77 in the next Test in Barbados set a pattern for him to bat at No. 6 and, more often than not, rely mainly on tail-enders for resolute, back-to-the-wall heroics against all comers. His 77 was top score in the West Indies first innings total of 304, in the Barbados Test, in reply to England's 355. When, in the early stages of the match, West Indies were in grave peril at 126 for six, Chanderpaul rallied heroic support from two bowlers – Ambrose (44) and Benjamin (43) – in partnerships that gave their team at least a fighting chance in the match. The chance was not grasped, for England won by 208 runs; but Chanderpaul's example had inspired in the tail-enders exactly the sort of fighting spirit that would eventually become a template of his mascot role for West Indies.

As for his 75 not out in the Fifth England against West Indies Test in St Johns, Antigua, in April 1994, it was made partly in association with Brian Lara's 375, then the world record for the highest Test score; but this record was overtaken by Australia's Matthew Hayden (380) in 2003, and later surpassed by Lara himself who scored 400 in the Fourth Test against England in April 2004. During his 375, although Lara shared in preceding partnerships of 179 with Adams, and 183 with Arthurton, it was in the later stages of this historic innings which lasted for two full days that. according to Wisden, "he [Lara] needed shepherding by the impressively mature Chanderpaul" [WEB, Almanack Archive Home 1995] in a partnership of 219 that took him [Lara] to his coveted goal.

In his book *Beating the Field: My Own Story* Lara admits the encouragement given to him by Chanderpaul: "Chanderpaul was constantly speaking to me, urging me to keep my concentration and not give it away. For a nineteen-year-old he showed amazing maturity and I shall always be grateful to him for the part he played in my success." [Quoted in Vijay Kumar, *418 to Win*, 119] Chanderpaul's batting in early 1994 makes it clear that as the world tended to focus attention on his eccentricities (the black stripes on his face to ward off glare; his officious use of a bail to mark his guard; his unusual, bent-over stance, with his legs splayed open and his face turned more toward point than the bowler – his so called crabby technique) it was more by dint of unrelenting occupation of the crease, and studious accumulation of runs, that he could stake out a path to glory.

In 1994, out of three Tests between West Indies and India, Chanderpaul appeared only in one: a drawn match at Nagpur in early December, when he made 15 runs and bowled twenty overs taking one wicket for 63 runs. In a two-Test rubber against New Zealand, in February, 1995, in addition to bowling a few overs, Chanderpaul contributed 69 to the drawn First Test at Christchurch, and chipped in with another innings of 61 not out in the Second Test at Wellington which West Indies won by the crushing margin of an innings and 322 runs. In a rubber with England in 1995, Chanderpaul appeared only in the Fifth and Sixth Tests, in August, producing scores of 18 and 5 not out in the Fifth, and 80 in the Sixth, for a tour aggregate of 103 and average of 51.50. Against New Zealand, again, this time in the Caribbean, two Tests brought him a reward of 131 runs for an average of 42.75.

Chanderpaul's first big challenge was a full tour of Australia from November 1996 to February 1997 when he appeared in all five Tests.

In the first innings of the First Test at Brisbane, he hit 82 and was bowled for 14 by McGrath in the second innings. More in character was the Second Test in Sydney where, facing a target of 340 in the fourth innings of the match, West Indies capitulated with 215, and Chanderpaul who had displaced Adams to bat at No. 5, achieved top score (71) after a brave if futile salvage operation with Hooper that yielded 117 runs for the fourth wicket. He scored with such unaccustomed freedom and authority that, at one stage, Warne had to be removed from the attack. His first 50 came off 38 balls although, in the end, Warne was brought back and devised a huge leg-break that turned in and hit Chanderpaul's wicket. Thanks mainly to a brilliant haul of nine wickets by Ambrose, West Indies won the Third Test at Melbourne. Chanderpaul contributed another top score of 58 that gave his team a small if crucial first innings lead of 36, but elevated to No. 3 in the batting line-up, he did not shine in the next two Tests, and West Indies lost the rubber 2:3.

The discouraging effect of four draws on India's tour of the Caribbean during March/April 1997 was relieved by a West Indies victory, despite its narrow margin of 38 runs, in the Third Test at Kensington Oval, Barbados. It is a memorable match in that India was set a final target of only 120 runs, and still fell short on a pitch of variable bounce. More memorable still, at least from Chanderpaul's point of view, was his first innings score of 137 not out (his first century in nineteen Tests) after he had acquired thirteen previous scores between 50 and 82. He devoted seven and a half hours to his chanceless 137 which included twelve boundaries.

For the next eleven series, until April 2002, when India visited the Caribbean again, Chanderpaul's batting seemed to go through a purgatory of doubt and dismay. Evidence from these arid years bears out his claim of working at his game with unceasing regularity. Six innings from three matches of a tour of Pakistan in November/December 1997 produced one notable score of 95, an aggregate of 153 and an average of 25.50, while five Test matches from England's tour of the Caribbean in January/March 1998 supplied only 272 runs, except that they included Chanderpaul's second century (118 runs) made in February 1998, in the first innings of the Fourth Test at Bourda, where he was afterwards thronged by grateful countrymen because it was the only Test century they had witnessed from a Guyanese, in their homeland, since Clive Lloyd's magnificent 178 against Australia in 1973. Although he was dropped at 9, Chanderpaul's century lasted six and a half hours, contained one six and fifteen fours, and included a partnership of 159 all of which proved vital to victory for West Indies who also won the rubber 3:1 with one drawn match.

The West Indies tour of South Africa from November 1998 to January 1999 was even less productive for Chanderpaul, ten innings netting him a mere 266 runs at an average of 26.60. His best results were two 70s, the first being 74 in the first innings of the opening Test at Johannesburg when, once again, he scored the most runs (out of 261) in another long (four and a half hours) determined knock. He also made 75 in the Durban Test at the end of December, but it was a dismal series in which West Indies lost all five matches.

An important aspect of this early stage of his career is that there was no fixed position for Chanderpaul who was moved around from almost every position from an opener to No. 6. The sense of being rudderless came out in his batting during his next eight encounters, over three years, between January 1999 and January 2002. There was only one score of 70 against New Zealand at Wellington in December 1999, and one of 89 against Pakistan in Antigua in May, 2000; there was also 73 at Edgbaston in England in June, 2000, and 74 against Zimbabwe in Harare, in July 2001; but these innings are well spaced out. What is important is that his shifting around in the batting line-up, serving as a general dogs body, seemed to unsettle him. Not until April 2002 at the beginning of India's five-match tour of the Caribbean did Chanderpaul finally settle down at No. 6 in the batting line-up, ready for the real take off of his career.

In addition to his similarity with Sobers in starting off as a bowler before becoming a specialist batsman, the record shows that Chanderpaul and Sobers perform best at No. 6, except that Sobers was regarded as a specialist in almost everything from batting and bowling to fielding, catching or whatever else. After appearing higher in the batting order early in his career, and consulting with Worrell, as already mentioned, Sobers switched to No. 5 or No. 6, and after 1965, almost invariably to No. 6. In his greatest tour, to England in 1966, he never shifted from No. 6 in eight Test innings, with spectacular results – a Bradmanesque aggregate of 722 runs and average of 103.14. His most spectacular achievement was in the Second Test at Lord's when

West Indies were in dire distress at 95 for five (effectively 9 runs for five wickets because of a first innings deficit of 86) and Sobers and his cousin David Holford contrived, whether through science or magic, a partnership of 274 runs that produced a draw. The transformation in Chanderpaul's results at No. 6 is almost as career-changing.

India's 2002 Caribbean tour which comes soon after completion of the first one-third of Chanderpaul's 153 Test matches, is pivotal since it marks the point when he has more or less decided on essentials of his batting: intense concentration, studious attention to the state of play, and undisturbed occupation of the crease. Most of all, he is reconciled to his role as a standard bearer who can provide resistance when misfortune looms. But in the Second Test of this 2002 series when India set West Indies a reasonable target of 313 runs to get in favourable conditions, in the fourth innings, Chanderpaul and Gayle had put on 73 for the fifth wicket when Gayle got out leaving his team 76 runs short with five wickets remaining. The long tail then collapsed leaving West Indies still 37 runs short of victory, and consigning Chanderpaul to isolation on 67 not out. Chanderpaul suffered in this way a few times, but evidently thought he and his team had more to gain from his chosen batting order.

A glance at Chanderpaul's tour statistics reveals the importance of the India series to his career: 7 innings, 562 runs, three centuries, and an average of 112.40. In the First Test at Bourda which ended in a draw because of rain, Chanderpaul achieved his third century and what was then his highest score – 140. He and Hooper (233) were together for six hours and eleven minutes during a stand of 293. India won the Second Test, and West Indies returned the compliment with victory in the Third Test in Barbados by ten wickets, thanks to another partnership between Hooper and Chanderpaul (101 not out) this time for 215.

The high-scoring Fourth Test in Antigua was drawn with both Hooper and Chanderpaul each returning an identical score – 136 runs (Chanderpaul's fifth century). The difference was that Hooper's effort required 401 minutes and 278 balls, while Chanderpaul's utilised 675 minutes and 510 balls. A win by ten wickets in the Fifth Test, in Jamaica, gave West Indies victory in the rubber 2:1 with two matches drawn. Such was the brilliance of Chanderpaul's form in the series that he snatched two further 50s (58 and 59) in this final match. In terms of statistics alone, results from this India rubber transformed Chanderpaul into one of the increasingly rare jewels still maintaining its lustre in the fast fading crown of contemporary West Indian cricket.

On a two-match tour of the Caribbean, in June 2002, New Zealand won the First Test in Barbados by 208 runs due mainly to reckless batting in the West Indies first innings of 107, when only Chanderpaul weathered the collapse with 35 not out. The second match was drawn and was followed, in October, by a West Indies tour of India in which the hosts won the three-match rubber 2:0 with one draw. When India won the First Test in Mumbai by an innings and 112 runs, resistance came once again mainly from Chanderpaul whose 54 in the first innings was the highest out of a total of 167. Chanderpaul was also the last man out and, in the second innings of 188, again remained the lone survivor of the carnage with 36 not out. In the Third Test at Kolkata, a drawn match, Chanderpaul was more impressive with 140 in the West Indies first innings of 497. Such was his mastery of India's spin attack that he struck four 4s and one six in two consecutive overs from Kumble.

If India's tour of the Caribbean in April/May 2002 gave Chanderpaul's cricket fresh impetus, the Australia tour, one year later, confirmed that it was no fluke. Never mind that Australia won the rubber 3:1, nor that one of their victories was in the First Test match at Bourda where Chanderpaul's innings of 100, made off their bowling, is now ranked as the fourth fastest in Test history! It was not its size for there are bigger scores: it was the completely unexpected combination of spectacle and drama with irony, calmness and control. When Chanderpaul came in with the score at 53 for five, not all that different from the 95 for five that Sobers encountered at Lord's in June 1966, we expected calmness, control and sobriety mixed with stout, unyielding defiance in the midst of a solemn vigil. Instead, we got a hundred in sixty-nine minutes, fourth only behind hundreds by Vivian Richards (56 balls), and Australia's Adam Gilchrist (57 balls) and Jack Gregory (67 balls).

The irony of Chanderpaul's epic innings is that its speed and abundance of sixes and fours seem to contradict his more phlegmatic demeanour as corroborated by comments from Mike Brearley, former captain of England. Using a metaphor from boxing Brearley writes: "He [Chanderpaul] is like an awkward southpaw who cleverly negotiates his opponent's attack, swaying this way and that, while delivering deft touches, landing like afterthoughts. He kills by a thousand scratches," [Brearley, *The Observer*, 16 June 2007] implying perhaps that rather than employing full blooded strokes, Chanderpaul is more of a deflector, nudger and tickler.

To be fair, Chanderpaul's awkward stance, as if he is about to fall over at any moment, together with his phlegmatic approach, do give that impression. But it is deceptive or at least misleading; for Chanderpaul has almost as full a range of strokes (except the falling hook) as Kanhai. Chanderpaul is something of a Jekyll and Hyde figure, in that we can never tell when he will switch from his introverted approach to more extroverted stroke play.

Rashness or adventure are alien to Chanderpaul who prizes more classical virtues of control, order, brevity and understatement. When he chooses to he can dish out sixes and fours as in his Bourda 100, or summon up grace and suppleness in deploying strokes of perfect timing and placement. Make no mistake, his Bourda 100 was no flash in the pan, due to some aberrant rush of blood, but a product of cerebral deliberation and thought. Chanderpaul does not bludgeon, pummel or pound. Minimum force is used and, wherever possible, the ball is directed or steered. Control and safety are guiding stars. Chanderpaul's batting is the handiwork of a classical master executed without frill or fuss, purely for the sake of itself. There is a certain nobility in a man who can insinuate himself so completely in work or art.

Chanderpaul's is the purest form of art, as James previously enunciated, a dramatic spectacle like theatre, ballet, opera and dance. For example, what James perceives is that the dramatic spectacle of watching Brad Hogg and Jason Gillespie bowling to Chanderpaul at Bourda, "in its own way grasps at a more complete human existence." [James, *Boundary*, 206] This is not mere abstraction. To a devotee of the dramatic art of cricket, as seen in Chanderpaul's Bourda innings in April, 2003, when a ball is bowled with skill or guile and struck with fitting timing, fluency and grace, the joint *reciprocal* activity (of bowler, batsman and fielder) conveys an impression of order, completeness and symmetry, of a natural fitness of things falling into place, as if by divine will.

Because of injuries in the Bourda Test Chanderpaul did not play in the next match in Trinidad which Australia won, as they did again in the Third Test in Barbados. For the Fourth Test in Antigua, cock-a-hoop

Australia were looking for another win that would complete a "whitewash" of their Caribbean antagonists. It is what adds spice to their complete reversal of fortunes in the Fourth Test, as the entire West Indies team joined ranks to turn the tables and achieve a memorable victory. And once more, of accredited batsmen, it was Chanderpaul alone left standing almost to the very end. By some freak, both teams made exactly the same score – 240 – in their first innings. Then, centuries by the two Australia openers put their team well ahead with a total of 417 that left their opponents with the dismaying task of achieving 418, a total never before seen in the fourth innings of a Test match.

When their captain Brian Lara was out at 165 for four West Indies saw the writing on the wall. But Sarwan and Chanderpaul steadfastly resisted with a stand of 123 runs before Sarwan was caught and bowled by Brett Lee for 103. As if that was not calamity enough, the incoming batsman Ridley Jacobs was caught by his fellow wicket-keeper at the same score. The ball had touched Jacobs's elbow and the crowd, moved to anger more by disappointment than disagreement with the dismissal, created another disturbance, briefly interrupting the game. That Chanderpaul could withstand such turmoil on top of the tension of the uphill task of getting another 130 runs, without reliable partners, is an essential part of his contribution to a team traditionally mocked for their predilection to cavalier "calypso-collapso" cricket!

Time was not a problem: an entire day remained, as Chanderpaul soldiered on to the end of the fourth day carrying the total to 371 for six, and his own score to 103. Early on the last day, he fell to Brett Lee after adding one run only, and the fate of the game was left in the hands of two bowlers Omari Banks (47) and Vasbert Drakes (27). The situation was a virtual replay of the finale of the Third Test against England in Barbados during Chanderpaul's début series in 1994 when he had brought his team to the brink of success but, despite their superhuman effort, Ambrose and Benjamin fell short of the finish line. This time, though, Banks and Drakes bravely defied the enemy to add another 26 runs and win an unforgettable victory. Chanderpaul won the 'Man of the Match' award.

Chanderpaul's aggregate from the three Australia matches is 257, and although his average of 42.53 is less than half as good as his average in the preceding India series in October 2002, it is more memorable. On a tour to South Africa in December 2003 and January 2004 Chanderpaul hit his ninth hundred (109) including one six and twenty fours in the second Test at Durban in December, 2003. His three matches in South Africa brought him a total of 286 runs for an average of 47.66. But England swept all before them winning three out of four matches in their Caribbean tour in March/April 2004, and Chanderpaul's figures plunged alarmingly to a total of 101 runs from six innings that included two noughts. His average of 16.83 also seems a temporary aberration that gave way to a return of prosperity in Bangladesh's short tour of May/June 2004 when Chanderpaul's chalked up his tenth Test century (101 not out) in Jamaica, in June 2004.

Chanderpaul's previous visits to England, in 1995 and 2000, were short and moderately successful. In July 2004, the first of four Tests in England brought out his true colours. England ran up a blockbuster total of 568 runs and West Indies had reached 139 for five before Chanderpaul entered the fray. He acted virtually as a one-man army after Lara got out cheaply, on a dubious decision, and only Gayle of the remaining West Indies players managed anything over 50. Chanderpaul met the full brunt of the England assault from Hoggard, Harmison, Jones and Giles batting through the entire lower half of the innings for 128 not out.

Not only that, after England threw down a challenge of 478 runs to get in the fourth innings, West Indies were again floundering at 172 for four after Lara was clean bowled by Giles, and Chanderpaul stepped into the breach with a score of 97 not out. West Indies fell short by 210 runs, but Chanderpaul's heroic combativeness was indisputable even if he did not achieve success for his team, or glory for himself by so narrowly missing the signal honour of two not out centuries at Lord's, cricket headquarters. He had remained unbeaten after ten hours and fourteen minutes of continuous occupation of the crease during the match; certain proof of his dauntless, defiant approach and unrelenting will to survive.

For integrity of will, and sheer grit and grind in confronting pressure, it would be hard to find Chanderpaul's equal in world cricket. Other batsmen are known for stubborn obduracy or stonewalling, but they are not main batsmen on whom the team regularly depends for sustenance. Here is another similarity between Sobers and Chanderpaul: as a front line batsman, while he was West Indies captain in the late 1960s and early 1970s, it is remarkable how often the team also failed when Sobers failed. Since Chanderpaul failed to repeat his heroics of the Lord's Test in the remaining three Tests, England won all three with convincing margins. Chanderpaul had one more good innings (76) in the Third Test at Old Trafford but benefited from his 225 runs in his Lord's marathon, and came out with his best tour statistics so far in England – 437 runs for an average of 72.83.

In a situation reminiscent of the Packer era when Clive Lloyd and other West Indies players temporarily abandoned Test cricket for World Series Cricket in Australia, in 1978, Captain Lara and six team-mates were absent from the West Indies team at the start of the South Africa rubber at Bourda, Guyana, in March, 2005, because of a dispute with the West Indies Cricket Board about sponsorship. As in 1978, a new West Indies team had to be assembled. Chanderpaul was appointed captain, and batting first in the First Test, West Indies ran up a huge total of 543 for five with double centuries from Wavell Hinds (213) and Chanderpaul (203 not out).

The slow, cautious and careful accumulation of Chanderpaul's style is once more evident from a contrast between his runs and those of Hinds: Hinds faced 297 balls and hit thirty-four fours and two sixes, while Chanderpaul received 369 balls and hit twenty-three fours. Even allowing for Chanderpaul's added responsibility as captain, the difference of Hinds' more attacking and adventurous play is obvious. South Africa, meanwhile, mainly through the fabled, all-purpose wizardry of Jacques Kallis, engineered a draw, and Chanderpaul, who got in thirteen overs of his own bowling for 25 runs and no wicket, was named 'Man of the Match'.

Although West Indian players, including Lara, who missed the First Test returned for the rest of the series, Chanderpaul continued as captain. South Africa won the Second Test in Trinidad and the Third in Barbados, while the Fourth in Antigua, which was drawn, produced a surfeit of runs. St John's, Antigua was where Lara had made both his 375 and 400. The ground was replaced by a freshly built one, but not before Gayle unfurled his triple century (317) in the Fourth Test against South Africa in 2004. Batting first, South Africa compiled 588 for 6 declared to which West Indies replied with 747, including Gayle's 317, and centuries from Sarwan and Chanderpaul, both with an identical 127. Chanderpaul amassed 450 runs in the series for an average of 90.00, while the results of his first stint at captaincy, with two losses and two draws, looked rather less promising.

On a brief tour of two Tests by Pakistan, in May/June 2005, the tourists won the First in Barbados and lost the Second in Jamaica. Chanderpaul excelled with two scores of 92 and 153 not out in the Barbados Test leading to his series total of 273 and average of 91.00. Another two-Test series in Sri Lanka, in July 2005, registered two further losses. In the First Test in Colombo, West Indies were 18 for three in their first innings when Chanderpaul retrieved the situation with a knock of 69 that led to a total of 285. In the second innings, West Indies were again in dire straits at 21 for five, when Chanderpaul intervened with a tenacious 48 not out that helped his team to set Sri Lanka a target of 172, although it was scarcely enough to deny the hosts. Chanderpaul's role in the team was underlined when he failed to contribute much in the Second Test in Kandy and West Indies lost by 240 runs.

A three-Test tour to Australia in November 2005 registered three further losses under Chanderpaul's watch as captain. West Indies were overwhelmed by 379 runs in the First Test at Brisbane, by nine wickets in the Second Test at Hobart, and by seven wickets at Adelaide. In three Tests, in March 2006, New Zealand also cashed in with two victories out of three matches, although the result in the First Test in Auckland was close. Set 291 to win, West Indies had a flying start from Chris Gayle and Daren Ganga, and then collapsed for 263. The team's fragility had become obvious, and Chanderpaul did not enjoy captaincy. He was as reticent in speech as he could be phlegmatic in batting, and his resignation as captain after the New Zealand tour was not surprising.

The reason Chanderpaul gave for resigning was his desire to concentrate on his batting; but his record of ten losses and four draws must also have been a factor. As he told Anna Kessel in an interview: "When I gave it [the captaincy] up it felt like a big weight off my shoulders ... You don't have time to focus on your own game, it's too much." More to the point, as he also tells Kessel: "I'm a private person ... I'm reserved, not outgoing." [Kessel, *The Observer*, 3 May 2009] With his demanding work ethic it is not surprising that captaincy or leadership did not suit Chanderpaul. His ethic calls for someone who constantly responds to his team's needs with infinite personal resources of patience, persistence and discipline rather than the skill of motivating others.

The similarity between Chanderpaul's and Kallicharran's appointment as captain has already been noticed. These were not "normal" appointments in the sense that the outgoing captain announced his resignation, and gave the West Indies Cricket Board enough time to select a replacement. Chanderpaul's appointment was precipitated by a dispute between the players' association (WIPA) and the WICB about players' contracts just as Kallicharran's appointment was invoked by a disagreement between the players' association (in 1978 not yet as militant as the WIPA) and the WICB about World Series Cricket. In the ethnic quagmire surrounding cricket and society in the Caribbean, one cannot rule out ethnic factors also playing a role in the selection of two expendable Indian players who could be dismissed with ease when normalcy resumed. It is revealing how Lara and Lloyd both automatically resumed their post as captain without a ripple of comment as if they were simply re-assuming a natural, pre-established order.

It is perhaps going too far, but when Wes Hall encouraged Lloyd to regard Kanhai's captaincy appointment as merely temporary because Kanhai would soon make way for a younger man, one wonders if it was not a similar idea of the expendable Indian plantation labourer at work in the Caribbean social subconscious. We know from his interview with Anna Kessel that Chanderpaul was relieved to give up the captaincy. Kallicharran, on the other hand, thought he was ill-used when Lloyd resumed as captain. It is not strange that these ethnic suspicions should involve Lloyd (African-Guyanese) and Chanderpaul and Kallicharran who are both Indian-Guyanese, nor that the Guyanese President should be implicated in the appointment of Lloyd as captain.

Lara resumed as captain on India's tour of the Caribbean in June 2006 for a four-match rubber of which the first three matches were drawn while India won the Fourth Test in Jamaica by 49 runs. In a rare event, in the First Test in Antigua, five Indian-Caribbean players were picked – Daren Ganga, Ramnaresh Sarwan, Chanderpaul, Denesh Ramdin and Dave Mohammed. Chanderpaul had only one good score throughout – 97 not out in the Third Test in St Kitts. And in Jamaica West Indies were given a reasonable target of 269 to win but were foiled by Kumble's haul of six wickets in the last innings. Chanderpaul collected 291 runs from the four matches at an average of 41.55. West Indies tour of Pakistan for three matches in November 2006 was roughly similar to India's tour, except that Pakistan won two matches and the third was drawn. Out of five innings Chanderpaul had two scores over 50 including 81 in the First Test at Lahore. His five innings amounted to 205 runs for an average of 41.00.

Just as India's tour to the Caribbean in 2002 was of critical importance to Chanderpaul's career in settling his position in the batting order and increasing his productivity, so was the tour of England that he now undertook with West Indies to England in May/June 2007. This time, what changed was the retirement of the most brilliant West Indies batsman of the contemporary era, Brian Lara, which took place one month before Chanderpaul's fourth tour to England. Lara's loss created both a gap that could not be filled, and an opportunity for Chanderpaul to shine. Another change was the appointment of Sarwan as West Indies captain, the first Indian-Caribbean captaincy appointment untrammelled by some unusual circumstance like Chanderpaul or Kallicharran holding the fort temporarily, or Kanhai as a stop-gap before the return of Lloyd. Chanderpaul had shown signs of less consistent productivity before the 2007 England tour. Now, although he missed the Second Test in Leeds because of injury, he revelled in two centuries and three fifty-plus scores in the three remaining Tests.

After heavy scoring from England in the first innings of the First Test at Lord's, and Chanderpaul's own contribution of 74 to the West Indies first innings reply, rain intervened and the Second Test at Lord's ended in a draw. In his first spell as captain, Sarwan seriously injured his right shoulder on the first day of the Leeds Test, and was ruled out from playing during the rest of the tour. Daren Ganga took over as captain. Whether all this or Chanderpaul's added absence in the Leeds Test had anything to do with it, West Indies were routed by an innings and 283 runs at Leeds, the heaviest defeat in their history.

The Third Test at Old Trafford looked as if it was heading the same way before it took a slightly different turn: West Indies still lost, but by only 60 runs. England batted first and made 370 to which West Indies replied with 227, Chanderpaul top scoring with 50. After their second innings, England set the visitors a daunting target of 455 on a treacherous pitch with bounce for both fast bowlers and the England spinner Monty Panesar. That West Indies contrived 394 runs on such a surface was largely due to Chanderpaul's seven-hour, undefeated vigil of 116 runs.

What defines Chanderpaul's achievement here is not building a monumental score to frighten the enemy, or dominating the situation with an arrogant display of rampant superiority, but their exact opposite: quiet, thoughtful acknowledgement of threat from overwhelming odds and steely determination to resist without budging an inch. It is part of Chanderpaul's inner machinery that combines an understated, diffident manner with unbending resolve. If heroism appears in different forms, surely this is one of them. Michael Vaughan, the opposing captain at Old Trafford said, with something like awe, that he could not remember a better innings than Chanderpaul's 116 not out. It is one thing to receive the appreciation of a friend, but unsolicited admiration from your enemy is rare indeed!

Tony Cozier, who regards the match as one in which, "this weakened derided team [West Indies] roused itself to fight back," comments on Chanderpaul's role in the brave if vain West Indian resurgence: "He [Chanderpaul] is not known as 'Tiger' for nothing. There is no grittier fighter in the game and, with Lara now gone, he must be the hub of the batting." [WEB, Tony Cozier, 'Taking the Positives', 13 June 2007]

The next match, the Fourth Test, at Chester-le-Street, underlines Chanderpaul's role as the hub of West Indies batting. Batting first, West Indies posted a total of 287 of which Chanderpaul contributed nearly half – 136 not out; it took him nearly seven hours, and the next highest score was 44. England's reply of 400 established a lead of 113 runs which put pressure on their opponents for a big score in their second innings to keep themselves in the game. Instead West Indies were flummoxed by Panesar's spin which accounted for five of their wickets as they stumbled to 222 in their second innings. Once more Chanderpaul's 70 was not only the highest score in their second innings, but their lifeline: apart from Chanderpaul's 70 and two other scores of 52 and 43, all that the seven remaining batsmen could muster among them was 39 runs.

Chanderpaul was named 'Man of the Match' in the Fourth Test, as well as 'Man of the Series'. He had compiled 448 runs in three Tests for an average of 148.66, and had two consecutive not out innings of 116 and 136 lasting more than 1000 minutes. Together with similar feats in 2002 (three consecutive not out innings of 67, 101 and 136) against India, and in 2004 (two consecutive not out innings of 128 and 97) against England, Chanderpaul is the first batsman to remain unbeaten after more than a thousand minutes of continuous batting on three occasions. Such statistics can sometimes be meaningless, but in Chanderpaul's case, as the hub of a team caught up in the midst of painful rebuilding, the value of his batting to West Indies, especially in the second half of his career, is inestimable.

Daren Ganga who took over as captain of West Indies in England after Sarwan's injury, speaks as an insider immediately after the Fourth Test Match at the end of the series: "Shiv [Chanderpaul] is a team player, he's someone who goes there and fights for the team. His batting in this series [2007] has been tremendous. He's somebody who can carry our batting and we all need to take a page out of his book, the manner in which he commits himself to cricket." [WEB, Andrew McGlashan 'West Indies Getting Closer', June 19, 2007] Chanderpaul's dedication has a ring of Geoffrey Boycott's staunch loyalty to England.

For their three-match tour of South Africa from December 2007 to January 2008 Gayle replaced Sarwan as West Indies captain, and West Indies won the First Test in Port Elizabeth by 128 runs. They made 408 in the first innings thanks to 94 from Samuels and 104 from Chanderpaul. The score was a mere 33 for five wickets after one hour's play when these two came together and contrived a brilliant recovery. Chanderpaul's century (his seventeenth) meant he had equalled a record held by Everton Weekes and Andy Flower of Zimbabwe, of seven 50s in consecutive Test matches. Faced with a target of 389 runs in the last innings, South Africa reached only 260 to give West Indies their first victory in South Africa.

The Second Test at Cape Town was more to Chanderpaul's taste since he spent five hours and fifteen minutes on 65 runs which turned out to be the top score in a West Indies total of 243. South Africa's reply of 321 earned them a small lead of 78. In their second innings, West Indies made 262, after another five-hour marathon top score of 70 from Chanderpaul which left South Africa with a target of only 185 runs which they reached with ease. But the spectacle of Chanderpaul barricading one wicket as his private domain, for hours on end, was becoming monotonous, and drew a predictable reaction from Graeme Smith, the South Africa captain: "Chanderpaul, he's like a tick you can't get rid off. He doesn't kill you, he just wears you down." [WEB, Neil Manthorp, 'South Africa against West Indies 2007-08', January 2008] Smith's image of a tick slowly sucking the blood of an animal until it dies, rather than someone dealing the beast one quick and merciful death blow, agrees with Brearley's idea of an equally slow killing through scratches; but whilst Smith's image, coming from a current opponent, understandably betrays irritation, Brearley whose playing career ended long ago, can afford more detachment and see Chanderpaul's tactics as a clever ploy in an ongoing contest.

South Africa won the Third and final Test at Durban where Chanderpaul made 0 in the first innings, his first 0 since 2005; but he was suffering from 'flu and did not bat in the second innings. Still, the tour established his role of dauntless defender as proved by his aggregate of 247 and average of 82.33. The visit to South Africa was followed by a two-match visit of the Sri Lankans to the Caribbean. Chanderpaul did not prosper in the first match at Providence, the new cricket ground in Guyana, where Sri Lanka won by 121 runs. Maybe it was the old idea again of the team failing when Chanderpaul failed; for in the Second Test in Trinidad where West Indies was set a target of 253 runs, they achieved it mainly because of a partnership of 157 between Sarwan (102) and Chanderpaul (86 not out). Chanderpaul's total from the two Sri Lankan matches was 130 for an average of 43.33.

Australia's three-match tour of the Caribbean was next, beginning with the First Test in Jamaica which Australia won by 95 runs. There is no other match that reveals Chanderpaul's fundamental qualities of single-minded persistence and limitless patience more perfectly than this match at Sabina Park, Jamaica, in May 2008. Australia batted first and put up 431 runs to which the hosts replied with 312. Even this inadequate reply would not have been possible without Chanderpaul's legendary obduracy in facing up to the enemy, while some of his team-mates squandered their wickets away. When he had reached 86, however, he was struck on the back of his helmet by a Brett Lee bouncer that knocked him flat on the ground where he lay unconscious for minutes while he was attended by a doctor and a physio.

After such a blow, no one expected Chanderpaul to continue his innings. But he quietly took guard and continued with the job, confirming his own modest and frequently expressed response when congratulated for some extraordinary batting exploit: "I'm only doing my job". This is less the mantra of a man modestly apologising for his limitation than a quiet but firm assertion of what he saw as his life's ambition. Upon resuming his innings, the crowd cheered each run like they were celebrating new life, a veritable resurrection; and when he reached his century, cheers proved insufficient and turned into tears of joy. Tony Cozier reports, "every man, woman and child rose to acclaim a sporting performance they will remember for as long as their memories do. Amy [Chanderpaul's wife] was not the only one shedding tears. So were big men without a hint of embarrassment." [WEB, Tony Cozier, 'Courage Under Fire', 25 May 2008] A majority of spectators at Sabina Park are African-Jamaicans who form about double the population of the rest of the English-speaking Caribbean, and since the main theme of this book is cricket as an instrument of unity and identity in the region, we cannot miss the significance for regional co-operation and unity in the spontaneous rapture of Sabina Park spectators for an Indian-Guyanese batsman.

Chanderpaul had come in with the score at 196 for four and, more than six hours later, was last man out for 118. When critics complain about his endless patience, defensive play and obdurateness, they should also notice that in this innings, for instance, six of Chanderpaul's team-mates made less than 10 runs each. While it may not be wrong to talk about killing by scratches or ticks that wear you down, where in the world are there people, in whatever vocation, whose devotion to duty is as selfless as Chanderpaul's in this match! Perhaps five or six hours spent watching a Chanderpaul vigil can be a trial, but surely securing one end in cricket should not be devalued if it helps either to win a game or fend off defeat! Nor is Chanderpaul unique in holding an end, when necessary, at expense of scoring. Despite his credentials as a super-patriot, English selectors once dropped Boycott from the England team for what they considered slow scoring.

The Second Test in Antigua was drawn. Australia posted 479 in the first innings and West Indies replied with 352, Chanderpaul's contribution being 107 not out with five team-mates this time scoring less than ten runs each. By declaring at 244 for six wickets in their second innings, Australia set the hosts a target of 372, and West Indies responded with 266 for five when time ran out. It seems monotonous, but once again, were it not for Chanderpaul's 77 not out in the second innings, things could have been very different. With his 77 not out Chanderpaul becomes the first batsman with unbeaten fifty-plus scores in both innings of a Test match on three occasions.

In the Third Test in Barbados, West Indies replied to Australia's 251 with 216, and one could almost guess both that Chanderpaul was 79 not out and that six of his team-mates made less than 10 runs each. Australia's second innings score of 439 for five left West Indies with a target of 475, and although it was a tall order, they made a gallant effort to reach it, but Chanderpaul was adjudged lbw when he was 50. Hawkeye, the computer system that records the trajectory of deliveries, later reported that the ball would have gone over the stumps, but even if the decision was in Chanderpaul's favour it is unlikely he would have got the necessary support to reach 475 and victory. West Indies' 387 was still a gallant effort, although Australia won the rubber 2:0 with one draw. Chanderpaul, meanwhile, registered a tour total of 442 runs and his second best tour average – 147.33.

Two Tests against New Zealand in December 2008 were drawn. In the first at Dunedin two days were lost to rain, but New Zealand still completed 365 in their first innings, while West Indies made 340 in the course of which Chanderpaul deployed another rescue mission. West Indies were 173 for 6 when he entered and added 76 in a partnership of 153 with Jerome Taylor. This was repeated in the Second Test at Napier when Chanderpaul (126 not out) and Nash added 163 together which took their score from 74 to 237 and a final figure of 307. Chanderpaul made 0 in the second innings but Gayle's 197 ensured a draw. Chanderpaul's total in these two matches was 202 and his average 106.50.

Five Tests were next played against England in the Caribbean between February and March 2009. In the first in Jamaica, West Indies won a memorable victory by an innings and 23 runs, largely due to a remarkable spell of fast bowling from Jerome Taylor who captured five wickets for 11 runs in England's second innings of a paltry 51. England had made 318 in the first innings and West Indies replied with 392 to which Chanderpaul contributed only 20, but Taylor's inspired bowling exacted retribution from England who, in 2004, on the same ground, had bowled West Indies out for 47 to win by ten wickets. The Second Test at North Sound, the new ground in Antigua, was abandoned as mentioned before, and the Third Test was played on the old St John's ground which lived up to its reputation of nurturing high scores. England ran up 566 in their first innings and dismissed West Indies for 285, then added 221 in their second innings forcing West Indies to eke out a draw with 370 for 9 in their second innings. It was not quite up to the high drama of his usual heroics, but Chanderpaul still did his bit with 55.

England ran up another big total of 600 for six wickets declared in the Fourth Test in Barbados which drew a West Indies riposte of 749 for seven, mainly due to Sarwan's 291, although Chanderpaul also slipped in a cameo 70. Such high totals left little time for a decisive conclusion as the match ended in a draw with England on 279 for three. Eager for an equalising win England posted another formidable total of 546 for six declared in the first innings of the Fifth Test in Trinidad while West Indies responded with 544, mainly due to a partnership of 234 from Chanderpaul (147 not out) and Nash. Not giving up that easily, England rattled up 237 for six declared and had West Indies reeling at 114 for eight before they were saved by the bell. Thus West Indies earned their first series victory since 2004, one match to nil with three draws, and Chanderpaul clocked-up a series total of 299 for an average of 54.80.

Two Test matches in England in May 2009 introduce a brief and less productive period of Chanderpaul's career, with predictable repercussions for his team. Cold, blustery weather in early May might have had something to do with the loss of two Tests by West Indies at Lord's by ten wickets and at Chester-le-Street, in the Second Test, by an innings and 83 runs. Although Chanderpaul contrived one score of 47 in the second innings of the Second Test, from what we have seen of him before, it was uncharacteristic that all he could scrape together out of four innings was 74 runs and an average of 18.50.

But three Tests in Australia, in November and December 2009 were little better. In the First Test at Brisbane, Australia won by an innings and 65 runs with Chanderpaul making 2 runs in each innings. The second match, in Adelaide, was drawn. Australia settled for caution instead of going for a target of 330 runs in the fourth innings, and Chanderpaul mustered 62 and 27. In the Third Test, in Perth, where Gayle hit a whirlwind century and West Indies did their best to reach a target of 359 in the fourth innings, they failed by merely 36 runs. Chanderpaul who had injured a finger in the Adelaide Test did not play in Perth and was left with a total of 93 in three Tests for an average of 23.25.

In South Africa's tour of the Caribbean in June 2010 Chanderpaul's gloom lifted slightly with a couple of good scores. South Africa established dominance early in the First Test in Trinidad with a substantial lead, then added 206 in their second innings making it impossible for the hosts to get back into the game. With two totals over 500 and some rain delay in the Second Test in St Kitts, a decisive result was not possible. West Indies replied to a South Africa first innings total of 543 with 546 in which Chanderpaul (166) shared a stand of 220 with Nash. South Africa won the Third Test in Barbados after bowling West Indies out for 231 and replying with 346. The West Indies second innings score of 161 was not enough and would have been worse without Chanderpaul's 71 not out when, again, six of his fellow players made less than 10 runs each. Not since England's tour of the Caribbean in early 2009 had Chanderpaul returned such good tour figures – 300 for an average of 75.00.

Three Tests against Sri Lanka, in Sri Lanka, during November/December 2010, were all drawn due mainly to the weather. At the time, Sri Lanka was No. 3 in International Cricket Council ratings. West Indies, who were ranked No. 7, were lucky to escape both in the Third Test at Pallekele which was completely washed out, and in the Second Test at Colombo where they were 12 for 2 chasing a total of 202 when the fourth day's play was rained off. Gayle's triple century ensured a draw in the First Test in Galle, and Chanderpaul finished the ill-fated series with a total of 94 and an average of 31.33. West Indies then took on Pakistan in a one-off, low-scoring and close-run Test in Providence, Guyana in May 2011. After scores of 226 from West Indies, and 160 from Pakistan in the first innings, West Indies followed up with 152 (Chanderpaul 30 not out) in the second innings, and Pakistan who could only muster 178 lost by 40 runs. Chanderpaul's average in the match was 63.

The first of three matches played by India in their tour of the Caribbean during June/July 2011 is the second occasion with five Indian-Caribbean players appearing together in a Test match – Chanderpaul, Sarwan and Ramdin (wicket-keeper) along with two bowlers, Ravi Rampaul and Devendra Bishoo. In the First Test, in Jamaica, India scored 246 and West Indies 173 in the first innings, but when set 326 runs to win in their second innings West Indies merely came up with 262 and lost by 63 runs. The remaining two matches were drawn as India won the series 1:0, but in the Third Test in Roseau, Dominica, Chanderpaul registered his first century (116 not out) for a whole year. In the series altogether he compiled 241 runs for an average of 44.20.

In two matches against Bangladesh in October 2011, the home team came close to winning the first at Chittagong, but were foiled by bad weather. After leading by 124 runs in the first innings of the Second Test at Mirpur, West Indies set Bangladesh the impossible task of getting 508 runs and dismissed them for 278 runs thus winning by 229 runs. In both matches Chanderpaul compiled 126 runs for an average of 63. While abroad West Indies then continued with three Tests against India in November 2011. In the First Test at Delhi they led by 95 runs in the first innings thanks to a sterling 118 by Chanderpaul out of a total of 304. But they collapsed in the second innings to 63 for six before being boosted by 47 from Chanderpaul and 42 from Captain Sammy to reach 181. That left a target of 276 for India which they achieved and won by five wickets. Following their huge first innings total of 631, India won the Second Test at Kolkata by an innings and 15 runs. All West Indies had to offer in resistance were two scores of 153 and 463. Chanderpaul was injured and did not appear in the Third Test at Mumbai which was drawn. His aggregate for two matches was 216 for an average of 54.00.

In the Australia series of three Test matches in the Caribbean which began in Barbados, in early April, 2012, West Indies started brightly with a first innings total of 449 (Chanderpaul 103 not out) and Australia replied with 406, but West Indies collapsed for 148 in their second innings, and despite a valiant effort by their bowlers to restrict Australia in their second innings, Australia won by three wickets. Because of inclement weather, Australia tried to force another win or, at least a decisive result, in the Second Test in Trinidad by declaring their second innings closed for eight wickets, and setting West Indies a lower target than possible; but a draw became inevitable. In the Third Test in Roseau, Dominica, West Indies made a gallant effort to reach their target of 370 runs but failed by 75 runs, and Australia won both the match and the series 2:0 with one draw. Chanderpaul had a good series with four fifty-plus scores, and an aggregate of 346 runs for an average of 86.50.

Because of his steadfast dedication to his craft, tenacity and strokes of classical purity, Shivnarine Chanderpaul remains not only the best Indian-Caribbean batsman, but one of the best batsmen ever seen. MARTY MELVILLE/AFP/GETTY IMAGES

Three Tests followed in England in May/June 2012. In the first, at Lord's, England established a lead of 155 in the first innings, and although West Indies resisted bravely with a second innings score of 345, it left a target of only 191 which England easily achieved for five wickets. Chanderpaul, meanwhile, again collected two fifty-plus scores. The Second Test at Trent Bridge began the same way with England establishing a first innings lead of 58, but this time West Indies succumbed to England's fast bowlers in a second innings that yielded only 165 runs and left a target of only 111 which England reached easily to win by nine wickets. The final Test, the Third, at Edgbaston, is the match with six Indian-Caribbean players mentioned in the first paragraph of Chapter One of this book. The match was drawn and England won the series 2:0 with one draw. Chanderpaul who did not play at Edgbaston finished with series figures of 235 runs and an average of 78.33.

In two Tests against New Zealand, in Antigua and Jamaica, in July/August 2012, Chanderpaul did not fare very well, emerging with a total of 52 runs from three innings for an average of 26.00. He had the opposite fate in two Tests against Bangladesh in November 2012 when he posted scores of 203 not out, 1, and 150 not out for a series total and average of 354. In the First Test at Mirpur, West Indies declared at 527 for four, but the hosts hit back with 556, and a first innings lead of 29. A West Indies second innings total of 273 set Bangladesh a target of 245 on the last day and they fell short by 77 runs. In the second Test at Khulna, West Indies ran up another huge total of 648 (Chanderpaul 150 not out) which gave them a first innings lead of 261. Following on, Bangladesh could only muster 287 and West Indies won by ten wickets, which gave them an outright series victory of 2:0.

With a career total of 11,219 runs, and an average of 51.93, Chanderpaul is so far the second highest Test run-getter among West Indian batsmen, after Brian Lara who leads with 11,953 runs. Chanderpaul comes ninth in world ratings, again after Lara who comes fifth. Chanderpaul's twenty-nine centuries also come second to Lara's thirty-four among West Indian batsmen; but seventeen of his centuries are unbeaten, a world record, only one ahead of India's Sachin Tendulkar. Like Kanhai and Kallicharran, Chanderpaul has not registered many large scores, and his rate of converting fifties into hundreds is the lowest of the three: Chanderpaul's twenty-nine hundreds out of sixty-

Shivnarine Chanderpaul celebrates 11,000 Test runs on 5 December 2013 during the First Test against New Zealand at Dunedin. MARTY MELVILLE/AFP/GETTY IMAGES

two fifties come to 46.77 per cent, compared with a similar calculation of 57.14 per cent for Kallicharran, and 53.57 per cent for Kanhai.

As a Caribbean cricketer, for entertainment value alone, Chanderpaul may not measure up to Lara, Richards, Sobers or Kanhai, but for reliability and tenacity he is probably without peer in the world except, perhaps, for the South African Jacques Kallis (13,289 runs) who holds the highest average of the top ten batsmen in the world – 55.37. Currently, Chanderpaul ranks third among the top ten cricketers in the world in the ratings of the International Cricket Council. Indeed, Chanderpaul has held the ICC Number One ranking in cricket three times – July 2008; May 2009; and April 2012.

The First Test between India and West Indies in Mumbai in November 2013 is regarded as historic because of Tendulkar's unique record of reaching his 200th Test milestone. By coincidence, it is also the match in which Chanderpaul became the only West Indian batsman to play in 150 Test matches. This achievement prompted a glowing editorial in *Stabroek News*, Guyana's leading newspaper:

> Just think about it: the quiet man [Chanderpaul] from the village of Unity, from a country with a population of a mere 750,000 has been consistently ranked the best in the world, through dedication to his craft, an exemplary work ethic and sheer professionalism. If this is not a source of national pride and inspiration for us all, young and old, then we don't know what is... The greater achievement is that it is also a similar source of pride to the entire Anglophone Caribbean as well. [*Stabroek News*, 15 November 2013]

It is curious that, at least since Lara's retirement, West Indies should rely on a player with credentials so untypical of the maroon colours he flourishes. Fellow Guyanese, Arnon Adams, notices the paradox of, "the world's best batsman in what is, by far, the weakest of the more established teams of world cricket." In the same article, Adams also mentions Chanderpaul's "monumental concentration" and, "unbelievably dogged determination," and casts him as a pivotal figure forcing his team-mates to confront the reality of changing times to which they have so far been blind:

The fact too, that the accolade of the world's best test batsman has been claimed by an unlikely West Indian – an advocate of patient, painstaking accumulation of runs rather than a dashing exponent of the art of breathtaking stroke-play – say a Richards or a Lara – is perhaps a poignant message to Caribbean cricket – a message from an ageing champion – that times have changed and that Caribbean cricket needs to be reordered to pay much more attention to focus than to flashinesss. [WEB, Arnon Adams, *Stabroek News*, 19 August 2008]

The premium Chanderpaul places on patience, protection of his wicket, and accumulation of runs suggests a fundamental concern with a Creole, West Indian need for psychological if not physical or economic security, best expressed by the archetypal Indian-Caribbean hero, Mohun Biswas, who, in V.S. Naipaul's novel, *A House for Mr Biswas*, wages unyielding struggle for security in the midst of dismaying Caribbean mixing and multiplicity. While Biswas has become a universal symbol of human resilience, his story is rooted in the fluid, shifting matrix of Caribbean nationality. Adams hints at this, perhaps subconsciously, when he notices Chanderpaul's "contribution to the quest to unify the Caribbean – by Guyanese and, as well, by descendants of slaves, indentured labourers and, to a lesser extent, by the descendants of other waves of immigrants."

Adams hits the nail on the head; he wisely interprets the significance of Chanderpaul's crowning virtue – unceasing cerebral vigilance. Brearley's "scratches that kill" do not imply a preference for pushes, prods and nudges or furtive deflections. No batsman with more than ten thousand Test runs under his belt relies on such subterfuge. Many of Chanderpaul's runs do come from ones and twos. His scratches are careful and studious lines in the drawing of a practised artist who patiently takes time to wait, watch and ponder, before going about his business as if it is nothing more than another day's work. Chanderpaul does not frown on stroke play; it is just that the strokes must conform to the classical control and purity of his style: planned, ordered and shaped by his shrewd cricketing brain. Chanderpaul is cerebration itself. Bold splashes, rash moves, acting on impulse are not his way. The Barbadian historian and statistician Keith Sandiford once told me in correspondence that if the head of Chanderpaul were put on the body of Kanhai we would get the perfect cricketer.

Instead of such wishful thinking, however, what we have is a cricketer who may forever appear as something of an enigma because of his introverted reticence, both in speech and action. Because of steadfast dedication to his craft, intestinal fortitude, and strokes of classical purity, Chanderpaul remains not only the best Indian-Caribbean batsman, but one of the best batsmen ever seen. In the knowing words of a former West Indies fast bowler and Chanderpaul's erstwhile team-mate: "No more single-minded batsman has traversed the West Indian cricketing landscape since Brian Lara's debut [1990] than Shivnarine Chanderpaul." [Ian Bishop, *Wisden Cricketer's Almanack*, 2006] In the same place, in addition to single-mindedness, Bishop adds raw courage: "This writer, who played several Test series with him [Chanderpaul] has seen more esteemed team-mates shrink in the face of the fastest bowling, but never Chanderpaul."

While Brearley, Smith and Bishop all shed light on aspects of Chanderpaul's genius, Tony Cozier, who witnessed each stage of Chanderpaul's cricketing sojourn since its commencement in 1994, sheds most light on the mystery of his enigmatic reach into a more universal realm of the human spirit: "Throughout the thirteen years since he [Chanderpaul] entered the West Indies team as a fragile nineteen-year-old, he has set an example for every batsman, present team-mates and those to follow, that an innings is to be treasured almost as dearly as life itself." [WEB, Tony Cozier, 'Courage Under Fire', 25 May 2008] Call it what you will – unflinching courage, stern doggedness, or mere cussedness – at its best, Chanderpaul's batting proclaims a selfless, inborn, universal capacity of the human spirit, "to seek, to strive, to find and not to yield". [WEB, Alfred Lord Tennyson, *Ulysses*]

CHAPTER 8

Ramnaresh Sarwan: A simple sport can unite West Indian people

Ramnaresh Sarwan, a right-handed batsman and right-arm leg-break bowler, was born in Wakenaam, Guyana on 23 June 1980, and was vice-captain of West Indies in 2003, when he was invited to captain a Demerara team against a Berbice team, in Guyana. The game was organised by the Guyana Indian Heritage Association as part of a Jahaji Cricket Festival, and Sarwan missed it because he was in the US on holiday and could not return to Guyana in time for the match. When asked for a public apology by the organisers, Sarwan told *Stabroek News* that he did not know that the organisers were involved in playing politics. He said: "As a representative of the West Indian cricket team and the current vice-captain, I do not support anything that divides us as a people, especially in a country like Guyana where I expect support of all Guyanese when I am on and off the field." [WEB, *Stabroek News*, 14 September 2003]

In the same interview with Sean Devers, Sarwan said: "I feel we are one people with different views, cultures, religions and so on and cricket has taught me a lot about how a simple sport can unite so many West Indian people with so many differences in their lives." [WEB, Sarwan/Sean Devers] From Ramadhin to Sarwan the main theme of *Indian-Caribbean Test Cricketers and the Quest for Identity* has been to reflect on Sarwan's belief as stated in the title of this chapter, and present the accomplishments of Indian-Caribbean Test cricketers as steps in a quest for West Indian identity.

Sarwan became the youngest ever First Class West Indian cricketer when he started playing for Guyana, aged fifteen, in the regional Red Stripe Cup competition. He has so far played in eighty-seven Test matches, compiled 5842 runs for an average of 40.01, and captured twenty-three wickets. He had an impressive début in Test cricket against Pakistan, in Barbados, in May, 2000, when he produced two not out scores of 84 and 11 in a drawn match facing bowlers of the calibre of

Wasim Akram and Saqlain Mushtaq who claimed five wickets for 121 runs in the first innings of the match. Initial reaction to Sarwan's début was very positive and Ted Dexter, a former captain of England, has been pilloried for predicting that the young Guyanese had a bright future ahead with a possible Test average of fifty-plus.

While not a huge success, Sarwan's first tour of England in August 2000 confirmed that he had promise: at least one of his six scores was over fifty. In the Third Test at Old Trafford he was brought in for the injured Chanderpaul and was lbw twice. The Fourth Test at Leeds was more promising after West Indies collapsed for 172 in the first innings, and Sarwan made 59 not out. He also carried his bat in the second innings of the match when he, Adams and Campbell were the only West Indies batsmen able to reach double figures while five of their team-mates each made 0. He came up with only 5 and 27 in the last match at the Oval, but he had just returned from his girlfriend's funeral in Guyana which, he claims, deeply affected his cricket.

The ill-effects of this bereavement seem to have followed Sarwan on his first tour of Australia, from December 2000 to January 2001, when he appeared in the first two and the fifth of the scheduled Test matches, all five of which were won by Australia. For Sarwan it was a baptism of fire with scores of 0, 0, 2, 1, 0 and a sixth score of 51 in his final visit to the crease – the second innings of the Fifth Test in Sydney. Sarwan's personal problem may not have had anything to do with it, but the poor showing of the West Indies team as a whole (Australia having won the series 5:0), caused the team to take on the services of sports psychologist, Dr Rudi Webster. Whatever the psychological motivation of his team-mates, Sarwan evidently had to cope with very disappointing and uncharacteristic results from his six innings on the Australia tour – 53 runs and a negligible average of 8.83.

Sarwan's next series, South Africa's tour of the Caribbean in March/April 2001, shows signs of improvement. At his home ground, Bourda, in Guyana, he was run-out for 91 in the second innings of the First Test, an innings noted by Tony Cozier for its "handsome cuts and drives". It would have been his first century, but he and Hooper were accelerating in order build a safe total, and declare before trying to bowl their opponents out. Neither did Sarwan get his century nor did West Indies succeed in forcing a win, and the match ended in a tame draw. Although he did not pass fifty again in the three remaining South

Africa matches, Sarwan had shown his worth, and his four Tests against South Africa had yielded 238 runs for an average of 29.75. West Indies lost the series 1:2 with two matches drawn, but won a fresh series of two Tests against Zimbabwe 1:0 with Sarwan showing clearer signs of improvement in the form of two fifty-plus scores and a total of 175 runs for an average of 87.50.

Three matches on his first tour to Sri Lanka did not produce the elusive century but, as in Chanderpaul's case, only in reverse, Sarwan moved from a lower to higher position in the batting order with better results. While Chanderpaul prospered in his role as a middle order batsman, Sarwan settled into his function at No. 3 as the team's leading storm trooper. This is the crux of the matter: that he seemed so well equipped technically, in terms of natural footwork, instinctive timing and elegant stroke play, but had not produced scores expected from a premier batsman.

Batting at No. 3 instead of No. 5 or No. 6, in all three Tests in Sri Lanka, Sarwan turned in three fifty-plus scores, an aggregate of 318, his highest series total so far, and an average of 53. In the First Test at Galle he made 88 and 30, and in the Third Test at Colombo – 69 and 66. But Sri Lanka won all three matches. In the first innings of the Third Test Sarwan and Lara added 194 for the third wicket, and in the second innings of the same Test, 141. Another aspect of this moderate success is that up to the Zimbabwe tour, immediately preceding this one to Sri Lanka, Sarwan was run-out three times in five series implying perhaps inexperience or erratic judgment.

His first fully fledged five-match series, India's tour of the Caribbean in April/May 2002, brought him four fifty-plus scores, but visiting journalists spotted a contradiction between someone who plays with such aplomb and grace and yet fails to produce a single century. West Indies won the India series 2:1 with two draws, and Sarwan registered a total of 317 for an average of 45.40. In three short series beginning with New Zealand's two-match visit to the Caribbean in June 2002, New Zealand won the First Test in Barbados, while the Second in Grenada was drawn.

On the visit of West Indies to India for three matches in October 2002, India won the First Test in Mumbai by an innings and 112 runs, and the Second in Chennai by eight wickets, while the Third in Kolkata was drawn. Sarwan's best performance was in Chennai, with the top score of 78 – a five-hour effort. But the three India Tests brought Sarwan no more than 138 runs for an average of 27.60. Finally, in the first of two Tests against Bangladesh in December 2002, Sarwan got a century when, in reply to Bangladesh's first innings total of 139, West Indies posted 536 of which Sarwan contributed 119, the highest score. The century had taken him twenty-eight Tests and forty-eight innings, and his two Bangladesh Tests had brought him 149 runs for an average of 49.66. For those who dismiss Bangladesh as easy pickings, here is Sarwan's defence: "Of course my century against Bangladesh was special to me. Who cares if it was against one of the weaker Test teams. You know how long I have been trying to get a Test century and just falling in the eighties and nineties." [WEB, Sarwan/Devers]

During Australia's tour to the Caribbean in April/May 2003, Sarwan missed the First Test in Guyana which Australia won. Australia also won the next two Tests in Barbados and Trinidad. But the Fourth Test in Antigua, which West Indies won by three wickets, proved to be the most memorable, not so much because of the West Indies victory, or because of Sarwan's personal achievement of 105 (his second century) but because the West Indies score of 418 in the fourth innings was the largest fourth innings total yet made to win a Test match. It surpassed the 406 for four from India's defeat of West Indies in the Third Test in Trinidad in 1976. But for Sarwan it was the satisfaction of his second Test century and his partnership of 123 with Chanderpaul which together established the chief building block to support their historic victory.

Two Tests were played in Sri Lanka's brief visit to the Caribbean in June 2003. The First in St Lucia was drawn while in the Second, in Jamaica, fairly low scores – Sri Lanka (208) and West Indies (191) – precipitated a final innings in which West Indies required 212 runs to win. It took the combined wiles of Sarwan and his captain Lara, in a spectacular stand of 161 runs, to lead West Indies to victory by 128 runs. Sarwan's contribution was 82 and he was out when, with the score at 211, and one run was needed for victory, he went after yet another spectacular shot. It was something Rohan Kanhai might attempt for the sake of entertainment, but never Shivnarine Chanderpaul. In another short two-match tour of Zimbabwe in November 2003, West Indies narrowly escaped defeat in the First Test in Harare, which was drawn, but in the Second Test in Bulawayo, a first innings score of

481 to which Sarwan contributed 65, enabled them to clinch victory by 128 runs.

A four-match tour of South Africa from December 2003 to January 2004, seemed to move Sarwan to more solid ground with two centuries and one score over fifty out of eight innings. South Africa won the First Test at Johannesburg by 189 runs, and the Second in Durban by an innings and 65 runs with one full day to spare. Sarwan hit one innings of 114 although it was in a losing cause. He also had scores of 44 and 69 in the Third Test at Cape Town which was drawn, but South Africa won the Fourth Test at Centurion with another huge margin of ten wickets. Sarwan scored his fourth century (119 including eighteen fours) even if he couldn't rally the troops around him. His tour aggregate (392 runs) was the highest he had so far achieved, accompanied by a respectable average of 49. Except for inevitable gaps in the productivity of such a mercurial batsman this South Africa tour seemed to announce greater maturity.

In the next series, England's four matches in the Caribbean during March/April 2004, England was dominant, winning the first three matches and drawing the fourth in Antigua. Sarwan registered his second pair (two noughts) in the First Test in Jamaica, and did little better in the Second Test in Trinidad. He made contributions of 69 and 5 in the drawn Test in Barbados and one of 90 in the final Test in Antigua where he revelled in a partnership of 232 with Lara. Still, his figures for the tour were disappointing – a total of 192, and an average of 27.45. A two-match tour of the Caribbean by Bangladesh revived him by providing the highest score of his career – 261 not out in the Second Test in Jamaica, where he won awards both as 'Man of the Match' and 'Man of the Series'. His aggregate and average for the Bangladesh tour were impressive, both 301.

Four Tests in England in July and August, 2004 didn't much help matters as West Indies were crushed in all four. England's first innings' totals tell almost the whole story: 568; 566; 330; 470. Sarwan resisted only in the first innings of the Second Test at Edgbaston with 139, his sixth century, and in the second innings of the Third Test at Old Trafford with 60. His sixth century helped him to post a series total of 267 and an average of 37.37.

The South Africa tour of the Caribbean for four Tests in April 2005 was more productive for Sarwan who extracted two centuries from five innings although it didn't stop the tourists from riding roughshod over their hosts and winning the rubber 2:0 with two draws. Sarwan did not appear in the First Test in Guyana because of the sponsorship dispute, but in the second innings of the Second Test in Trinidad, after he and Lara returned, he remained undefeated in an innings of 107 out of a total of 194 when eight of his team-mates contributed altogether a grand total of 11 runs, and South Africa won by eight wickets. In the Fourth Test in Antigua, when West Indies replied to South Africa's 588 with 747 Sarwan chipped in with his seventh century – 127. Out of three Tests he accumulated 249 runs for an average of 62.25. In the next series, a brief tour of the Caribbean by Pakistan for two matches, the home team won the First Test and the visitors the Second. Sarwan had 55 in the second innings of the Second Test, in Jamaica, and a series total of 70 runs together with an average of 17.50.

A sterner test awaited West Indies in their next tour of Australia for three matches in November 2005. Australia won all three matches, and Sarwan salvaged only one fifty-plus innings in the Third Test, in Adelaide, when he scored 62 in the second innings. The total of his scores in all three matches amounted to 164 with an average of 27.33. Then followed a West Indies tour of three matches in New Zealand in March 2006. The First Test, in Auckland, in March 2006, shifted from one side to the other throughout, until West Indies were finally faced with a target of 291 in the fourth innings, and were 48 without loss at the end of the third day. Fortune then seemed to favour them, but the next day Sarwan was hit a nasty blow on his helmet by the New Zealand fast bowler Bond and retired hurt. In the end, West Indies lost by 27 runs. Sarwan didn't appear in the remaining two Tests for he was sent home, not because of the blow from Bond, but because of a leg injury. On the strength of his results from one match only he scored 66 runs for an average of 33.

By June 2006, Sarwan was fully fit for India's Caribbean tour of four matches beginning with the First Test in Antigua. In the first innings, Sarwan contributed 58 to a West Indies score of 371 before they were given ninety-five overs to reach a target of 392 runs in their second innings. At the end, in the final hour of the match it was left to two tail-enders to fend off 19 balls to ensure a draw with their score at 298 for nine. Sarwan did not fare well in the Second Test, but registered his ninth century – 116 – in the Third Test, in St Kitts, which ended in a third draw on the tour. In the Fourth Test in Jamaica, India left West Indies 269 for victory in the fourth innings, and Sarwan's 51 raised brief hopes of a win which were later shattered by a six wicket haul from the Indian spinner Kumble.

In November 2006, Sarwan appeared in two out of three Tests in Pakistan. In the First, in Lahore, West Indies simply could not cope with a first innings total of 485 from the hosts, and in the Third Test in Karachi where the Pakistan batsman Mohammad Youssuf recorded a century in each innings of the match, the tourists again were up against it; and when required to come up with 444 runs in the fourth innings, fell short by 199 runs. It is no exaggeration to record that the injury-prone Sarwan retired hurt after being hit on the foot by Pakistan's fast bowler Gul, and had to be content with a total of 61 runs from the two Tests and an average of 15.25.

So far as Indian-Caribbean cricketers are concerned, the First Test between England and West Indies at Lord's in May 2007 represented something of a breakthrough since it was not only the first time when an Indian-Caribbean cricketer, Sarwan, was appointed captain in a genuine manner (unlike Kanhai, Kallicharran and Chanderpaul), but when an Indian-Caribbean, Daren Ganga, was also named vice-captain. In the Lord's Test, West Indies mounted a spirited reply of 437 to England's massive first innings score of 553 for five declared, although eventually bad weather did not permit any other result than a draw. If Sarwan's injuries so far seem hard to believe, while fielding on the boundary in the Second Test at Headingley, Leeds, he fell over and hurt his collar bone badly enough to be again sent home and miss the rest of the tour which now continued with Ganga as captain. Evidently, whether due to misfortune or carelessness, Sarwan's career has suffered from more than his due share of injuries.

It is almost a surprise for Sarwan to complete two full matches on Sri Lanka's brief tour to the Caribbean in March/April 2008, uninterrupted and in fine style, recording his tenth century as well. Sri Lanka had a good start of 476 in the first innings of the First Test in Providence, Guyana, which allowed them to set a challenging target of 437 for West Indies in the fourth innings. The home team made an effort but fell short by 121 runs. However tables were turned in the Second Test in Trinidad when West Indies made light work of reaching a winning total of 253 for four wickets. After being away from cricket for ten months it was satisfying to see Sarwan resume play in such good form: his four innings consisted of 80, 72, 57, 102, a total of 311 for an average of 77.75, the second highest average he had so far achieved. He also won the 'Player of the Series' award and, at last, seemed to have to have hit his stride.

Ironically, Sarwan's failure in two matches in New Zealand in December 2008 (20 runs for an average of 6.66), served as a prelude to the greatest success of his career so far – in five Tests played by England in the Caribbean during February/March 2009. Not only did he amass his highest series total ever (626 runs and an average of 106.50), it was the sort of success his supporters had always expected but he never quite delivered, whether because of the impulsiveness of his fast disappearing youth, or recurring fitness problems.

In the first innings of the First Test in Jamaica he notched up his twelfth century – 107 – and since this was the match when Jerome Taylor bowled England out for 53 in their second innings, West Indies did not need to bat a second time. With his 107 Sarwan reached 5,000 runs in Test cricket, the youngest West Indian cricketer to do so. As we know, the Second Test at the new ground in Antigua was abandoned as a draw. In the Third Test at the old Recreation Ground, Sarwan missed the distinction of scoring a century in each innings of a single Test match when he posted 94 in the first innings, and 106 in the second innings of the match. For all that, West Indies were still in peril and, as in the Antigua Test against India in June 2006, two tail-enders, this time Powell and Edwards, held out against England for ten overs, and shepherded West Indies to 370 for nine and a draw.

Sarwan's 106 was his thirteenth century and equals a world record for the most centuries in the fourth innings which he shares with India's Sunil Gavaskar and Australia's Ricky Ponting. In the Fourth Test in Barbados, Sarwan did even better by scoring 291, the highest score of his career, and one that should silence doubters who saw his 261 over Bangladesh as easy pickings.

It is not that Sarwan thrives only against weak opposition, for he is credited with more than one century against Australia as well as England. As mentioned above, the truth is that he has failed to deliver on expectations that he raised from the time Dexter made his so far ill-fated prediction at his début match. As Andrew McGlashan writes: "This is the type of surge that his talent has always suggested could

In a region fragmented by insularity, ethnicity, colour, class and politics, Ramnaresh Sarwan's passionate affirmation of cricket as a force for West Indian unity is reassuring.

MARK GRAHAM/AFP/GETTY IMAGES

happen since he [Sarwan] made his début ... But a career average of 41 ... represents someone who hasn't been quite able to rise above the mediocrity by which he has often been surrounded." [WEB, Andrew McGlashan, 28 February 2009]

Sarwan's surge against England in February 2009 represents the peak of his career so far. He again appeared in two Tests against England, later in the year, in May 2009, and added a fifteenth century to his record, but it only brought him a series total of 136 runs and an average of 34. This is very similar to his next venture in Australia, in December 2009, when back spasms made him miss the First Test in Brisbane. He played only in the Second and Third Tests which brought in 88 runs and an average of 22. Two more two-match series at home, one with Pakistan, contributed only a total of 54 runs (average 13.50) while the other with India turned in even more derisive returns of 29 runs (average 7.25).

Sarwan was not a regular bowler: as a leg-spinner his twenty-three wickets appeared in dribbles, one in each of six matches, and two in each of five matches; although, once, against Bangladesh, in May 2004, in St Lucia, he managed seven wickets in one Test match. Alas, it now seems that even Sarwan's main Test career, as a specialist batsman, has reached some sort of crossroad. If his batting betrays signs of inconsistency, partly because of unusually persistent fitness problems, we surely cannot forget that he is capable of stroke play of grace, fluency, polish and silken elegance.

He also has leadership potential, and in a region fragmented by insularity, ethnicity, colour, class and politics, his passionate affirmation of cricket as a force for West Indian unity is reassuring. Also as a former West Indies captain, he reminds us in his Sean Devers interview, of his continuing reliance on strong and intimate support from the whole West Indian community: "We [players] know it hurts the fans when they see us lose and I can tell you it hurts us even more. We have a young team and we are working hard to win more matches and we need the fans to rally round the West Indian team." [WEB, Sean Devers, *Stabroek News*, 14 September 2003]

No doubt Sarwan's pronouncement that forms the title of Chapter Eight sounds somewhat hollow, especially since it comes from a player whose career has been dogged by such disappointing stops and starts. It cannot be denied that identity and nationality prove elusive in the

Anglophone Caribbean because of historical, geographical, ethnic, economic, cultural and political factors. It leaves the quest for identity unfinished, on going. Yet, as *Indian-Caribbean Test Cricketers and the Quest for Identity* proves, for all its lack of total effectiveness, the sport of cricket has so far made greatest headway toward overcoming the historic insidiousness of disorder, discontinuity and divisiveness in the Anglophone Caribbean.

Appendices

APPENDIX 1

John Major, More Than a Game: The Story of Cricket's Early Years, London, Harper Collins, 2007

Written by Sir John Major who was leader of the Conservative Party and Prime Minister between 1990 and 1997, *More Than a Game: The Story of Cricket's Early Years* is the first book on the game by a British Prime Minister. *More than a Game* surveys the development of cricket from its origin in England, in the middle of the sixteenth century to the game's Golden Age, the two decades immediately preceding the First World War. Nor is the story of cricket as straightforward as it sounds; for although Sir John dismisses alternative theories of cricket's origin and wields a somewhat pugnacious style, no doubt honed by long practice at fending off barbed inquiries from members on the other side of the House, he also admits that: "[cricket's] birth is shrouded in legend and mystique." [18]

Sir John draws on documentary evidence about cricket chiefly from administrative, ecclesiastic, legal or other records. Assuming that cricket evolved out of earlier ball games in England, he tells of two men being fined for playing cricket instead of going to church on Easter 1611 and, in 1624, of another man being hit (and killed) by the batsman's stroke when trying to catch the ball. Another incident is of a minister charged for playing cricket with lower class people, implying that the game initially attracted players mostly from the lower or working class. But by the 1640s, cricket had begun to climb socially and, by the eighteenth century, could claim an upper class or aristocratic following.

The narrative in *More than a Game* progresses chronologically in a step-by-step, easy-to-follow fashion. Here is the picture around 1700: "[cricket] was still a rustic sport, poorly endowed and ... confined to the South of England. Teams had no set number of players. Rules were haphazard ... Dress was variable. Bats were curved. Two stumps [with a connecting bail on top] was still the norm. Bowling was underarm and along the ground ... Drake-style, but no faster." [39] If bowling was underarm from the beginning, change was imminent, not only in bowling or other technical aspects of the game, but in English society itself. Here, this time, is the author as political historian: "In 1700 England was on the eve of an empire that would carry to the world a language, a system of law, a parliamentary tradition and ... above all cricket." [38] By the 1750s, clubs were formed, notably Hambledon in Hampshire, and cricket games had become great, bustling, social and commercial events with much gambling, betting, eating and drinking.

So far as mechanics of the game are concerned, rules were becoming codified: the two stumps were to be twenty-two inches high and six inches apart; and in a game, in 1775, when a bowler beat a batsman's defence three times and stared in agony as the ball passed harmlessly between the two stumps each time, it was agreed to add the third central stump that we have today. Around the same time, the modern bat or something like it with a flat front was also born. Over five centuries, like other social or cultural practices, cricket reached its contemporary form through trial and error, experimentation and gradual change; and whether the change is from two stumps to three, from under-arm to round-arm, then over-arm bowling, from four-ball to six-ball overs, or from five-a-side single-wicket games to the current two-wicket, eleven-a-side game, we can follow each stage in *More Than a Game* through a lively, often witty text, enriched by copious quotations, references and anecdotes, not to mention lavish photos, some in colour, including some of ladies in beautiful ankle-length dresses playing cricket as early as 1779.

There is also splendid coverage, again including excellent photos, of rich and powerful patrons who dominated the game for a century and a half, until the emergence of county clubs and eventually the County Cricket Championship in 1890. To cap it all, 1787 saw the arrival of the Marylebone Cricket Club (MCC), soon to become, for almost two centuries, arbitrator and law-giver of cricket the world over. Predictably, there is much on the origin of Wisden's Cricketer's Almanac, the Gentlemen versus Players fixture, and on the (literally) outsize figure of W.G. Grace who, apparently, was called a "cheat" by the Australian fast bowler "Demon" Spofforth in the first Test that Australia won in England (1882). So much for bad blood between Aussies and Poms!

There is much else in *More than a Game* either about individual games, grounds and players, or about the fascinating connection between cricket and English literature – I never knew, for example, that Dr Johnson played cricket. Spofforth's comments on W.G. Grace illustrate the author's effort, if not to be fair, at least to achieve candour in discussing moral, social or political issues historically embedded in the game. Thus, despite his distinguished Conservative credentials, Sir John shows an admirable sense of fairness in acknowledging racism in British officials toward Indians in British colonial India. He also admits: "The social case for cricket is convincing. It can uplift the morale of communities, even nations ... It has socially healing properties," [392] and he cites approvingly C.L.R. James's view that: "cricket had a magic that was a guiding light for the dispossessed and disenfranchised." [390]

In *More Than a Game* cricket's social healing properties have already helped to remove the notion of class privilege between Gentlemen and Players in England, abolish South African apartheid, moderate religious rivalry in India, and hasten West Indian independence. All this surely proves that cricket is more than a game, even if its magic has not so far sparked the radical and comprehensive social and economic changes still needed in South Africa, India and the West Indies.

APPENDIX 2

Ray Goble and Keith A. P. Sandiford, 75 Years of West Indies Cricket 1928-2003, *London, Hansib Publications, 2004*

75 Years of West Indies Cricket 1928-2003 celebrates the first seventy-five years since West Indies first began playing Test cricket in 1928, but it achieves much more than that: a succinct, historical and statistical account of the game in the West Indies, from its arrival in the region during the second half of the nineteenth century to the present day. The volume does even more: by avoiding a chronological analysis of cricket in the West Indies as a whole, *75 Years* sheds rare and welcome light on the development of cricket in individual territories within the English-speaking Caribbean. As Professor Emeritus, Baldwin S. Mootoo writes in his Preface to the volume, this territory by territory approach: "gives us a better appreciation of the development of the administrative structure that has led to the present West Indies Cricket Board Inc."

75 Years is divided into two Parts, the first of which consists of seven chapters of commentary. The first chapter offers a general survey of the game in the Caribbean; four others consider each of the so called "Big Four" territories – Barbados, Guyana, Trinidad and Tobago, and Jamaica; the sixth deals with the remaining islands collectively, and the seventh with West Indians who played cricket for other countries. Chapter Eight is devoted to World Records established by West Indian cricketers. There is also an Appendix with seven sub-headings, giving such essential information as the dates of birth and death of West Indies cricketers and records about their Test debut. Most, if not all, of Part I is written by Barbadian Keith A.P. Sandiford, Professor Emeritus of history at the University of Manitoba.

Part Two, meanwhile, is written by Ray Goble, who is a cricket and football statistician from England, and also co-author of *The Complete Record of West Indian Test Cricketers* (1991). Section One of Part II, which consists of about two-thirds of the entire volume, furnishes complete statistics of all West Indies Test and One Day International cricketers. This alone is something of a feat in collecting records that provide a compact summary of performances by all West Indies cricketers at the highest level. In "Additional Statistics," in Section Two of Part II, there are also such rare records as "Summary of Early Match records 1896-1928", and "Players' Unofficial Tests Before 1928". All this, plus the batting and bowling averages of One Day Internationals, confirm that *75 Years* provides the most comprehensive and up to date statistical coverage that we so far have of West Indies cricket. But the appeal of *75 Years* is less as a compendium of cricket records than as a full-fledged treatise on West Indies cricket in which Ray Goble's statistics serve as the complementary half of the volume by providing evidence of the commentary and analysis of Professor Sandiford in the first half.

Homage is paid to the West Indies team which, first under Clive Lloyd, then Vivian Richards, dominated Test cricket between 1980 and 1995. What is more interesting though is Professor Sandiford's analysis of factors that restricted the development of West Indies cricket during much of the twentieth century. Professor Sandiford speaks of parochialism, racism and snobbery in West Indian attitudes, of divisions both between different islands or territories, and between social classes, or people of different race and colour. For instance, the domination of West Indian cricket by Barbados, Guyana, Jamaica, and Trinidad and Tobago meant that cricketers from the "small islands" of Antigua, St Kitts-Nevis, St Vincent, Grenada and St Lucia were generally excluded from selection for the West Indies team until the 1960s. This is ironic since it is partly the extraordinary contribution of "small island" cricketers such as Vivian Richards, Richie Richardson, Curtly Ambrose and Andy Roberts, all of whom are from Antigua, that enabled West Indies to achieve international success in the 1980s and 1990s.

Perhaps what was most restrictive in the early years was the absence of any regular, inter-regional competition that exposed West Indian cricketers to a high level of competition in matches lasting several days. To some extent, the inter-colonial matches between different West Indian territories filled this need, but they lacked the organised regularity of the Shell Shield competition which started in 1965/66. The absence of such competition before the 1960s encouraged habits of what Professor Sandiford calls Saturday afternoon cricket: "impatient batting, incompetent fielding, deplorable catching, and uninspiring leadership." [14] A quick examination of Test match records between 1928 and 1960 confirms the damaging effect of Saturday afternoon habits on West Indian performances. Here is only one example: "between 1951 and 1957, the West Indies played 31 Tests, winning only eight and losing thirteen, with four of their victories coming at the expense of lowly New Zealand." [142] In this period, in ten matches against Australia, West Indies won once and lost seven times, although, at the time, the West Indies team could boast of such celebrated players as the three Ws, Ramadhin and Valentine.

Yet, even the early, Saturday afternoon decades of West Indian cricket produced its heroes. If Learie Constantine fits the Saturday afternoon paradigm *par excellence* with short spells of super-energetic fast bowling, and brief bouts of blistering batting, George Headley flatly contradicts it, for Headley's career batting average of 69.86, in Professor Sandiford's words, is: "the best by far of any West Indian." [114] Not only that, Headley's 2,230 runs on the West Indies tour of England in 1933 still remains the highest aggregate in a single season of any West Indies batsman touring England. It goes to show how valiantly West Indians struggled against the restrictions that they faced.

APPENDIX 3

Clem Seecharan, Muscular Learning: Cricket and Education in the Making of the British West Indies at the End of the 19th Century, *Kingston, Jamaica, Ian Randle, 2006*

African slavery sustained a plantation-based economy in the English-speaking West Indies for more than two centuries before it was abolished in 1834, and indenture, which succeeded slavery, lasted for eight decades, ending during the First World War. But, even after the First World War, the plantation-based economic structure bequeathed by these two cruel practices and their criteria of social organisation – race, colour and class – ensured that Whites, comprising only a small ethnic group, continued to hold sway over a majority of the West Indian population, consisting largely of descendants of African slaves and Indian indentured workers. White dominance prevailed in everything, in politics as in business, in work as well as play; and the argument in Professor Seecharan's most recent book *Muscular Learning: Cricket and Education in the Making of the British West Indies at the end of the 19th Century* is that, before 1900, the Black or African-descended population had already begun to redress this imbalance of White hegemonic power through the game of cricket.

Elite secondary schools established in British West Indian colonies, particularly Barbados, were patterned on British public schools and administered by Oxbridge teachers who inculcated a tough-minded, Christian-inspired ethic of education (muscular learning) that gave students the means to transform both the unrepresentative nature of West Indian cricket and, ultimately, the injustice of the colonial system itself. This ethic, Victorian in essence, advocated *mens sana in corpore sano*, a sound mind in a sound body, or, as Professor Seecharan describes it: "the virtues of scholarship and physical training" [37] which included values such as discipline, team spirit, fair play and selfless service that could take Black men beyond the artificial, race-drawn boundaries of colonial society.

Professor Seecharan takes his cue from C.L.R. James and his treatise *Beyond a Boundary* which poses the Kiplingesque question, "What do they know of cricket who only cricket know?" In other words, cricket was not just a game, but a possible means of national transformation. Following the Gospel According to St James, Professor Seecharan claims that cricket, or rather its aura of British educational, moral and cultural principles, could shape a West Indian intellectual temperament that would be receptive to the ideals of liberal democracy and the politics of gradualism, in pursuit of West Indian social, cultural and political self-development. Exemplars who are cited of successful muscular learning through the values of cricket are James himself, Arthur Lewis of St Lucia, Norman Manley of Jamaica, Grantley Adams of Barbados and Eric Williams of Trinidad and Tobago.

The first three chapters of *Muscular Learning* discuss various elite West Indian schools and the careers both of revered British teachers such as Horace Deighton and Arthur Somers-Cocks, and distinguished West Indian intellectuals such as Dr Robert Love, Dr Theophilus E.S. Scholes, Colin Jackman Prescod, Sir Conrad Reeves, Joseph Ruhomon and Edward Blyden. Chapter Four considers the first tour by English cricketers to the West Indies in 1895 when R. Slade Lucas's team took on White West Indian clubs mainly, although matches were also played against Barbados, Trinidad and Demerara, as Guyana was then known.

Chapter Five covers tours by two teams of English cricketers in 1897, one team led by Lord Hawke, the Yorkshire captain, MCC affiliate and passionate cricket proselytiser, and the other by Arthur Priestley. Then, Chapter Six records the first tour of England by a West Indies team, made in 1900, and is fleshed out with an extensive Appendix containing a review of the tour by Trinidad-born Sir Pelham (Plum) Warner, and scorecards of all matches. Two concluding chapters, Seven and Eight, expand on the effectiveness of political gradualism.

In 1895 and 1897, the English touring teams won most of their matches. Lord Hawke's team, for instance, lost only two matches, both against Trinidad. Since Trinidad was the only team that included Black players, five in all, it was evident that Black players made a difference which sent a clear signal of the potential of multi-racial West Indian cricket. In particular, the performance of two Black Trinidad fast bowlers, Woods and Cumberbatch, who bowled out Lord Hawke's team for totals of 58 and 63, each bowler claiming five wickets in the first match, and five and three wickets respectively in the second, laid the foundation of a tradition of superb West Indian fast bowling.

On their tour of England in 1900, the West Indies team which included five Black players, played seventeen matches of which five were won, eight lost, and four drawn. Not distinguished results perhaps; but we must remember the White, Anglo-centric, colonial context whereby the (mainly White) West Indies team were, at best, regarded as poor relations to more skilled and sophisticated Englishmen. Still, the fact that a Black batsman C.A. Ollivierre, from St Vincent, topped the West Indies batting averages, and went on to play county cricket for Derbyshire, while Lebrun Constantine, Learie's father, scored the first century by a West Indies player in England, supports the main thesis of *Muscular Learning* that cricket had made a breakthrough, and that: "education and cricket were at the core of the agenda for civil and political rights." [206]

Whether his thesis is convincing or not, we are swept away by the author's supercharged plethora of facts and figures, and his wide variety of quotations and references to West Indian history and society around 1900, much of it reproduced verbatim from rare or forgotten newspapers and journals of the period. That Professor Seecharan has laboured mightily is obvious from his hugely informative text, impressive bibliography, and the irrepressible vigour and ebullience of his style in *Muscular Learning*. His bold inclusion of the Indian-Guyanese Joseph Ruhomon among his pantheon of West Indian intellectuals also confirms the originality and eclecticism of his approach to West Indian history.

APPENDIX 4

Winston McGowan, The Origins and Development of Guyanese Cricket: The 2004 Walter Rodney Chair Lectures, *Guyana, Pavnik Press, 2006*

The Origins and Development of Guyanese Cricket: The 2004 Walter Rodney Chair Lectures consists mainly of two lectures given by the author in 2004: "as a part of the events commemorating the 75th anniversary of the involvement of West Indies in international cricket." [p.vi) The first lecture "The Origins of Guyanese Cricket From Early Times to 1928" covers the period from the mid-nineteenth century when cricket was first played in Guyana and the Caribbean to the year when a West Indies team played their first international or Test match. The second lecture "Guyanese Cricket: The Last 75 years from 1928 to 2003" then brings the record more or less up to date.

According to Professor McGowan, cricket was probably first played in Guyana by British residents, plantation owners and their White employees before the game spread to Blacks and Coloureds, Portuguese, and later to Chinese and Indians. This ethnic chronology is not merely random, but a direct product of the structure of nineteenth century Caribbean plantation society in which White owners and their employees formed the ruling class, Blacks and Coloureds occupied a middle position, while indentured immigrants like the Portuguese, Chinese and Indians appeared as the lowest class.

The first and most important cricket club in Guyana, the Georgetown Cricket Club (GCC), was formed in 1858, its members drawn, as one would expect merely twenty years after the end of slavery, from a colonial elite of British proprietors, attorneys, plantation managers, wealthy merchants and senior Government officers. Since GCC shared the Parade Ground in Georgetown with other groups, and felt uncertain about its future use, they moved in 1885 to Bourda, a ground destined to become the hallowed home of inter-territorial and Test cricket in Guyana until 2007 when the venue of Providence was inaugurated.

For more than half a century, until the British Guiana Cricket Board of Control was formed in 1943, the Bourda club presided over the destiny of cricket in Guyana. And even after 1943, in spite of the emergence of other clubs, for example, several Portuguese clubs, the British Guiana Cricket Club, catering to Black and coloured professionals, several Chinese clubs, and the British Guiana East Indian Cricket Club, GCC maintained national control over Guyanese cricket by the sheer dominance of its members' business and commercial contacts, social prestige and financial resources. GCC's historic dominance was crucial, stretching beyond providing a venue for inter-territorial or Test cricket to influencing the actual selection of teams representing Guyana.

Still, even if ethnically restricted, Guyanese cricket flourished under GCC leadership which encouraged competition both with local and foreign teams, for instance, playing host to Bermudan cricketers in 1859, or touring the US and Canada in 1886. In 1887/1888 the Club also crossed swords with the visiting "Gentlemen of the USA," and between 1895 and 1926 played host to several touring English teams. No wonder Professor McGowan can write: "British Guiana occupies a pivotal place in the origins and development of this inter-territorial cricket in the Caribbean." [12] Alas, it seems the Club's playing skills did not quite match their enthusiasm for organising the game: up to 1928, out of eighteen inter-territorial matches, Guyana won only two; they lost seven out of eight games to Barbados, and nine out of ten to Trinidad. For all that, Guyana produced one or two outstanding players in this early period, for example, the Barbadian-born all rounder C.R. "Snuffie" Brown, and Edgar Wright, an English-born Inspector of Police, who scored the first century in Caribbean first class cricket, and was described by C.L.R. James as: "the first great name in West Indian cricket." [20]

All this illustrates the unequal colonial conditions in which cricket has to foster resistance and nation building. After all, in 1928, the British Guiana cricket team: "consisted entirely of players of African descent and those of mixed race, all of whom were residents of Demerara, especially Georgetown," [32] – this, in a country in which Demerara is the smallest of three counties! Ethnic exclusiveness had combined with the dominance of an urban centre like Georgetown to disfigure the democratic development of politics, economics, culture and sport as it also did in other British Caribbean colonies. If there is an underlying theme in *The Origins and Development of Guyanese*

Cricket, it is that cricket was the most effective instrument for challenging this disfigurement.

By the 1950s, not only had cricket spread outside Georgetown but, in addition to Butcher, (African) the county of Berbice had produced Indian cricketers like Baijnauth, Kanhai, Solomon and Madray who had become internationally known and were accepted as household names throughout Guyana. Not only that, Georgetown's historic claim to dominance was challenged by the appearance of grounds in Berbice like those at Rose Hall and Albion where first class matches began to be played. The author admits that, to date, there is still limited involvement of Chinese, Amerindians and women, or people from the county of Essequibo in cricket. But, as we have seen from his information about Berbice cricket, solid steps have already been taken to achieve a Guyanese cricket team and general cricketing practices more representative, in ethnic and social terms, of Guyana as a whole.

Despite the volume's modest size, 83 pages, *The Origins and Development of Guyanese* Cricket yields rich dividends in information about Guyanese history, cricket and nationality – the result of energetic research that delves into dusty, half-forgotten files of newspapers and periodicals to ferret out priceless discoveries or make unsuspected revelations. How else would we know that the Demerara Cricket Club whose membership, for a half-century or more, has come from the Black lower middle class, was originally a Portuguese club! Or that, in 1956, Guyana was reputed to have the best batting side in the Caribbean! All this illustrates the rich serving of cricket lore on which we will feast in Professor McGowan's splendid work.

APPENDIX 5

*Stephen Camacho, Winston McGowan, Ian McDonald, Ron Legall,
Cricket at Bourda: Celebrating the Georgetown Cricket Club,
Georgetown, Hand-in-Hand Group of Companies,
Sheik Hassan Printing Inc., 2007*

Older than Kingston Cricket Club in Jamaica (1863), Pickwick Cricket Club in Barbados (1882), or Queens Park Oval in Trinidad and Tobago (1896), the Georgetown Cricket Club (GCC) began life in 1858 at the Parade Ground, Middle Street, Georgetown, where it shared facilities with the public until it moved to its historic home at Bourda. *Cricket at Bourda: Celebrating the Georgetown Cricket Club* marks the 150th year of the Club's existence as well as the central role of both the Club and Bourda in the history of cricket in Guyana. The book consists of commentaries by Camacho, McGowan and McDonald, and statistics and pictures presumably by Legall. Clarence A. F. Hughes Chairman of the volume's sponsor – Hand-in-Hand Companies – contributes a "Foreword" acknowledging cricket's "vital role in uniting Guyanese, uniting all West Indians," and the volume's usefulness "in recalling and moulding the nationhood to which we aspire." There are also brief congratulatory messages from Neil Singh, President of the GCC, and Chetram Singh, President of the Guyana Cricket Board.

"Brief History of GCC and Reminiscences," the longest commentary, is by Camacho who tells us that on 26 December 1885, the Club was formally opened at Bourda, and in 1887, it hosted the first Inter-colonial cricket match in Guyana (formerly British Guiana) with the auspicious result of Guyana beating Barbados by 108 runs. As mentioned in previous books, the Club was the supreme cricket authority in the country, socially and economically an elevated institution, rather like MCC in England, that served by common consent as law-giver, facilitator and enforcer. In Camacho's words, the Club, "arranged domestic cricket and ran and financed Inter-colonial tournaments and International matches." [3]

So entrenched was the power and prestige of GCC that it represented Guyana on the West Indies Cricket Board of Control which existed since 1928, and even though a Cricket Board of Control for Guyana was eventually established in 1943, GCC's guiding hand was still at the helm since the Board's first three Presidents were GCC members. All this may be reported by Camacho with due praise and admiration for GCC; but it also reflects typically oligarchic control by a White, upper class elite in a British Caribbean colony before independence in the 1960s.

Yet Camacho speaks convincingly out of strong personal connections with GCC: his maternal grandfather George Cyril Learmond toured England with the West Indies cricket team in 1900 and 1906 and, apart from numerous other family connections, his father George Camacho was President of GCC, and served as captain of the Club and Guyana in both cricket and hockey. Most of all, Camacho himself became President of GCC in 1968 and, to his credit, approved of the dismantling of the old, colonial oligarchic structure of the club and the transformation of: "the membership of cricket clubs [which] had been compartmentalised along lines of ethnicity and social position." [51]

In the first of four contributions "Bourda and its Heroes," Winston McGowan recalls notable matches or performances at the ground, and players from E.F. Wright and John Hampden in the 1880s to our contemporary Shivnarine Chanderpaul who has so far compiled 758 runs at Bourda in seven Test appearances, including one double century, three separate hundreds, and an average of 108.28. McGowan follows up with a fuller biographical sketch "Edward Wright: Unrecognised Guyanese Cricket Hero" and a second sketch "Lance Gibbs: Bowler par Excellence" which reviews the career of the best bowler so far produced by Guyana.

Fitting tribute is paid to Gibbs's outstanding achievements such as his eight wickets for 38 runs against India in Barbados, in March 1962, and his generally "tigerish' or combative attitude to cricket. In "The Historic 1930 Bourda Test" McGowan evokes highlights of the first Test match played in Bourda or Guyana. This 1930 Test yielded the first victory for West Indies in Tests, and was also the first occasion that a Guyanese – Marius Fernandes – captained the West Indies team. Not until 1973, when Rohan Kanhai succeeded Garfield Sobers, would the West Indies captaincy again pass to a Guyanese.

In his first commentary, Ian McDonald pays tribute to seven cricketers who were inducted to Guyana's Cricket Hall of Fame in 1999 – Basil Butcher, Roy Fredericks, Lance Gibbs, Rohan Kanhai,

Clive Lloyd, Joe Solomon and Clyde Walcott – all of whom he regards as national heroes. His second contribution re-creates the context of Clive Lloyd's magnificent 178 against Australia at Bourda in April 1973, in McDonald's words: "one of the very great Test innings of the modern era." McDonald celebrates Lloyd's transcendent courage in deploying such an innings in the process of emerging from a bad patch in his career. In "Rohan Kanhai – Batsman Extraordinary," after he lists qualities which he might expect in the world's greatest batsman – statistical distinction, reliability, tenacity, persistence, athletic genius, elegance, power, control – McDonald selects Kanhai as the "batsman who had something of all the greatness, and in their total combination." [84] In his final essay "Five Great Berbician Cricketers" McDonald extols the merits of Kanhai, Butcher, Solomon, Fredericks and Kallicharran, all of whom he regards as being, "touched with genius."

The statistical data that supplement these commentaries include the following: complete scorecards for all the thirty Test matches played at Bourda from 1930 to 2005; a list of batsmen who made Test centuries at the ground; and lists of bowlers who took five wickets in an innings or ten or more wickets in a Test match at Bourda. Splendid pictures of individual players and teams round off a comprehensive catalogue of facts and figures that cannot fail to jog the memory of cricket lovers, Guyanese most of all, who will savour salient memories and pay homage, as memory slowly fades into the romance of heroic deeds and valiant feats witnessed on hallowed ground within sacred precincts.

APPENDIX 6

Hilary McD. Beckles, Ed., The First West Indian Cricket Tour, Canada and the United States in 1886, Jamaica, Canoe Press, 2007, With The Tour of West Indian Cricketers, August and September, 1886 "A Memory" *by One of them – L.R. Fyfe*

As Professor Beckles writes in his Introduction, the aim of his book is: "to promote growing interest in the game [cricket] in the Americas." It helps his purpose too that the volume appeared shortly before the Cricket World Cup tournament, hosted by West Indies in early 2007, when the eyes of the world were focused on a region – the Americas (including the Caribbean) – where cricket was popular among Canadians and Americans in the middle of the nineteenth century. No doubt it seems surprising today, but in 1886, when West Indian cricketers made their first international tour, to Canada and the US: "cricket culture was more developed in Canada [than in the West Indies] and ... clubs in the United States had adopted a professional approach." It is even more surprising to learn that in 1867 Sir John A. MacDonald, Canada's first Prime Minister, had declared cricket as Canada's national game!

The United States of America was established as an independent nation in 1783, and the Dominion of Canada in 1867 as newly created nations which, along with the West Indies, shared a common culture as former British colonies. The chief difference within this Anglo-centric cultural community was that, in 1886, Canada and the US were self-governing democracies with populations mostly of European descent while the West Indies remained British colonies with a population mainly descended from African slaves. Since West Indian society was dominated by a tiny elite of (White) British plantation owners, business men and officials, the all-White West Indies cricket team whose members paid their own expenses for the tour – one thousand pounds – did not include any Black West Indians; for the truth is that the 1886 tour was less concerned with cricket than with fostering Anglo-centric links between people of common British ethnic origin. More importantly, as sugar producers constantly faced by economic crisis, the West Indians were eager to: "seek out new commercial partners and build sustainable markets."

APPENDIX 3

Preparation of *The First West Indian Cricket Tour* encouraged by the American and Canadian diplomatic corps in the West Indies, carries a "Foreword" by the Hon. Peter Mackay, Canadian Minister of Foreign Affairs, and Minister of the Atlantic Canada Opportunities Agency. A second section consists of a brief "Preface" and Acknowledgements by Professor Beckles who adds an Introduction followed by pictures of the tour and a full reprint of an account of the tour by L.R. Fyfe, one of the West Indies players, first published in 1887 by the Argosy Press in Demerara. (now Guyana)

The tour itself lasted through August and September 1886 when the West Indies cricket team played thirteen matches against Canada and the US. The West Indies won six matches, lost five and drew two, although their loss of four out of seven matches against the US suggests that the US had the strongest of the three teams.

Fyfe's account is undoubtedly the centre-piece of the volume since it restores an authentic voice from the past and supplies basic facts, for instance, that Guy Wyatt the Demerara captain first conceived the idea of the tour; that certain players were not available for business reasons; that the absence of Demerara players such as Wright, Henery, Goodridge and Garnett greatly weakened the West Indies team; and that only Jamaica, Barbados and Demerara were represented, and Trinidad not at all.

If the account does not maintain the interest it might have had one hundred and twenty years ago, one reason is that the author reproduces results, commentaries and scorecards, quoted verbatim from 1886 press reports of the thirteen matches played that year, and this prompts him to avoid making: "any but casual references on special points in regards to the matches in this narrative." [6] So what we get is a mere chronicle of social events along with a rather tedious catalogue of repeated examples of generous hospitality that the West Indians received from their Canadian and American hosts.

But limited appeal as an historical artefact is handsomely redeemed by the analytic depth and insight of Professor Beckles's Introduction which may detract a little from the formal shape of the volume by repeating some facts from Fyfe's narrative, but adds far more in perspective and context by considering events in hindsight long after they occurred. The Introduction reveals information about interesting or neglected issues. For example, if cricket was so popular in the US until at least the 1850s when it was regarded as "the principal ball game" in the country, why did it lose out so comprehensively to baseball by the early 1900s? Neither the visit of two English teams to the US in 1868 and 1872, nor the West Indies tour in 1886 could forestall the encroaching popularity of baseball which, according to Professor Beckles, became decisive as early as the Civil War (1861-1865) when it was difficult to obtain cricket equipment and maintain pitches. Other factors were the ease of playing baseball almost anywhere once four bases were set; the spiralling increase of native-born Americans; and the great influx of European immigrants to whom cricket was foreign.

So far as Canada is concerned, from 1870 to 1894, seventy-five cricket clubs flourished; and in 1849 the first match between Canada and the US took place; while, between 1859 and 1900, of forty-two games played in Canada against international teams, the home team won only once. It is the decline of cricket in North America, the comprehensive dominance of baseball in the US and declining interest in Canada, that justifies Professor Beckles's attempt to promote cricket in the Americas in 2007. For he correctly perceives a revival of interest in the game, both in Canada and the US, stimulated principally by the large scale influx of immigrants from cricket-playing British Commonwealth countries during the last quarter of the last century.

APPENDIX 7

Arnold Bertram, Jamaica at the Wicket: A Study of Jamaican Cricket and its Role in Shaping the Jamaican Society, *Kingston, Jamaica, Research and Project Development Ltd., 2009*

The very size of Arnold Bertram's *Jamaica at the Wicket: A Study of Jamaican Cricket and its Role in Shaping the Jamaican Society* (685 pages), together with its ambitious title, suggest a task of Herculean proportions. There are certainly plenty of dates, statistics, scores and anecdotes; also a chronological survey of historical events, biographical portraits and extensive commentary and analysis. But, if anything, the author's own description of his book seems a little self-effacing: "a modest contribution to the continuing documentation of cricket as a primary cultural institution and its place in the Jamaican social process."(xiii) *Jamaica at the Wicket* achieves far more than mere documentation; it analyses and justifies links between Jamaica's progress in cricket, and critical stages in the island's social, political and economic development from 1778, when Jamaican cricket is first mentioned, in Thomas Thistlewood's diary, to the present day.

The game took root in the 1850s when: "British soldiers, educators, administrators and other professionals, along with Jamaican students educated in Britain ... successfully exported cricket to Jamaica." [20] The first cricket clubs on the island were formed by 1857, and Kingston Cricket Club (KCC), later to become headquarters of Jamaican cricket, in 1863. When a West Indies cricket team toured Canada and the US, in 1886, the seven Jamaican players in the seventeen-man squad were naturally all White, and all members of KCC. For in this early period, barely fifty yeas since slavery was abolished, a sharp divide still existed between Blacks (former slaves) and Whites (former masters), and since cricket was an elite (White) activity, Black Jamaicans – then 78.5 per cent of the population – were excluded from the game.

Another disadvantage to its cricket development, during this colonial period was Jamaica's failure to participate in regional competition with its sister British Caribbean colonies until 1896. As Bertram observes: "Jamaica, one of the earliest British colonies in the West Indies, was the last colony to enter inter-colonial cricket tournaments which had been going on since 1846 when a team from British Guiana visited Barbados." [93] The failure was geographical: Jamaica was separated from the Southern Caribbean colonies by more than a thousand miles of sea, and transportation by ship was slow and difficult, so Barbados, British Guiana and Trinidad had already played eighteen matches among themselves by 1896.

Foreign competition for Jamaica first came through touring goodwill English teams, for example, one led by Slade Lucas in 1895, another by Sir Arthur Priestley in 1897, one by Lord Brackley in 1905, and yet another by A.W. Somerset in 1911. But in a: "most important initiative in the development of the game in Jamaica," [112] a Senior cup competition was inaugurated after Priestley's tour, drawing in both cricket clubs and leading schools like Jamaica College, Wolmer's and St Georges College. One step, critical to the growth of Black cricketers, was the establishment of Calabar Elementary School by the Baptist Missionary Society of Great Britain in 1820. This led, in 1893, to the formation of the Jamaica Cricket Club, a Black club that later changed its name to "Lucas" in tribute to Slade Lucas who had sent them cricket gear from England.

In 1901, "Lucas" was admitted to Senior Cup competition, and by 1925 "Lucas" and Clovelly – another Black club – dominated the Senior Cup. At this stage in his narrative Bertram's general thesis really hits its stride. He reminds us, for instance, that undemocratic Crown Colony government ended in 1884 and that: "the rise of Black players [was] achieved against the background of a broader campaign for the expansion of democratic rights and racial equality." [111] A Black man Dr Joseph Robert Love pioneered the creation of a new political and racial consciousness which, by the 1930s, produced: "a tradition of greatness established by Jamaicans on the international stage." [179] The tradition included such distinguished Black achievers as John Brown Russwurm, Theophilus Scoles, Marcus Garvey and, most of all, the batsman George Alphonso Headley.

Headley's career forms the centrepiece of *Jamaica at the Wicket*. His arrival coincided with what the author calls: "the golden age of Jamaican cricket" [235] from 1925 to 1939, which was then followed by a post-Second World War period when the social base of cricket expanded to include children from middle and working class families as students in elite schools. Bertram sings Headley's praises for inspiring all this: "his [Headley's] genius indicated their [Jamaicans'] possibilities in a world which historically condemned them both to discrimination and servitude." [268]

Headley, after all, is regarded as equal to the Australian Sir Donald Bradman as the greatest of all batsmen. But a note of defensiveness comes through Bertram's narrative when he contrasts Bradman's admiring reception in his homeland with the experience of Headley facing: "continued domination by a White minority in post-Emancipation Jamaica." [404] Still, after Independence, Bertram acknowledges that a sculpture of Headley's head was unveiled at the National Stadium in Jamaica, and he received both the Norman Manley Award and the Order of Distinction from the Jamaican government.

If Headley is the leading light, lesser stars are not neglected in *Jamaica at the Wicket*, for example, the Holts (father and son) and perhaps the brightest star of all, O.G. 'Collie' Smith, whose lowly origins: "symbolised the hopes and aspirations of the displaced peasantry and the urban working class." [312] Allan Rae, Gerry Alexander, Roy Gilchrist, Frank Worrell and the generation following them – Lawrence Rowe, Courtney Walsh, and Michael Holding – are all given their due. Cricketers are convincingly linked to social, political, racial and economic factors that influence their performance not only in Test matches or regional competitions, but nowadays, alas, also in globalised international competitions that encourage them to be more concerned about individual financial gain than about their historic role as agents of national development.

APPENDIX 8

Hilary McD. Beckles, A Nation Imagined: First West Indies Team: The 1928 Tour, *Kingston, Jamaica, Ian Randle Ltd., 2003*

A Nation Imagined: First West Indies Team: The 1928 Tour is a commemorative volume that celebrates the 75th anniversary of West Indian entry into Test cricket in 1928, when three Test matches were played against England, in England. Before 1928, only England, Australia and South Africa – all White or White-dominated countries – were admitted to an international or Test-playing cricket fraternity whose activities were regulated by the Marylebone Cricket Club (MCC) headquartered at Lord's cricket ground in London. Although, by the 1950s, the Second World War dealt a mighty blow to European imperial pretensions, empire still prevailed in the 1920s, for instance, through Anglocentric domination of cricket. *A Nation Imagined* analyses the beginnings of West Indian cricket within this global, Anglocentric context that permitted Sir Cavendish Boyle to welcome members of the 1906 West Indies cricket team to England as "children of Britain" and part of a chain that "binds the sons of Great Britain with the children of Greater Britain" [16].

The first noticeable aspect of *A Nation Divided* is its strange shape and format. The volume looks more like a decorative packet of faded postcards than a book. Either that, or a picture album of some kind. The author acknowledges this "slightly unorthodox design" under "Acknowledgements." The fact that the volume is twice as long as it is wide, and consists of barely seventy-five pages of thick glossy paper confirms its unusual appearance. Still more unusual are the volume's two parallel texts: the first, an historical commentary by Professor Beckles on left-side pages only of the book, and the second an assortment of newspaper reports, pictures and scorecards of matches on the right-hand pages only. Each text has its own pagination, Professor Beckles's in Roman numerals, and the other in italics. But the commentary on the left-side pages do not always match the exact reports, pictures or scorecards on the opposite side.

APPENDIX 8

One sees the intention behind the design: for the pages of Professor Beckles's analysis to be illustrated and reinforced by the pictorial and statistical "evidence" on the pages directly opposite. The result, alas, is one of discontinuous reading that calls for much page turning in an effort to match up commentary with statistics. Still, this is not a great inconvenience in such a short book, and we should thank Vaneisa Baksh and her colleagues Anya De Souza and Jeffrey Pataysingh for the design which is certainly eye-catching.

Taking his cue from Benedict Anderson's seminal work *Imagined Communities: Reflections on the Origin and Spread of Nationalism* (1991), which suggests that citizens of modern nation states rely on imaginative works for their shared sense of nationality, Professor Beckles argues that cricket offers West Indians a symbol of their most sustaining sense of national togetherness. He focuses on three tours that West Indies teams made to England in 1900, 1906 and 1923. By including some Black players, these teams began to erode the colonial structure of local, White, racist domination of cricket in the West Indies; and when West Indies finally gained Test status in 1928, Professor Beckles claims that the ensuing series "was understood in the West Indian world as the prime symbol of a nation imagined" (Introduction).

According to Professor Beckles, the 1900 West Indies tour of England was the "beginning of modern non-racial West Indian 'international' cricket," [p.14] and, by the 1923 tour, West Indian cricketers "began to assume the identity as popular symbols of a nation imagined" [p.23]. But the 1928 tour results were disappointing: West Indies lost all three Test matches, each by the margin of an innings, and out of thirty other matches, they won only five, lost twelve and drew thirteen. Whatever explanations are given for it, this apparently spineless submission to England, the imperial oppressor, somewhat detracts from cricket's claim of being the prime symbol of West Indian nationality.

Yet the successful introduction of more democratic principles into the racist structure of West Indian cricket during the tours of 1900, 1906 and 1923, is clearly demonstrated by Professor Beckles; and we know that following further West Indies defeats by England, in England, in 1933 and 1939, and a celebrated, if dubious victory over England in 1950, West Indian cricket joined with politics and literature, during the 1950s, to inspire political independence of the Anglophone

Caribbean in the 1960s. So the indispensable role of cricket as a prime mover of West Indian nationality is beyond dispute.

The truth is that the 1928 tour was only one step, albeit a backward one, in the long-term process of the evolution of a West Indian national identity. But the commemorative demands of the 75th anniversary of West Indies Test cricket encourage a rousing celebratory tone in Professor Beckles's writing, and betray a hint of imposing theory on fact, for example, when he complains of the "startling" or "phenomenal" absence of Indian players from the 1928 West Indies Test team. Here, Professor Beckles protests too much by betraying perhaps too earnest a desire to demonstrate cricket's role as "the region's first expression of popular mass culture" [2].

To expect Indian participation in Test cricket in the 1920s, 30s or 40s, rather underrates the malign and deep-seated influence of race and class in the Caribbean, and an ingrained social stigma against "coolies", especially in Guyana and Trinidad, where most Indians had settled. But this is mere cavilling. The pictures alone in *A Nation Imagined* are full of rare and marvellous information, and, in combination with its newspaper reports, excerpts and scorecards, constitute nothing less than an enthralling evocation of the early history of cricket in the West Indies; and when this is further added to Professor Beckles's insightful and revealing commentary, what we have is a simply sumptuous volume on West Indies cricket, one to be treasured, even if it is hugely overpriced.

APPENDIX 9

Clem Seecharan, From Ranji to Rohan: Cricket and Indian Identity in Colonial Guyana 1890s-1960s, *Hertford, UK, Hansib Publications, 2009*

In his book, *From Ranji to Rohan: Cricket and Indian Identity in Colonial Guyana, 1890s-1960s*, Professor Clem Seecharan surveys a variety of thoroughly researched sources including, most interestingly, buried, forgotten, or largely unknown information exhumed from Guyanese newspapers, journals and personal contacts. His main argument is that cricket was: "indispensable to the construction of identity in this polyglot [Guyanese] colonial environment," [18] and that Indian-Guyanese, like African-Guyanese who arrived in the colony centuries before them had, by the 1960s, assimilated the game into their national psyche.

When the first Indians arrived as indentured plantation labourers in Guyana, in 1838, most of were unfamiliar with basic elements of Guyanese culture such as the English language (or its Guyanese variant), Christianity, and Western habits of dress, food, sport and so on. Five or six decades later, however, some members of a small Indian middle class had emerged, many of them Christians, for example, Joseph Rohomon, the Wharton brothers, and Veerasawmy Mudaliar. Inspired by achievements on the world stage of distinguished Indians such as Prince Ranjitsinhji, a cricketer of rare genius, Dadabhai Naoroji, the first Indian elected to the British parliament, and Swami Vivekanda who had addressed the world's Parliament of religion in Chicago in 1893, Professor Seecharan argues that these men produced pioneering efforts that made them: "central to the process of redefinition of Indo-Guyanese Indian-ness." [22]

That the redefinition appeared most visibly through cricket was not accidental since the game was: "a defining idiom of Creole society" [74] and the most readily available access into the heart and soul of Guyanese society. Stalwarts in the early development of Indian-Guyanese cricket, for instance, were Thomas Flood, businessman, and J.A. Luckhoo a lawyer, both Christians. Soon, in 1914, the East Indian Cricket Club (EICC) was established, and one or two Indian-Guyanese players chosen to represent Guyana in inter-colonial cricket, for example, J.A. Veersawmy a dynamic fast-medium bowler and cricket writer, Charlie Pooran a right-handed batsman, R.B. Rohoman a slow bowler, and Chatterpaul "Doosha" Persaud, the most gifted Indian-Guyanese batsman of his era who scored heavily in local Parker Cup matches during the 1930s, and probably possessed the calibre for Test cricket, except that he failed in trial matches for the 1939 West Indies tour to England and never got another chance to prove himself.

By the 1950s, as Indian-Guyanese cricketers marched forward, politics raised its ugly head with growing agitation for freedom from colonial rule which provoked the calamity of Britain's suspension of Guyana's Constitution in 1953. Professor Seecharan does not flinch from making a connection between Dr Cheddi Jagan, the political hero, even if a failed one by his account, and Rohan Kanhai, the batting genius, through their common birthplace in plantation Port Mourant, and their shared background with cricketers from the ancient county Berbice) such as Sonny "Sugar Boy" Baijnauth, Sonny Moonsammy, Leslie Amsterdam, Saranga Baichu, Joe Solomon, Ivan Madray and Basil Butcher. It was a turbulent time when the period from 1955 to 1957 became both a "watershed in the colony's cricket" [p.122] and a decisive moment in Guyana's failed political history because of a tragic split in Dr Jagan's People's Progressive Party.

The title of Chapter Four of *From Ranji to Rohan* "Rebellion and Racial Bitterness: the Age of Rohan Kanhai" admirably captures the spirit of these times by portraying Kanhai's batting as a triumphant gesture of defiance against the humiliation of indenture and the failure of Guyanese political aspirations. Kanhai's batting, in short, atoned for the limitations of Indian-Guyanese political history. Professor Seecharan expatiates on Kanhai's batting triumphs during the West Indies tour of India/Pakistan in 1958/59 when he scaled two of the highest peaks of his career: his 256 against India in Calcutta in 1958 (his highest score) and 217 against Pakistan shortly afterwards.

Deploying painstaking research, Professor Seecharan also quotes lavishly from Australian cricket gurus Jack Fingleton and Richie Benaud who, following Kanhai's exploits in Australia in 1960/61, boldly declared him the best batsman in the world at the time. To such glory showered on one of their own, Kanhai's fellow plantation dwellers reacted with something akin to religious ecstasy: "He [Kanhai] was at the centre of their [Indian-Guyanese] lives ... they had actually elevated the man [Kanhai] into the pantheon of Hindu gods." [p.178] Also:" he [Kanhai] made them [Indian-Guyanese] feel they had earned the right to belong to the West Indies." [186]

If cricket speeded up the process of Creolisation for Indian-Guyanese it did not solve the deep-seated problem of ethnic conflict between Indian-Guyanese and African-Guyanese that still bedevils Guyana's future: "Cricket in British Guiana helped to bridge the incomprehension across the African/Indian racial chasm; but it deepened that divide." [234] This is the Guyanese sphinx whose riddle has defied solution from the bravest and best so far. *From Ranji to Rohan* may not solve the riddle, but it offers illumination by revealing much previously hidden information about cricket in colonial Guyana, together with reflections about: "so many of our outstanding cricketers withering on the vine." [242]

The volume provides details, for example, about forgotten players like Sonny Moonsammy and Ivan Madray whose careers did wither on the vine, and even of Basil Butcher who became a successful Test batsman, but whose career was negatively influenced by his role as an African-Guyanese from Port Mourant. More importantly, the volume records the crucial influence on the development of Guyanese cricket by Robert Christiani as Personnel Manager at Port Mourant, and of Clyde Walcott as cricket organiser for the Sugar Producers Association. It also offers such information that, in the 1940s, Baijnauth, "was the first Indian from a plantation [in Berbice] to represent British Guiana." [147] It all lends support to Professor Seecharan's argument that, by Kanhai's heyday in the 1960s, "cricket was now unambiguously central to Indian-Guyanese identity." [156]

APPENDIX 10

Kenneth Ramchand with Yvonne Teelucksingh, The West Indies in India: Jeffrey Stollmeyer's Diary, 1948-1949, *Macoya, Trinidad, Royards Publishing Company Ltd., 2004*

Except for when he came down with chickenpox for a couple of weeks, Jeffrey Stollmeyer not only composed his *Diary* but regularly mailed sections of the text to his wife, in Trinidad, while he was vice-captain of the West Indies team, playing cricket throughout their tour of India, from October 1948 to March 1949. Astonishing! Accounts of cricket tours by professional journalists are common enough, but not by players. That and the fact that the *Diary* now appears in public, more than fifty years after it was written, surely make it probably unique in annals of cricket history and literature!

India's legendary poverty is never far from Stollmeyer's mind in his *Diary*. At Ratham Railway Station he encounters: "Frightful-looking people, victims of small-pox, many blind, emaciated, leprous, syphilitic" [49]; "a servant steals several suits and shirts from one player's (McWatt's) suitcase" [80]; Calcutta is pitiable, "an infernal city" [172], and he curses India when he gets chicken pox [155]; he also speaks disparagingly of the "strange country" [179] he is in, and of: "the way their [Indian] minds work" [105]. At the same time, he lavishes praise on the grandeur and splendour of the hospitality offered the West Indies team by the Maharajah of Patiala. Such candid and intimate social observations and opinions are the stock in trade of genres like memoirs, journals, diaries or travelogues.

But Stollmeyer's *Diary* is primarily concerned with cricket and cricketers, West Indian as well as Indian; and the volume provides a detailed account of the nineteen First Class matches that West Indies played in India, of which they lost only one, and their five Test matches of which they won one and drew four. That West Indies won seven and drew sixteen of their twenty-four matches in India tells virtually the whole story of the tour: slow wickets and un-enterprising Indian cricket. As we see from his earlier comments, Stollmeyer can be scathing: "the type of cricket dished out by most of the Indian side is very discouraging from the spectators' viewpoint" [152]. He also laments what he calls, "the usual Indian trait, 'lack of guts'" [162], and claims that one of the best India batsmen Lala Amarnath runs away from fast bowling. But Stollmeyer does not blame the Indians only for a tour that is: "grossly mismanaged on all sides" [236]: the West Indies manager Donald Lacy is declared to be, "incompetent in the extreme" [148]. At the same time, he provides perceptive portraits of West Indian players, and vivid reports of their struggle against poor living and travelling conditions, or playing facilities.

Yet the true appeal of a diary is less its objective reporting than the diarist's subjective self-revelation; and beneath the factual record in Stollmeyer's *Diary*, of Weekes's four consecutive Test centuries in India, the perils of Indian umpiring, or the author's penchant for horse racing and cinema going, there is an underlying, self-revealing theme: that John Goddard lacks enough tactical ability in field placing, making bowling changes, even in social skills as a speaker, to be a successful captain; and that if West Indies are to win on their forthcoming tour of England, in 1950, which the author thinks entirely possible, it should be under his – Stollmeyer's – captaincy. Stollmeyer harps on Goddard's tactical and strategic inadequacy throughout his narrative. He also harps on George Headley's seeming pretence of being too ill to play which leads Professor Ramchand to suggest in his useful, if lengthy Introduction: "What was really going on with Headley in India cries out for research and analysis." (xviii)

Headley's problem did not start in India, in 1948, nor in the West Indies, in 1947, when he showed similar reluctance to play against England: it started in the 1930s when Headley was the top batsman in the world, equal to Bradman. As much as Constantine, before him, Headley resented others being appointed as captain of the West Indies team over him, chiefly because they were White – Rolph Grant in 1939, Goddard and Stollmeyer in 1947/48, and Goddard in 1948/49. Nor were Headley's credentials in tactics wanting, as we hear from Stollmeyer himself in his book *Everything Under the Sun*: "he [Headley] had a greater tactical sense than any cricketer with whom I have played." [p.37] Stollmeyer's derision of Headley as a "tourist" in his *Diary* is demeaning to the supreme master among West Indian batsmen, however understandable it may be within the colour-conscious, West Indian social code that still flourished during the 1930s and 1940s. What also needs research is the rivalry between Goddard and Stollmeyer, which may help to explain the hidden fragility of the much vaunted, West Indies triumph in England in 1950, their debacle in Australia in 1951/52, and much else in West Indies cricket up to 1957.

Stollmeyer makes no secret of his own political views when he describes the opinions of his opening partner Allan Rae as: "strangely anti-conservative" [202], and suspects that Rae may be: "guilty of reading the wrong books." [202] As a product of White privilege in colonial Trinidad, Stollmeyer's elitist taste for horse racing, hot baths, reading and diary writing is all of a piece with the leisured, patrician elegance of his leg side play. We should be grateful to all those who collaborated in this lavish production of the *Diary*, despite minor printing or spelling errors, for example, in names like Karl Nunes [p.xv] Duleepsinhji [218], and Grimmett [240]. Most of all, we should be grateful that the events of Stollmeyer's *Diary* which, "were not intended for public consumption" [iv] are, at last, available to public view. For an aficionado of cricket to come upon these events in *The West Indies in India, Jeffrey Stollmeyer's Diary 1948-1949,* is like an archaeologist wandering into some forgotten shaft on a neglected excavation site in Egypt, only to discover royal treasures more precious than rubies.

APPENDIX 11

John Figueroa, West Indies in England: The Great Post-war Tours, *London, Kingswood Press, 1991*

West Indies in England focuses on ten series of Test matches that West Indies played in England from 1950 to 1988. The volume opens with three general chapters of roving discussion, followed by eight chapters on the Test matches themselves, before ending with four further chapters of general discussion. Nor are the Test matches considered in chronological sequence. Instead, the author ranges back and forth between selected matches, giving free rein to his opinions, insights, memories and preferences. Rather than a formal cricket treatise, *West Indies in England* thus emerges more as a free-ranging and rather indulgent assemblage of cricket reminiscences from a well-known, Jamaican literary critic, poet and academic, who was also cricket correspondent for various newspapers and the BBC.

Professor Figueroa deserves praise for a comprehensive Appendix with full scorecards and averages of all the tour matches played by West Indies, in England, from 1950 to 1988. This, no doubt, is one way of backing up what he says in his text which remains paramount, especially his reminiscences which are an irreplaceable repository of West Indian cricket lore. Who today remembers, for example, that on the 1950 West Indies tour of England, the three main West Indian fast bowlers, Lance Pierre, Hines Johnson and Prior Jones, took a meagre 91 first class wickets between them, compared with a staggering total of 250 between Ramadhin and Valentine alone! Or that in the historic Second Test, at Lord's, on the same tour, the West Indies captain, John Goddard, bowled a spell of six overs, all maidens, for no wicket! Thus do commonplace recollections appear as genuine revelations! As for his explanation of the evanescence of Kenny Trestrail's promised brilliance, namely that Trestrail lacked the right temperament for Test cricket, and might have possessed "a certain cussedness" [62]. Professor Figueroa strikes an almost forgotten chord of recognition in those of us fortunate enough to have seen Trestrail bat.

Such opinions are entertaining even if controversial, and *West Indies in England* would not be the same without them. While the author acknowledges the achievement of Frank Worrell's team in the early 1960s, and of Clive Lloyd's in the 1980s, as two of the highest peaks in West Indian cricket, he is positively euphoric about the West Indies 3 to 1 victory over England, in 1950, which he regards as: "perhaps the greatest contribution which West Indies have made to the great game" [131]. He also claims that this 1950 team was the best that ever toured England from the West Indies [66]. This, despite a counter claim from Tom Graveney that the 1963 West Indies team "was one of the best of all sides that ever visited England, including the 1948 Bradman team" [66], and a confession from Sir Garfield Sobers that the 1963 team was "the best team I ever played on" [67].

When, to justify himself, Professor Figueroa argues that, in 1950, West Indies beat a powerful England team consisting of players such as Hutton, Washbrook, Compton and Sheppard, he may forget that Compton was injured and played in only one Test, as did Washbrook and Sheppard. He also appears to ignore England's frenzied switching of players such as Edrich, Doggart, Dollery, Parkhouse, Berry, Jenkins, Laker and Shackleton from one Test to the next, a tactic that surely betrays instability and weakness rather than strength. Undeterred, however, Professor Figueroa describes the 1950 West Indies team as "a microcosm of what might be a brave new world" [104]. But this reverential attitude to the 1950 West Indies team is no idiosyncratic whim of the author's: it is deeply imprinted in the West Indian psyche. The trouble is that it relies less on facts than on a spontaneous and somewhat wishful sense of triumphalism that attempts to atone for centuries of West Indian enslavement, exploitation and colonialism by British rulers.

Professor Figueroa gives this away in his description of the 1950 victory as "showing to people ever so sure of themselves, and of their right to win that the mighty can fall – even in their own territory" [131]. In 1950, West Indies scarcely formed a team, being more of a collection of talented individuals; and, instead of beating a powerful England team, they faced a weakened, post-war England side that had already been mauled by Australia in 1948. Furthermore, reverence surely gives way to fantasy when Professor Figueroa argues that Goddard's 1950 side was superior to Frank Worrell's in 1963; for, despite its lack of a stable pair of opening batsmen, Worrell's team remains the most varied and balanced that ever shouldered arms for West Indies; and it was indisputably the best led.

Evidently, Professor Figueroa's comments on West Indian cricket in the 1970s and 80s are less eye-catching than those of earlier decades when he was personally acquainted with players and commentators alike. His real achievement in *West Indies in England* is historical, for example, his explanation that the stereotype of cavalier West Indian cricket comes from the amateur origins of the game in the West Indies, or his authoritative identification of Sir Learie Constantine as the supreme exemplar of cavalier cricket because of his "generous, if exhibitionist inclination to entertain the fans" [27].

So far as his writing goes, Professor Figueroa's liberal use of repetition, anecdotes, humour, even Latin quotations, may sometimes betray traces of exhibitionism, name-dropping, irrelevance or mere gossip. As a cricket historian too, his acute awareness of the historic cricket rivalry between England and West Indies induces the note of defensiveness already seen in his gloating remarks about the West Indies victory in 1950. There is also a seemingly retaliatory desire, in *West Indies in England,* to expose English attitudes of superciliousness, condescension or hypocrisy in cricket. Yet, paradoxically, this emotional element is what elevates Professor Figueroa's volume, from a mere record of assorted cricketing reminiscences, to a stimulating, arresting and revealing narrative of some of the most deeply felt of all West Indian longings, resentments and satisfactions.

APPENDIX 12

John Arlott, Days at the Cricket,
London, Longmans, Green and Co. Ltd., 1951, pp.199

The Second Test at Lord's, from 24th to 29th June 1950, is the most memorable of all West Indies cricket matches. No other match, among those in the 1930s, immortalising peerless deeds by George Headley, contests in the 1950s and 60s, reflecting unique virtuosity from Garfield Sobers, or victories in the 1980s or 90s establishing global West Indies dominance, captures what seemed like the pure splendour of an heaven-blest miracle bestowed to the West Indies team at Lord's in 1950; and it would be hard to find a better on-the-spot account of the match than John Arlott's *Days at the Cricket.*

Although West Indies had toured England in 1928, 1933 and 1939, and played one three-match Test series in each year, their failure to win a single Test betrayed the impudence of their puny challenge from a remote colonial outpost against the metropolitan might of imperial Britain. But talented new players who surfaced after the Second World War had helped West Indies win against England in West Indies in 1947, and against India, in India, during 1948/49.

West Indies also opened their 1950 England tour with promisingly huge totals in preliminary county matches. But in their first Test at Old Trafford, in early June, they suffered humiliating defeat by 202 runs. This probably explains the chastened spirit with which openers Rae and Stollmeyer took guard in the West Indies first innings at Lord's on 24th June. Their styles contrasted sharply: Arlott notes Rae's dour determination: "the certainty, purpose, and accustomed air of a man in his own garden plot" [42] while he thought Stollmeyer's elegant strokes: "had the quality of a court ceremony." [42] After seeing off the English pace bowlers, Stollmeyer was lbw for 20 to left-arm spinner Johnny Wardle, leaving the lunchtime score at 102 for one wicket.

After lunch, Worrell was bowled by Bedser for 52, and both Rae and the incoming Weekes were dropped in the slips off Bedser before Weekes (63) was also bowled, again by Bedser. By end of play West Indies had reached 320 for seven with Rae, their lynchpin, 106 not out; and when, the next morning, Rae was caught and bowled by leg spinner Jenkins without adding to his score, the innings ended tamely on 326.

England's first innings was launched by stalwart retainers, Hutton and Washbrook, whose names went together like a stately English horse and carriage. They survived the West Indies fast pair of Jones and Worrell without alarm before Hutton was stumped by Walcott off Valentine for 35 with the score at 62. Then, abruptly, what so far seemed like a contest of mere mortals was instantly translated by the bowling of Ramadhin and Valentine into a mythic morality tale of gods; for nothing else can explain how two utterly untried West Indian youths, immediately before lunch, for instance, could bowl forty-six consecutive deliveries to two of England's top batsmen, without a single run being scored!

The consistency of Valentine's left-arm leg-breaks turning viciously into right-handed batsmen, and the almost supernatural mystery of Ramadhin's occasional leg-breaks being indistinguishable from his off-breaks transformed West Indies close fielders into a deadly noose throttling Washbrook who was stumped off Ramadhin for 36, and Doggart who was removed, lbw Ramadhin for nought. Then, from 74 for three, as one accurate maiden over followed another in solemn procession, the England batsmen became so overcome by accumulating terror that Arlott acknowledges this stage of the match as: "the longest and most tense period I have ever known in a cricket match." [54] Like a priest administering last rites, Arlott writes: "Edrich ... wore the sackcloth of unremitting defence with the militant pride of an anchorite." [54]

After enduring thirty deliveries, Parkhouse blindly cross batted Valentine and was bowled without scoring, while Edrich's prolonged agony was mercifully ended when he was caught at the wicket off Ramadhin for 8. At 86 for five, Ramadhin and Valentine had devastated England's first innings, and only desperate blows from the last England pair, Wardle and Berry, dragged their total to 151 – a deficit of 175. The scale of devastation is clear from Arlott's report that runs were scored from only 16 of Ramadhin's 222 deliveries, and also only from 16 of Valentine's 234 deliveries.

In the West Indies second innings, Rae was dropped twice and play ended on the second day at 45 for no wicket with Rae on 16 and

Stollmeyer 29. The next morning Jenkins quickly disposed of both openers, and Worrell played polished strokes before he too fell to Jenkins. With the score at 108 for three, captain Goddard, a left-hander, came in early to blunt the effect of Jenkins's leg breaks and googlies, but Jenkins disposed of him when the score reached 146 for four. During the morning Jenkins had taken four top West Indies wickets and let in at least a glimmer of English hope. Yet, when play ended at 386 for five, this hope had all but seeped away.

At 425 for six on the fourth day West Indies declared, setting England a seemingly impossible goal of getting 601 runs with two days left. The first six overs from Ramadhin and Valentine produced one scoring stroke only before Hutton was bowled by Valentine for 10, and by lunch when the score was 44 for one, Ramadhin and Valentine had bowled 18 overs for 19 runs scored by only seven strokes. It was bowling of unerring length and accuracy, and although Washbrook had no inkling which way Ramadhin was turning the ball, he bravely soldiered on to reach 114 not out by the end of the fourth day. On the final day, though, after facing six consecutive maidens, he had to face what was inevitable, and gave up the ghost as England stumbled to 274 – their first home defeat by the West Indies – by 326 runs. It was nothing more than a miracle, still celebrated today in calypsonian folklore, as the heavenly handiwork of "two little pals of mine, Ramadhin and Valentine!"

APPENDIX 13

Andy Ganteaume, My Story: The Other Side of the Coin, St James, Trinidad and Tobago, Medianet Limited, 2007

My Story: The Other Side of the Coin is the autobiography of Andy Ganteaume, a Trinidadian who was born in 1921 and played cricket (also football), but had a career of only one Test match when he opened the first innings for West Indies in their Second Test against England, at Queen's Park Oval, Trinidad, in February 1948. Ganteaume scored 112 runs and was then omitted from seven subsequent series (against India in 1948/49; England in 1950; Australia in 1951/52; India in 1952/53; England in 1953/54; Australia in 1954/55; and New Zealand in 1955/56) until he was selected for the West Indies tour to England in 1957; but he was still not picked in any of the five disastrous Tests in 1957 when West Indies were trounced 3:0. Thwarted, probably by foul rather than fair means, Ganteaume was then outshone as a player by a galaxy of new stars (Hunte, Kanhai, Sobers, Collie Smith), although he later became a West Indies selector and manager and is, along with Rodney Redmond of New Zealand, chiefly remembered today for the unique curiosity of his single Test match career century.

No doubt Ganteaume's failure to gain regular Test selection and the long gestation period of *My Story* – nearly sixty years – suggest a desire to get even. But if *My Story* only expresses a long-nursed sense of grievance, it could be dismissed merely as a rancorous display of pique rather than an anguished cry, *de profundis*, of righteous indignation and sober protest against criteria of race, colour and class that prevailed in British Caribbean colonies before Independence in the 1960s. *My Story*'s aim, according to the author, is: "to dispel the perception that I was removed from the West Indies team after making a first appearance Test century because my scoring rate was too slow, and also to give some sense of the period in which sportsmen like me had to operate." [p.2] Ganteaume's grandfather was Indian and his grandmother Black (African), and his book exposes West Indian ethnic snobbery and discrimination which, unlike South African apartheid, lacks South Africa's institutionalised legality and brutishness.

Historically, West Indian cricket insinuated its own racial criteria into class divisions inherited from the English game. Thus, like C.L.R. James, Ganteaume joined the Black club of Maple, while Queen's Park, the club that controlled cricket in Trinidad and Tobago, was reserved for Whites. The President of Queen's Park, Sir Errol Dos Santos, nicknamed "The Great White Lord", was also President of the West Indies Cricket Board of Control (WICBC) from 1954 to 1970 when he treated West Indian cricket as his private fiefdom. After democratic change had transformed the membership of Queen's Park Club, Ganteaume tells Dos Santos: "the time has come when it is no longer acceptable for a private club to run cricket for a country," and Dos Santos replies by asking slyly if he and his fellow Whites had not done a good a job, and by rhetorically inquiring if the MCC (Marylebone Cricket Club) had not run cricket in England. Dos Santos then: "walked away imperiously after saying: 'When you fellas mash it [Queen's Park Club] up, don't come back to me for help.'" [19] By Dos Santos's feudalistic and paternalistic standards the new (Black) cricket regime at Queen's Park Club were, in the author's words, "incapable and presumptuous" [19] to think they could run cricket in Trinidad and Tobago.

Dos Santos's snobbery/racism explains the dilemma of preparing the Test schedule when England toured West Indies in 1948/49, and George Headley was the most qualified West Indian to lead the team. As Ganteaume puts it, Headley: "had the impediment of being of African descent; 'the aristocracy' had to be kept up and the 'Establishment' boys had to have their share of the pie. The welfare of West Indies cricket was incidental." [p.27] So a plan of shared captaincy was hatched with Headley appointed captain for the first and fourth Tests in Barbados and Jamaica respectively, (White) Stollmeyer for the second in Trinidad, and (White) John Goddard for the third in Guyana. Ironically, injuries and unfitness scotched the plan, ending with Headley as captain in the first Test, Gomez in the second, and Goddard in the third and fourth.

As far as details of his Test appearance are concerned, Ganteaume: "was convinced that 'the Establishment' did not want me to play." [p.30] He perceives a "devious design" [29] to install (White) Kenny Trestrail as opening batsman in the Second Test, and although he is later told by selector (White) Edgar Marsden that he can play,

Ganteaume notes Marsden's: "resentment at having to announce something he didn't want to happen." [30] To crown it all, soon after reaching his century, in the midst of his innings, captain Gerry Gomez sends a written message to him and his partner Frank Worrell to: "press on now. We are behind the clock and need to score more quickly." [43] Soon afterwards he was out. Ganteaume argues strongly that his 112 in four and a half hours was not unusual compared with other centuries at Queen's Park Oval, for instance, the 133 in five and three-quarter hours by England's Jack Robertson, in the same match.

There is much else in *My Story*: historical sketches, cricket anecdotes and reminiscences, portraits of cricketers and friends, and a profusion of nostalgic photos. Perhaps some readers may be sceptical of the author's frequent reliance on his own subjective reactions, or personal observations and conversations – oral rather than written evidence. But this evidence is consistent, and corroborated by some of the most famous cricketers of the author's generation, for instance, Everton Weekes who speaks of "atrocities" and "injustices." [p.iv] It is evidence too conscientiously preserved, too candidly displayed and too confidently presented, for instance, reproducing a photo of the note sent out by Gomez, to be anything less than totally convincing.

APPENDIX 14

Linda M. Deane and Robert Edison Sandiford, Eds., Shouts From the Outfield: the ArtsEtc Cricket Anthology, *Bridgetown, Barbados, ArtsEtc Inc. 2007*

If admission by the editors of *Shouts from the Outfield: the ArtsEtc Cricket Anthology* that they are "two cricket-know nothings" tempts people not to buy and/or read their book, they would make a big mistake. For although Linda Deane and Robert Sandiford grew up outside the West Indies, in Britain and Canada respectively, they had Barbadian (Bajan) parents, through whom they imbibed what seems a genuine love of West Indian cricket. Ms Deane, at any rate, confesses to being captivated by: "the historical and socio-political significance of the game and its supernaturalness." [p.xiv]

Shouts from the Outfield contains twenty-one essays from mainly Bajan contributors whose comments or "shouts" about West Indian cricket from the public outfield are organised into three sections, the first of which "Silly at Mid-On: Commentaries" consists of general essays on cricket, including light-hearted touches that create a humorous tone. Adonijah's "Mad Dogs and Englishmen," for example, opens with an anecdote about a panic-stricken Bajan housewife whose urgent phone call to the Fire Service, reporting her house on fire, gets this response: "Sorry, lady, you got to call back later. Sobers batting now." [p.33]

Humour is one thing, but the Fire Service's passion for cricket smacks of something which comes out more clearly in Philip Spooner's "Laramania" in the form of a letter from C.L.R. James to Frank Worrell, after the latter was appointed captain of the West Indies team for their tour of Australia in 1960/61. At the time, the West Indies were still British colonies, and James urged Worrell to use his appointment as the first Black captain of the team to show: "that we [West Indians] are capable of managing our own affairs, and if you can demonstrate that, then we will go to 10 Downing Street [residence of the British Prime Minister] to discuss independence in this region." [p.49] Cricket, in other words, was a key to the West Indian political kingdom.

Ikael Tafari's 'The Drama of Cricket', the last essay in Section One, delves further into this political link. Relying on insights from Orlando Patterson's essay 'The Ritual of Cricket', Tafari analyses an incident in the Third Test match at Sabina Park in February, 1968, after West Indies had replied with 143 to an England first innings total of 376, and having followed on, had reached 204 for five in their second innings. Butcher was given out by Douglas Sang Hue, a Chinese-Jamaican umpire, and a riot ensued.

The crux of Tafari's argument – that cricket is: "a gladiatorial drama of consciousness depicting the primordial struggle between Prospero and Caliban – between coloniser and colonised." [64] All this may seem old hat, nowadays, long after Independence, and after the 1980s and 90s when the West Indies team achieved international cricket supremacy under Clive Lloyd.

Section Two, 'Border Cricket: Legends', offers comic relief consisting of five items, including an excerpt from Austin Clarke's Giller Prize-winning novel *The Polished Hoe* which mixes hilarity and historical reminiscence into a seductively revealing and entertaining blend. Best of all "Fete Match," a long (eleven-page) poem by Paul Keens Douglas, is a masterpiece of joyous whimsy that captures the farcical extravaganza of a Selvonesque cricket match in which the coin tossed up before the start of the match: "never came back down. Somebody teaf it." [121]

Section Three, 'Kensington Memories: Reminiscences', then closes *Shouts from the Outfield* with reminiscences by five authors of Kensington Oval, the Test match ground in Barbados. The first, "Kensington Memories," is by Tony Cozier the most distinguished cricket journalist and broadcaster to have emerged in the West Indies during the past three or four decades. As a Bajan, Cozier knows everything about his home ground, and comments on special moments such as its founding in 1922 by the Pickwick Cricket Club, its hosting of the inaugural West Indies home Test against England in 1930 and, in 1958, Hanif Mohammad's exploit of the longest Test innings ever played – sixteen and a half hours.

In "A Partnership to Remember" Keith Sandiford re-creates the context of the match-saving, record-breaking seventh wicket partnership of 347 runs between West Indies captain Denis Atkinson and wicket-keeper Clairmonte Depeiza, a fellow Bajan, in the Fourth

Test against Australia at Kensington Oval, Barbados, in 1955. Atkinson scored 219 and became: "the first cricketer to score a double century and capture five wickets in an innings in the same Test." [183] Depeiza, meanwhile, made 122.

Professor Hilary Beckles argues in "Tribute to Sir Gary Sobers" that Sobers's achievement was part of an historic "cricket revolution" [193] that began with early West Indian activists like J.J. Thomas and Paul Bogle, and continued with "radical cricketers" [192] like Learie Constantine and George Headley, before inspiring a "wider democratic movement" [193] through men like C.L.R. James, Frank Worrell and Garfield Sobers. If the editors of *Shouts from the Outfield*, mere cricket know-nothings, serve up such a delicious blend of history, politics, reminiscence and thoughtful reflection, lavishly spiced with humour, imagine what they might have served if they were cricket know-alls instead!

APPENDIX 15

Peter Oborne, Basil D'Oliveira: Cricket and Conspiracy: The Untold Story, *London, Little, Brown, 2004*

Basil D'Oliveira is not simply a biography of the South African batsman/bowler who represented England in Test matches between 1966 and 1972: the book is also about dark deeds of deception, bribery and treachery provoked by prejudice against the cricketer's race and colour. D'Oliveira was born in 1931 in Signal Hill, South Africa where he was officially classified as coloured or racially mixed. After 1948, mainly to protect White economic privilege, racial classification and segregation were rigidly institutionalised in South Africa to keep Whites apart from the rest of the population of Indians, Muslims, Africans and Coloureds. This system, known as apartheid or apartness, then formed the basis of the country's entire social and political structure.

Peter Oborne cites the example of the coloured spin bowler Owen Williams whose mother, brother and sister were classified as White, and therefore could not live in the same area as Owen and another brother and sister who were classified as Coloured. Nothing could be more unnatural and unjust, for non-Whites did not have voting rights, and the national cricket team consisted only of White players who enjoyed the best funding and playing facilities. So much for hypocrites who complained that opponents of apartheid *introduced* politics into sport!

There was clearly no future for a coloured cricketer in such conditions and, in 1960, through the urging of friends, particularly the Indian sports journalist Damoo Bansda, D'Oliveira contacted the English broadcaster and cricket writer John Arlott who helped him to get a coaching job with the central Lancashire League club of Middleton in England. His airfare to England came from money collected by Bansda and his friends in Signal Hill. At first, D'Oliveira struggled to adjust to English social and cricketing conditions. Accustomed to hard, matting wickets at home, he had difficulty with soft and wet English wickets on which the ball tended to stop, but he persevered and reached the top of the League's batting averages by the end of his first year. Eventually, he was able to settle down in England with his (coloured, South African) wife Naomi and two sons, and after three years in League cricket, moved on to play county cricket for Worcestershire. He also took out British citizenship which meant that he could play for England.

As D'Oliveira's cricket prospered, he never forgot that he was a standard bearer of hope for his comrades in Signal Hill, indeed for all non-White South Africans. What they wanted most of all was his selection for England. Imagine their joy when, in 1966, he was picked for England against West Indies and, in four Tests that summer, had scores of 76, 54, and 88, apart from taking a few wickets! More success followed against India and Pakistan in 1967, after which D'Oliveira's place was assured in the England team as a reliable, right-handed, middle order batsman and occasional, medium pace bowler. His series against the West Indies in 1967/68 was disappointing, but he was picked for the First Test against Australia in England, in 1968, and in a valiant if vain attempt to stave off Australian victory, contrived a superb second innings score of 87 not out. Yet, surprisingly, he was not included in the team for the next three Tests, and his crowning ambition, not to mention that of his countrymen in Signal Hill, to be picked for the forthcoming England tour to South Africa in 1968/69, appeared to be slipping away.

Meanwhile, during the 1968 Australia tour, D'Oliveira was the subject of feverish discussion between the South African government and MCC members who were selecting the England team. Under apartheid rules, South Africa did not play against non-White teams like India, Pakistan or the West Indies: in 1967, they even refused to play a (mainly White) New Zealand rugby team which included some Maori players. D'Oliveira's inclusion in the England team would therefore put the 1968/69 tour at risk; and Oborne leaves no doubt that some members of MCC colluded with South African Government officials to prevent D'Oliveira's inclusion. In what seems like desperation, an agent of the South African Government secretly offered D'Oliveira a bribe to accept a coaching job in South Africa, and announce his unavailability for the 1968/69 South Africa tour.

Meanwhile, D'Oliveira was reluctantly included in the Fifth Test against Australia in 1968, and produced a magnificent, match-winning innings of 158, which Oborne regards as the greatest ever played: "No other cricket innings has changed history. This one did. No other innings in Test history ... has done anything like so much good" [p.185] Now, surely, he had to be picked for England's South Africa tour. Yet, wonder of wonders, the MCC selectors omitted D'Oliveira from the England touring party! Two facts suggest conspiracy and treachery: the presence of a spy for South Africa at the selectors' meeting, and the later theft of the minutes of the meeting. But worse was to come for the conspirators when an English player who was selected subsequently dropped out from the tour party. It forced MCC into a corner. At last, unwillingly, they had to pick D'Oliveira as a replacement and call South Africa's bluff. It now forced South Africa into a corner: they rejected England's team, and MCC cancelled the tour.

The cancellation was the first telling blow against apartheid in South African sport, and it led to South Africa's exclusion from Test cricket, the Olympics and international sport in general. It also helped to hasten the collapse of apartheid and freedom of the imprisoned freedom fighter Nelson Mandela. Oborne, an English journalist, deserves our gratitude for narrating this deeply moving drama with consummate professionalism, episode by enthralling episode.

APPENDIX 16

David Sheppard, Parson's Pitch,
London, Hodder and Stoughton Ltd., 1964

In his aptly titled autobiography *Parson's Pitch* the Right Reverend Lord David Stuart Sheppard (1929-2005) who played cricket for Cambridge University, Sussex and England, was considered for the Anglican Primacy as Archbishop of Canterbury in 1991, but was apparently discounted by Prime Minister Margaret Thatcher's officials who thought he brought politics into sport, and Marxism into Christian theology. Born into a middle class family, Sheppard was educated at Sherborne School and Cambridge University where he first wanted to study law, but changed to theology. He became ordained in 1955, served as Bishop of Woolwich from 1969-1975, as Bishop of Liverpool from 1975 to 1997, and in 1998 was elevated to a life peerage. He remains the only ordained minister to play Test cricket. (Others played cricket before being ordained) Sheppard also wrote a second autobiography *Steps Along Hope Street* (2002).

It was during the match of Cambridge University against the touring West Indies team, in 1950, that I first became interested in Sheppard. He opened the Cambridge innings and scored 227 runs out of a total of 594 for four, only for West Indies to reply with a commanding 730 for three of which Frank Worrell made 160 and Everton Weekes 304 not out. Sheppard glows with admiration for Weekes, for example, his: "cutting and hooking anything short with tremendous power ... driving in all directions off the back foot which I had never really seen done before." [p.55] He also made his Test début the same year, with scores of 11 and 29 against the tourists in the Fourth Test at the Oval, which West Indies won to take the four-match rubber in triumphant fashion 3-1, their first series win in England.

From 1950 to 1956, Sheppard played against West Indies, India, Pakistan, New Zealand and Australia, scoring his first Test century (119) in the Fourth Test against India at the Oval in 1952; and his second century (113) in the fourth Test against Australia at Old Trafford in 1956. His third Test century, another 113, came in 1962, in

Melbourne, in the second Test against Australia. But as the author writes: "probably the best innings I ever played for England" [p.151] was his 62, the top score, in the drawn Oval Test match against Australia in 1956, when he had to contend with bowlers like Lindwall, Miller and Archer on a "sticky" wicket. Twice also, when Len Hutton was unavailable, he captained England, in the Second and Third Tests against Pakistan, in 1954, winning the Second and drawing the Third.

In a career that lasted from 1950 to 1963, Sheppard played 22 Tests scoring 1,172 runs for an average of 37.80, and in a First Class career for Sussex lasting from 1947 to 1962 he played in 230 matches, scored 15,838 runs for an average of 43.51. In 1952 he topped the batting averages during the English season with 2,262 runs at an average of 64.62, and in 1953 scored 2,272 runs for an average of 45.40. He was also named Wisden Cricketer of the Year in 1953. But it is obvious that Sheppard's cricket took second place to his ministry, which means that he was often called upon to play without due practice or readiness. For a time, he was even regarded as the rival of Len Hutton for the captaincy of England, and once went so far as to announce his unavailability for the tour to Australia in 1954/55 unless he was needed as captain.

The extent to which all this may have hampered his cricket is no doubt an intriguing question. Like Jack Grant who captained West Indies for three series in the 1930s before giving up cricket to become a missionary in Africa, we cannot know what untold sporting heights Sheppard might have scaled if he had put cricket before his ministry. Neither do we know if Sheppard's irregularity on the cricket field may have reduced the quality of his performance in games in which he actually played. There is a story, for instance, that during the Australia tour in 1962, when he also preached to packed cathedrals in each state capital, his fielding was marred by several dropped catches in Test matches. This was so worrying that when an Australian couple asked Mrs Sheppard whether her husband would be kind enough to christen their baby, she advised against it because of the possibility that he might drop the baby during the christening ceremony.

The one country Sheppard never played against was South Africa. He made no secret of his steadfast objection to the racist policy of South African apartheid. His ministry, he claimed, was based on Christ's admonition of service to one's fellow creatures, and it explains not only Sheppard's concern for the fate of Black South Africans but of deprived sections of society in Britain itself, and his undisguised admiration for West Indian, Indian and Pakistani cricketers. His insight, for instance into the potential of the India team – in the 1950s – when Indian cricketers were woefully inexperienced in international cricket, exhibits both acute foresight and a noble feeling of human brotherhood: "with all the talent among their players, India could become the most powerful cricketing country in the world." [p.105] Incredible as it seems, he had foreseen the likes of Tendulkar, Dravid and Harbajan Singh decades before their appearance.

But his principled resistance to the MCC's collaboration with the apartheid regime when D'Oliveira was excluded from the England team to tour South Africa in 1968 will forever remain the noblest of his deeds. Despite knowing from the South African Prime Minister himself that a tour which included D'Oliveira would be cancelled, some MCC members publicly claimed that D'Oliveira was excluded purely for cricketing reasons. Later, when Sheppard moved a motion of no confidence in MCC selectors, and was vilified by members who knew the real reason for D'Oliveira's exclusion, he silently endured vilification rather than expose the hypocrisy of his fellow MCC members.

WORKS CITED

Apple, Arnold, *Guyana Boy*, Oxford University Press, London, 1973

Arlott, John, *Days at the Cricket*, London, Longmans Green and Co. Inc., 1951

Beckles, Hilary McD. and Brian Stoddart, Eds., *Liberation Cricket: West Indies Cricket Culture*, Kingston, Jamaica, Ian Randle Publishers, 1995

Benaud, Richie, *A Tale of Two Tests*, London, Hodder and Stoughton, 1962

Birbalsingh, Frank, (Ed.), *Indenture and Exile*, Toronto, TSAR, 1989

   (Ed.), *Jahaji*, Toronto, TSAR, 2000

   (Ed.), *Guyana and the Caribbean*, Chichester, Dido Press, 2004

Camacho, McGowan, McDonald, Legall, *Cricket at Bourda*, Guyana Sheik Hassan Printery, 2007

Cardus Neville, *A Fourth Innings with Cardus*, London, Souvenir Press Ltd, 1981

Clarke, John and Scovell Brian, *Everything's that Cricket: The West Indies Tour 1966*, London, Stanley and Paul, 1966

Deane, Linda M. & Sandiford, Robert Edison, (Eds.), *Shouts from the Outfield, The ArtsEtc Anthology*, Barbados, ArtsEtc Inc., 2007

Figueroa, John, *West Indies in England: The Great Post-War Tours*, London, Kingswood Press, 1991

Ganteaume, Andy, *My Story*, St James, Trinidad and Tobago, Medianet Ltd., 2007

Gilchrist, Roy, *Hit me for Six*, London, Stanley Paul, 1963

Gibbes, Michael, *Kanhai/Gibbs*, Kanhai-Gibbs Benefit Committee, Victory Commercial Printers Trinidad

Goble, Ray & Sandiford, Keith, *75 Years of West Indies Cricket, 1928-2003*, London, Hansib Publications, 2004

James, C.L.R., *At the Rendezvous of History*, London, Alison and Busby, 1984

   Beyond a Boundary, London, Hutchison, 1963

Kanhai, Rohan, *Blasting forRuns*, London, Souvenir Press, 1966

Kumar, Vijay P., *418 to Win*, Chaguanas, Trinidad, Eniath's Printing Company Ltd., 2003

Landsberg, Pat, *The Kangaroo Conquers: The West Indies v. Australia, 1955*, London, Museum Press, 1955

Lloyd, Clive, *Living for Cricket*, London, Stanley Paul, 1980

Manley, Michael, *A History of West Indian Cricket*, London, Andre Deutsch Ltd., Revised Edition, 1990

Mittelholzer, Edgar, *A Swarthy Boy*, London, Putnam and Company Ltd., 1963

Ramchand, Kenneth, with Yvonne Teelucksingh, *The West Indies in India: Jeffrey Stollmeyer's Diary 1948*, Macoya, Trinidad, Royards Publishing Company Ltd, 2004

Richards, Vivian, *Hitting Across the Line*, London, Headline book Publishing PLC, 1992

Rodway, James, *The Story of Georgetown*, Georgetown, Guyana, Guyana Heritage Society, 1997 (Reprint 1903 Edition; Revised 1920)

Ross, Alan, *Through the Caribbean*, London, Pavilion Books Ltd, 1986. First Published 1960

Sandiford, Keith, *Sonny Ramadhin: His Record Innings by Innings*, Leeds, City Press, 2003

Selvon, Samuel, *The Plains of Caroni*, London, MacGibbon & Kee, 1970

Sobers, Garfield, *My Autobiography*, London, Headline Book Publishing, 2002

Stollmeyer, Jeff, *Everything Under the Sun: My Life in West Indies Cricket*, London, Stanley Paul, 1983

Swanton, E.W., *West Indian Adventure*, London, The Sportman's Book Club, 1955

West Indies Revisited, London, William Heinemann Ltd., 1960

Walcott, Clyde (with Brian Scovell), *Sixty Years on the Backfoot*, London, Victor Gollancz, 1999

Webber, A.R.F., *Those that be in Bondage: A Tale of Indian Indentures and Sunlit Waters*, Wellesley, USA, Calaloux Publications, 1988 (1917)

Williams, Eric, *Inward Hunger: The Education of a Prime Minister*, London, Andre Deutsch, 1969

Woolridge, Ian, *Cricket, Lovely Cricket: The West Indies Tour, 1963*. London, Robert Hale Ltd., 1963

Worrell, Frank, *Cricket Punch*, London, Stanley Paul, 1959

PERIODICALS, ARTICLES, WEB

Adams Arnon, 'Chanderpaul', *Stabroek News* (19 August 2008)

Bala, Rajan, 'Flashing Blade, A Canny Mind', WEB (2009)

Bailey, Trevor, WEB (21 August 2008)

Balachandran K., 'Ramdin', WEB (6 July 2006)

Best, Lloyd, Interview, *Trinidad & Tobago Review*, V.25, # 10, (6 October 2003) 18

Bowes, W.E., 'First Test Match', *The Cricketer*, V.38, # 4 (8 June 1957) 205 208-9,212-3,223-4

Brearley, J.M. 'Chanderpaul', *The Observer* (16 June 2007)

WORKS CITED

Cozier, Tony, 'Chanderpaul', WEB (November 2005)
   'Courage Under Fire', WEB (25 May 2008)
Devers, Sean, Interview/Sarwan, WEB (14 September 2003)
Ganga, Daren, WEB (27 September 2011)
Griffith, S.C., 'Second Test', *The Cricketer*, V.31, # 6 (8 July 1950) 281-2
Jodah, Lloyd, 'First Bollywod Action Hero', WEB
Kanhai, Rosanne, *Express Woman/Sunday Express* (2 September 2012) 10-11
Keating, Frank, 'First Tied Test', *The Guardian* (8 December 2010)
Lashley, Patrick, 'Joe Solomon', WEB
Manthorp, Neil, 'South Africa Against the West Indies 2007-8', WEB (January 2008)
McGlashan, Andrew, 'West Indies Getting Closer', WEB (19 June 2007)
Staff, *Cricket Lore* (November 1991) 36
Victor, D., 'The Plight of Spin Bowlers in the Caribbean', WEB (16 December 2008)
Wattley, Garth, 'D. Ramnarine', WEB (31 March 2012)
Wisden, WEB, Almanack Archive Home, 1995

Test career statistics up to Season 2012/2013

	M	I	NO	Runs	HS	Avg	100	50	Ct/St	Overs	Mds	Runs	Wkts	Avg	BB
Ali, Imtiaz (1975-1976)	1	1	1	1	1*	-	-	-	-	34	10	89	2	44.50	2-37
Ali, Inshan (1971-1977)	12	18	2	172	25	10.75	0	0	7	610-4	137	1621	34	47.67	5-59
Asgarali, Nyron (1957)	2	4	0	62	29	15.50	0	0	0	-	-	-	-	-	-
Bacchus, Faoud (1978-1982)	19	30	0	782	250	26.06	1	3	17	1	0	3	0	-	-
Baichan, Leonard (1975-1976)	3	6	2	184	105*	46.00	1	0	2	-	-	-	-	-	-
Barath, Adrian (2009-)	15	28	0	657	104	23.46	1	4	13	1	0	3	0	-	-
Bishoo, Devendra (2011-)	11	19	8	143	26	13.00	0	0	8	507.4	75	1582	40	39.55	5-90
Chanderpaul, Shivnarine (1994-)	153	261	45	11219	203*	51.93	29	62	64	290	50	883	9	98.11	1-2
Chattergoon, Sewnarine (2007-)	4	7	0	127	46	18.14	0	0	4	-	-	-	-	-	-
Deonarine, Narsingh (2005-)	17	28	2	710	82	29.08	0	5	15	245.5	49	698	24	29.08	4-37
Dhanraj, Rajindra (1994-1995)	4	4	0	17	9	4.25	0	0	1	181.1	32	595	8	74.37	2-49
Fudadin, Assad (2012-)	3	5	1	122	55	30.50	0	1	4	5	1	11	0	-	-
Ganga, Daren (1998-2008)	48	86	2	2160	135	25.71	3	9	30	31	2	106	1	106.00	1-20
Jaggernauth, Amit (2008-)	1	2	1	0	0*	0.00	0	0	0	23	0	96	1	96.00	1-74
Jumadeen, Raphick (1972-1979)	12	14	10	84	56	21.00	0	1	4	523.2	140	1141	29	39.34	4-72
Kallicharran, Alvin (1972-1980)	66	109	10	4399	187	44.43	12	21	51	66.4	14	158	4	39.50	2-16

TEST CAREER STATISTICS

Player	Tests	I	NO	Runs	HS	Avg	100	50	Ct/St	Overs	Mdns	Runs	Wkts	Avg	BB
Kanhai, Rohan (1957-1974)	79	137	6	6227	256	47.53	15	28	50	30.1	8	85	0	-	-
Madray, Ivan (1957-1958)	2	3	0	3	2	1.00	0	0	2	35	6	108	0	-	-
Mohammed, Dave (2004-2007)	5	8	1	225	52	32.14	0	1	1	177.3	20	668	13	51.38	3-98
Nagamootoo, Mahendra (2000-2002)	5	8	1	185	68	26.42	0	1	2	249	68	637	12	53.08	3-119
Nanan, Rangie (1980-1981)	1	2	0	16	8	8.00	0	0	2	36	7	91	4	22.75	2-37
Narine, Sunil (2012-)	5	5	1	38	22*	9.50	0	0	2	216.3	37	721	15	48.06	5-132
Permaul, Veerasammy (2012-2013)	3	4	0	37	14	9.25	0	0	1	99.4	13	320	10	32.00	3-32
Ragoonath, Suruj (1998-1999)	2	4	1	13	9	4.33	0	0	0	-	-	-	-	-	-
Ramadhin, Sonny (1950-1961)	43	58	14	361	44	8.20	0	0	9	2233.3	813	4579	158	28.98	7-49
Ramdass, Ryan (2004-2005)	1	2	0	26	23	13.00	0	0	2	-	-	-	-	-	-
Ramdin, Denesh (2005-)	55	93	13	2110	166	26.37	3	11	155/5	-	-	-	-	-	-
Ramnarine, Dinanath (1998-2002)	12	21	4	106	35*	6.23	0	0	8	582.3	169	1383	45	30.73	5-78
Rampaul, Ravi (2009-)	18	31	8	335	40*	14.56	0	0	3	573.4	111	1705	49	34.79	4-48
Sarwan, Ramnaresh (2000-)	87	154	8	5842	291	40.01	15	31	53	337	32	1163	23	50.56	4-37
Shivnarine, Sewdat (1978-1979)	8	14	1	379	63	29.15	0	4	6	56	10	167	1	167.00	1-13
Singh, Charran (1959-1960)	2	3	0	11	11	3.66	0	0	2	84.2	35	166	5	33.20	2-28
Singh, Rabindra (1998-1999) *for India*	1	2	0	27	15	13.50	0	0	5	10	4	32	0	-	-
Solomon, Joe (1958-1965)	27	46	7	1326	100*	34.00	1	9	13	117	39	268	4	67.00	1-20

1st Class career statistics up to Season 2012/2013

	M	I	NO	Runs	HS	Avg	100	50	Ct/St	Overs	Mds	Runs	Wkts	Avg	BB
Ali, Imtiaz	46	62	12	558	48*	11.16	0	0	22	1514.4	367	4129	157	26.29	8-38
Ali, Inshan	90	118	21	1341	63	13.82	0	3	43	3208.5	634	9491	328	28.93	8-58
Asgarali, Nyron	50	89	5	2761	141*	32.86	7	8	29	372.3	103	972	23	42.26	4-72
Bacchus, Faoud	111	182	13	5944	250	35.17	8	37	88	78.3	15	197	8	24.62	2-18
Baichan, Leonard	63	100	13	4504	216*	51.77	13	23	35	7	0	34	0	-	-
Barath, Adrian	53	95	5	3013	192	33.47	7	17	35	2	0	3	0	-	-
Bishoo, Devendra	45	80	20	625	47*	10.41	0	0	29	1729.3	282	5210	175	29.77	6-64
Chanderpaul, Shivnarine	315	514	95	23179	303*	55.31	68	116	177	809	143	2537	60	42.28	4-48
Chattergoon, Sewnarine	73	126	3	3750	143	30.48	5	21	56	102.5	19	256	10	25.60	4-9
Deonarine, Narsingh	112	193	20	6344	198	36.67	9	42	75	1501.2	271	4261	134	31.79	7-26
Dhanraj, Rajindra	78	101	36	550	47	8.46	0	0	29	2697.4	489	7995	295	27.10	9-97
Fudadin, Assad	63	105	10	3202	145	33.70	3	16	47	248	50	741	23	32.21	4-42
Ganga, Daren	172	302	29	10137	265	37.13	23	48	112	103.4	14	334	4	83.50	1-7
Jaggernauth, Amit	67	97	36	696	47	11.40	0	0	53	2433.3	552	6325	258	24.51	7-45
Jumadeen, Raphick	99	119	48	604	56	8.50	0	2	45	4120.4	1164	9686	347	27.91	6-30
Kallicharran, Alvin	505	834	86	32650	243*	43.64	87	160	324	1188.5	183	4030	84	47.97	5-45

1ST CLASS CAREER STATISTICS

Name	M	I	NO	Runs	HS	Avg	100	50	Ct/St	Overs	Mdns	Runs	Wkts	Avg	BB
Kanhai, Rohan	421	675	83	29250	256	49.40	86	120	325/7	266	40	1039	19	54.68	2-5
Madray, Ivan	6	8	0	73	28	9.12	0	0	5	217.2	31	622	16	38.87	4-61
Mohammed, Dave	73	109	15	1571	74*	16.71	0	5	39	2184	451	6317	233	27.11	7-48
Nagamootoo, Mahendra	102	156	20	2587	100	19.02	1	7	79	4133.3	947	10813	370	29.22	7-76
Nanan, Rangie 109	94	143	18	2607	125	20.85	1	9	61	3872.4	1072	8457	366	23.10	7-
Narine, Sunil	12	16	5	211	40*	19.18	0	0	10	445.2	98	1268	59	21.49	8-17
Permaul, Veerasammy	58	87	11	978	66	12.86	0	1	30	2016	507	5187	209	24.81	6-39
Ragoonath, Suruj	66	119	7	3261	128	29.11	2	24	36	7.5	1	16	0	-	-
Ramadhin, Sonny	184	191	65	1092	44	8.66	0	0	38	7302.1	2505	15345	758	20.24	8-15
Ramdass, Ryan	21	36	2	1042	144*	30.64	3	4	10	7.4	0	25	2	13.50	2-16
Ramdin, Denesh	117	193	27	5092	166*	30.67	11	23	304/27	-	-	-	-	-	-
Ramnarine, Dinanath	68	106	23	773	43	9.31	0	0	43	2615.4	673	6453	252	25.60	6-54
Rampaul, Ravi	62	91	16	1031	64*	13.74	0	2	18	1643.2	284	5485	182	30.13	7-51
Sarwan, Ramnaresh	215	364	26	13221	291	39.11	33	70	152	728	105	2351	56	41.98	6-62
Shivnarine, Sewdat	49	78	11	2182	131*	32.56	3	14	36	938	231	2449	67	36.55	4-29
Singh, Charran	11	15	3	102	29*	8.50	0	0	8	557.5	203	1149	48	23.93	7-38
Singh, Rabindra	137	180	28	6997	183*	46.03	22	33	109	2032.3	372	6188	172	35.97	7-54
Solomon, Joe	104	156	28	5318	201*	41.54	12	27	46	609.5	118	1950	51	38.23	4-28

INDEX

75 Years of West Indies Cricket, 1928-2003, 22, 190, 191, 235
Achong, Ellis "Puss", 18
Adams, Arnon, 169-170, 236
Adams, Grantley, 194
Adams, Jimmy 145-147, 174
Adelaide (Australia), 22, 37, 60-61, 82, 94, 99, 116, 155, 163, 178
African(s), 7, 11-13, 15-16, 22-24, 65-66, 73-74, 107, 116, 193, 197-198, 223-224, 229
   America, 22
   Amerindian and (mixed), 17
   Caribbean(s), 13, 36, 86
   Chinese (mixed), 18
   emancipation of, 12
   European (mixed), 11-12, 83
   freed, 12-13
   Guyanese, 15-16, 86, 156, 211, 213
   Italian, 66
   Jamaican(s), 29, 161
   slaves/slavery, 12, 24, 107, 116, 193, 202
   Trinidadian, 14, 23, 24, 109
Afro-centricity/Afro-centric, 22-23, 73-74, 107
Alexander, Gerry, 40, 49, 55, 57, 59-60, 78, 82-83, 87, 105, 107, 207
Ali, Imtiaz, 109-110, 113, 116, 119, 238, 240
Ali, Inshan, 108, 110, 113, 119, 238, 240
Ambrose, Curtly, 109, 112, 116, 145, 147, 152, 191
Amerindian(s), 7, 12, 21, 198
   and African (mixed), 17
Amsterdam, Leslie, 212
Antigua, 20, 122-124, 130-131, 137, 140-141, 145, 148-149, 151, 154, 156, 161-162, 167, 176-178, 180, 191
Antiguan(s), 20

Apartheid (see also South Africa), 5, 20, 57, 89, 99, 100, 102, 189, 223, 229, 230, 231, 233, 234
Apple, Arnold, 15-16, 235
Arlott, John, 32, 34, 220-221, 229, 235
Arnold, Geoff, 91
Asgarali, Nyron, 11, 103-105, 119, 238, 240
Atkinson, Denis, 21, 45-46, 105, 227-228
Australia, 7-8, 37, 39-41, 44-46, 48-49, 54, 56, 60, 62-63, 71-73, 75, 77, 82-84, 94, 96-97, 99, 105, 108-113, 116, 131, 133, 139, 141, 146, 154-155, 163, 174, 178, 181-182, 212, 216, 223, 226, 230, 233
   cricket team, 8, 22, 32, 36-41, 44-46, 49, 56, 60-61, 63, 67-68, 70-71, 73, 77-79, 81, 83-84, 86, 89-90, 94-96, 98, 101, 105, 108-113, 115-117, 125, 129, 131, 133, 136, 139, 141, 146, 148, 150-152, 160-163, 165, 174, 176, 178, 180-181, 188, 192, 201, 207-208, 212, 218, 223, 228, 230, 232, 233, 235

Bacchus, Faoud, 22, 112, 114-115, 119, 238, 240
Baichan, Leonard, 113, 119, 238, 240
Baichu, Saranga, 212
Baijnauth, Sonny 'Sugar Boy', 85, 198, 212-213
Bailey, Trevor, 24, 36-37, 44, 63, 75, 236
Baksh, Vaneisa, 209
Bangalore (India), 92, 98, 115
Bangladesh, 136-138, 165, 167, 176, 177
   cricket team, 125, 136-137, 153, 165, 167, 176-177, 180, 182
Banks, Omari, 152
Barath, Adrian, 11, 119, 135-136, 238, 240

Barbados, 12, 16, 19, 27, 36, 42-44, 59, 61, 66, 71, 74, 79-80, 95-96, 105, 108, 123, 131, 133, 136, 145, 147, 149-152, 154-155, 162-165, 173, 175-177, 180, 190-191, 193-194, 199-200, 203, 206, 224, 226-228, 235
   cricket team, 54, 74, 84, 108, 194, 197, 199, 206
Barker, J.S., 63
Baseball, 19, 204
Beckles, Dr Hilary, 17, 22, 202-204, 208-210, 228
Bedi, [Bishen], 101, 111
Beginner, Lord (aka Egbert Moore), 34
Benaud, Richie, 60, 78-79, 81-82, 212
Bertram, Arnold, 205-207
Beyond a Boundary, 17, 68, 193, 235
Bishoo, Devendra, 51, 119, 137, 139, 143, 164, 238, 240
Bishop, Ian, 109, 171
Bourda cricket ground (Guyana), 22, 43, 45, 54, 58-59, 67, 71, 84, 89, 92, 94, 96-97, 103, 105-106, 115, 123, 125, 129, 131, 147, 149, 150-151, 154, 174, 196, 199, 200-201, 235
Blake, William, 79
Blasting for Runs, 53, 235
Boycott, Geoffrey, 159, 161
Bradman, Sir Donald, 18, 36, 63, 67, 69, 75, 81, 112, 148, 207, 215, 218
Brathwaite, Edward, 23, 136
Brearley, Mike, 150-151, 160, 171
British Guiana Cricket Board of Control, 196
British Guiana Cricket Club, 197
British Guiana East Indian Association, 18
British Guiana East Indian Cricket Club, 197
British Guiana (see also Guyana)
   country, 12, 18, 27, 43, 85, 199, 213
   cricket team, 103, 197, 206, 207, 213
Burnham, Forbes, 71-74
Butcher, Basil, 53, 56, 59, 80, 82, 85-86, 107, 198, 200-201, 212-213, 227

Calcutta/Kolkata, 56, 82, 93, 98, 115, 136, 150, 165, 175, 212, 214
Caliban, 108, 227
Calypso cricket, 53, 60, 66, 86
Calypso music, 22, 34, 35, 53, 222
Calypso-collapso, 65, 152
Camacho, Stephen, 17, 67, 78, 87, 95, 199-200
Canada, 197, 202, 203, 204, 205, 226
Cardus, Neville, 65-66, 75
CARICOM, 21
Challenor, George, 66
Chanderpaul, Shivnarine, 5, 8-9, 22, 25, 119, 121, 131, 145-171, 174-176, 179, 200, 238, 240
Chattergoon, Sewnarine, 119, 136, 238, 240
Chennai (formerly Madras), 79, 93, 98, 175
Chinese, 7, 107, 196, 197, 198
   African (mixed), 18
   indentured, 15, 196
   Jamaican, 107, 227
C.L.R. James: At the Rendezvous of Victory, 17, 53, 63, 235
Christiani, Robert, 27, 34, 43, 66, 213
Clarke, Austin, 227
Clarke, Sylvester, 97, 100, 109, 116
Colombo (Sri Lanka), 45, 131, 133, 155, 164, 175
Columbus, 11
Comins, D.W.D., 18
Compton, Denis, 37, 218
Constantine, Lebrun, 195
Constantine, Sir Learie, 36, 65-66, 116, 192, 195, 215, 219, 228
Contractor, Nari, 61, 83
Coolie(s), 14-15, 17, 35, 85-86, 210
Cowdrey, Colin, 46-48, 62, 106
Cozier, Tony, 40, 109, 158, 161, 171, 174, 227, 237
Creole, 13, 18, 22, 65-66, 170, 211
   cricket, 18
Christian(s), 13, 193, 211, 232
Christiani, Robert Julian, 27, 34, 43, 66, 68, 213
Creole-English language, 8
Creolisation/Creolised/Creolising, 13-14, 16-18, 66, 120, 213
Cricket at Bourda, 67, 94, 199, 235
Croft, Colin, 100, 102, 109
Croft, Robert, 112

D'Oliveira, Basil, 100, 229-231, 234
Days at the Cricket, 220, 235

INDEX

Democratic Labour Party (DLP), Trinidad and Tobago, 14, 23
Deonarine, Narsingh, 11, 119, 130-132, 238, 240
Depeiza, Clairmonte, 45, 227-228
Dev, Kapil, 87
Devers, Sean, 173, 176, 182
Devonish, Hubert, 22
Dexter, Ted, 59, 62, 174, 180
Dhanraj, Rajindra, 109, 119, 121, 123, 238, 240
Dominica, 165
Dos Santos, Sir Errol, 54, 224
Douglas, Paul Keens, 227
Drakes, Vasbert, 152
Durban (South Africa), 148, 153, 160, 177
Duke of Norfolk's XI, 69, 84

East Indian Cricket Club (EICC), 18, 197, 211
Edgbaston cricket ground (England), 11, 18, 46-48, 50, 55, 59-60, 62-63, 75, 90, 104, 133, 137, 140, 148, 167, 177
Edrich, Bill, 30, 32, 37, 218, 221
Emancipation, 12, 58, 207
England, 11, 16, 20-22, 27-32, 34, 36-50, 54-56, 58-64, 67-68, 70-72, 83-84, 86-87, 90-92, 95-96, 99-101, 103-107, 110-113, 115-116, 121-123, 125, 129-130, 133, 140, 145-148, 150, 152-154, 157-159, 161-164, 167, 174, 177, 179-180, 182, 187-190, 192, 194-195, 199-200, 206, 208-209, 212, 215-225, 227, 229-233
Everything Under the Sun, 215, 236

Figueroa, John, 27, 29-30, 47, 65, 217-219
Flood, Thomas, 211
Flower, Andy, 159
Francis, George, 36
Fredericks, Roy, 85, 113, 200-201
Fudadin, Assad, 11, 119, 137, 140, 238, 240

Ganga, Daren, 119, 125-127, 155-157, 159, 179, 238, 240
Ganteaume, Andy, 19, 54-55, 58, 104-105, 109, 223-225
Garvey, Marcus, 206
Gatting, Mike, 117

Gavaskar, Sunil, 64, 180
Gayle, Chris, 136, 149, 153-155, 159, 162-164
Georgetown (capital), 17, 43, 54, 85, 86, 196, 197, 198, 199, 236
Georgetown Cricket Club (GCC), 17, 196, 199
Gibbes, Michael, 67, 75
Gibbs, Lance, 49-50, 67, 82-83, 85, 103, 109, 117, 137, 200
Gilchrist, Adam, 150
Gilchrist, Roy, 57-58, 107, 207
Gillespie, Jason, 117, 151
Goble, Ray, 22, 109-110, 116, 190-191
Goddard, John, 27, 34, 37-41, 46-47, 49, 54-55, 58, 105, 215, 217-218, 222, 224
Gomes, [Larry], 97
Gomez, Gerry, 27, 29, 30, 105, 224-225
Grace, W.G., 188-189
Graveney, Tom, 42, 218
Gray, Cecil, 4, 8, 38-39, 50
Gregory, Jack, 150
Grenada, 129, 175, 191
Griffith, Charlie, 61-62, 74, 117
Griffith, Herman, 36, 116
Griffith, S.C. (Billy), 31, 36, 237
Grout, Wally, 61, 78
Gupte, Subash, 56, 61, 83
Guyana (formerly British Guiana), 12-19, 22, 34, 36, 41, 43, 53-54, 64, 68, 71-72, 74, 77, 85, 87, 89, 92, 97, 105, 112-113, 115, 117, 119-120, 123, 129-131, 136-137, 143, 145, 154, 160, 164, 169, 173-174, 176, 178-179, 190-191, 194, 196-200, 203, 210-213, 224, 235-236
cricket team(s), 54, 74, 85, 87, 173, 196-200, 212-213

Hall, Wesley (Wes), 50, 62, 71, 74, 78-80, 117, 156
Hammond, Walter, 87
Harper, Roger, 103, 109
Hassett, Lindsay, 37-38
Hawke, Lord, 194
Hawkeye, 162
Headingley cricket ground (England), 62, 84, 95, 125, 179

Headley, George Alphonso, 65, 136, 192, 206-207, 215, 220, 224, 228
Hindu(s), 13, 213
Hit Me for Six, 57, 235
Holding, Michael, 109, 111-112, 116-117, 207
Holford, David, 70, 73, 123, 149
Hooper, Carl, 147, 149, 174
Hunte, [Sir Conrad], 62, 78, 83, 223
Hutton, Len, 34, 37, 43, 45, 59, 218, 221-222, 233

Indenture, 11-15, 24, 27, 41, 107, 170, 193, 211-212, 236
   Chinese, 15, 196
   Portuguese, 15, 196
Indenture and Exile, 45, 48, 73, 80, 235
Independence
   in the Caribbean, 15, 23, 121, 200, 209, 223
   in Trinidad and Tobago, 23-24
   West Indian, 35, 68, 120, 189, 226-227
   in Jamaica, 207
India, 7, 12-14, 20, 49, 56-57, 59, 71-72, 82-83, 86, 95, 98, 101, 105, 114-115, 135-137, 150, 152, 159, 165, 169, 175-176, 189, 200, 212, 214-216, 220, 223, 234, 236
   cricket team, 41-42, 44, 49, 56-57, 61-62, 68, 70, 79, 83, 86-87, 93, 95, 98, 101, 108, 110-115, 119, 121, 125, 129-130, 133, 135-137, 146-147, 149-150, 156, 159, 164-165, 169, 175-176, 179-180, 182, 200, 212, 214-215, 220, 223, 230, 232, 234, 239
Indian-Guyanese, 8-9, 12, 14, 16, 18, 41, 43, 63, 73, 86, 106, 156, 161, 195, 211-213
Indian-Trinidadian, 9, 12, 14, 23, 41, 106, 120
Indigenisation, 13, 16
International Cricket Conference (ICC), 99-100, 137-138, 169

Jacobs, Ridley, 152
Jagan, Dr Cheddi, 212
Jaggernauth, Amit, 119, 136, 238, 240

Jamaica, 8, 12, 16, 19, 27, 36, 42, 44, 59, 61, 64, 68, 83-84, 89, 92, 95-97, 107, 111-112, 115, 124, 131, 133, 136-137, 140, 149, 153, 155-156, 160, 162, 164, 167, 176-180, 190, 193-194, 199, 202-203, 205-208, 224, 235
   cricket team, 29, 54, 84, 103, 109, 191, 205-207
   government, 207
   post-Emancipation, 207
Jamaica at the Wicket, 206-207
Jamaica College, 206
Jamaica Cricket Club, 206
Jamaican(s), 8, 29, 57, 107, 205-206, 217
   African, 161
   Black, 205
   Chinese, 107, 227
   students, 205
James C.L.R., 17-18, 53, 63, 65-66, 68, 75, 151, 189, 193-194, 197, 224, 226, 228, 235
Johnson, Dr [Samuel], 189
Johnson, Hines, 30, 217
Jones, Prior, 30, 217, 221
Julien, Bernard, 71, 102, 111
Jumadeen, Raphick, 109-111, 113, 119, 238, 240

Kallicharran, Alvin, 5, 8, 25, 64, 89-102, 112, 119, 129, 156-157, 167, 169, 179, 201, 238, 240
Kandy (Sri Lanka), 124, 131, 155
Kanhai, Rohan, 4-5, 8, 11, 17-18, 23-25, 53-75, 77-80, 82, 84-87, 89-90, 92, 100-101, 103, 108, 119-120, 124, 129, 151, 156-157, 167, 169, 171, 176, 179, 198, 200-201, 212-213, 223, 239, 341
Kanhai, Rosanne, 4, 23-25, 74, 108, 120, 237
Karachi (Pakistan), 56, 93, 113, 125, 179
Keats, John, 67
Kensington Oval, 108, 123, 147, 227-228
Kessel, Anna, 155-156
Khan, Imran, 95
Khan, Ismith, 120
Kingston Cricket Club, 199, 205
Kitchener, Lord (Aldwyn Roberts), 34
Knott, Alan, 91
Kumar, Vijay, 146, 235

INDEX

Lahore (Pakistan), 56, 93, 113, 115, 130, 157, 179
Laker, Jim, 31-32, 38-40, 104, 218
Landsberg, Pat, 44-46, 235
Lara, Brian, 63, 95, 112, 127, 131, 136, 146, 152-158, 167, 169-171, 175-178, 226
"Laramania", 226
Lamming, George, 35, 53
Larwood, Harold, 112, 116
Laxman, V.V.S., 56, 130
Lee, Brett, 8, 117, 152, 160
Lewis, [Sir] Arthur, 194
Lillee, Denis, 75, 94-95, 101, 109, 111, 113
Living for Cricket, 74, 235
Lloyd, Clive, 20-22, 64, 70-75, 89-90, 92-93, 96-97, 99-101, 109, 111, 115, 117, 148, 154, 156-157, 191, 201, 218, 227, 235
Lord's cricket ground (England), 11, 30, 32, 34-35, 50, 55, 62, 68, 73, 84, 90, 96, 104, 110, 148, 150, 153-154, 157, 163, 167, 179, 208, 217, 220
Love, Dr Joseph Robert, 194, 206
Lucas, R. Slade, 194, 206
Luckhoo, J.A., 211

Madeira, 12
Madeirans [Portuguese], 7
Madray, Ivan, 53, 85, 105, 119, 198, 212-213, 239, 241
Major, Sir John, 187
Mandela, Nelson, 231
Manley, Michael, 21, 236
Manley, Norman, 194
Manthorp, Neil, 160, 237
Marshall, Malcolm, 109, 112, 116-117
Marshall, Roy, 21
Martindale, Manny, 36, 116
Marylebone Cricket Club (MCC), 31, 106, 188, 194, 199, 208, 224, 230-231, 234
May, Peter, 42, 46-48, 59-60, 106
McDonald, Ian, 67, 77-78, 87, 94-95, 199-201, 235
McDonald, Sir Trevor, 20
McGlashan, Andrew, 159, 180, 182, 237
McGowan, (Professor) Winston, 84-85, 196-200, 235

McWatt, Clifford, 43, 106, 214
Melbourne (Australia), 38-39, 45, 60-61, 81-82, 94, 147, 233
Menzies, Badge, 43, 106
Middlesex County Cricket Club, 66, 68
Miller, Keith, 37-38, 233
Mohammed, Dave, 119, 129-130, 156, 239, 241
Moonsammy, Sonny, 212-213
Mootoo, Baldwin S., 4, 190
Mumbai (India), 93, 98, 101, 121, 135, 136, 150, 165, 169, 175
Murray, Deryck, 97, 99, 112, 117, 124
Muslims, 13, 229

Nagamootoo, Mahendra, 119, 128-129, 239, 241
Naipaul, V.S.
  A House for Mr Biswas, 170
Nanan, Rangie, 109, 116, 119, 239, 241
Narine, Sunil, 11, 51, 119, 140-141, 143, 239, 241
New Zealand, 7, 20-21, 39, 54, 99, 123, 132, 134, 136, 142, 155, 178, 180
  cricket team, 39-40, 46, 49, 68, 70, 87, 89, 90, 101, 108, 110, 121-123, 125, 129, 131-132, 134, 137, 140-143, 146, 148, 150, 155, 162, 166-168, 175, 178, 192, 223, 232
  rugby team, 230
Noriega, [Jack], 110,
Norman Manley Award, 207
North America, 22, 121, 204
Nunes, Karl, 60, 216
Nurse, Seymour, 101

Oborne, Peter, 229-231
Old Trafford cricket ground (England), 27, 30-32, 61, 96, 117, 130, 154, 157-158, 174, 177, 220, 232
Oval, The (England), 36, 56, 62-64, 87, 90-91, 104, 108, 129, 174, 232-233

Packer, Kerry, 96, 97, 99, 100, 117, 154
Pairaudeau, Bruce, 54, 55, 105
Pakistan, 56-57, 59, 93-94, 99, 115-116, 125, 130, 140, 143, 147, 157, 179, 212

cricket team, 41, 49, 55-56, 83-84, 86, 93-94, 96, 101, 105, 113, 115-116, 124-125, 130, 137-138, 148, 155, 157, 164, 173, 178-179, 182, 212, 230, 232-234
People's National Movement (PNM), Trinidad and Tobago, 14
People's Progressive Party (PPP), Guyana, 212
Permaul, Veerasammy, 119, 142-143, 239, 241
Persaud, Chatterpaul "Doosha", 212
Pickwick Cricket Club, 199, 227
Pierre, Lance, 30, 217
Pollock, Shaun, 124
Port Mourant (Guyana), 53-54, 77, 80, 85-86, 89, 212-213
Port of Spain (Trinidad), 14, 24, 61, 120,
Priestley, Sir Arthur, 194, 206
Prior, Matt, 140
Providence (Guyana), 137, 160, 164, 179, 196

Queen's Park Oval cricket ground (Trinidad), 58, 89-90, 92, 96-97, 101, 103, 105, 108, 110, 113, 115, 223-225

Rae, Allan, 27, 30, 34, 109, 207, 216, 220-221
Ragoonath, Suruj, 119, 127, 239, 241
Ramadhin, Sonny, 5, 8-9, 11, 18, 24-25, 27-51, 53-55, 58-59, 65, 72, 83, 85, 89, 103-104, 106, 109, 119, 143, 173, 192, 217, 221-222, 239, 241
Ramchand, Kenneth, 41, 214-215, 236
Ramdass, Ryan, 119, 131, 239, 241
Ramdin, Denesh, 11, 119, 133, 134, 136, 156, 164, 236, 239, 241
Ramnarine, Dinanath, 119, 122-124, 237, 239, 241
Rampaul, Ravi, 11, 119, 137-138, 164, 239, 241
Ranjitsinhji, Prince, 211
Richards, Sir Vivian, 19-22, 24, 72, 74, 96, 107, 111, 116, 133, 150, 169-170, 191, 236
Richardson, Peter, 104
Rickards, Ken, 29

Ring, Doug, 38-40, 45-46
Roberts, Aldwyn (see Lord Kitchener)
Roberts, Andy, 20, 109, 112, 191
Robertson, Jack, 225
Rodriguez, [Willie], 62
Rodway, James, 16, 17, 119, 236
Rohomon, Joseph, 211
Rowe, Lawrence, 92, 94, 100-102, 207
Rudolph, Jacques, 130

Sabina Park cricket ground (Jamaica), 96, 103, 111, 160-161, 227
Sammy, [Darren], 165
Sandiford, Keith A.P., 4, 17, 22, 50, 109-110, 116, 171, 190-192, 227, 235-236
Sandiford, Robert Edison, 226, 235
Sang Hue, Douglas, 92, 98, 107, 227
Sarwan, Ramnaresh, 5, 9, 25, 119, 125, 136, 152, 154, 156-157, 159-160, 164, 173-182, 237, 239, 241
Seecharan, Clem, 4, 17-18, 86, 105, 193-195, 211-213
Selvon, Samuel, 35, 120, 227, 236
Shell Shield competition, 108, 116, 191
Sheppard, David, 218, 232, 233, 234
Shivnarine, Sewdat, 97, 115, 119, 239, 241
Singh, Charran Kamkaran, 58, 106-107, 110, 113, 119, 239, 241
Sixty Years on the Backfoot, 49, 71, 236
Skinner, Clarence, 28
Slavery, 11-13, 24, 116, 193, 196, 205
Smith, Graeme, 159-160, 171
Smith, O.G. 'Collie', 55, 207, 223
Snow, John, 95, 113
Sobers, Sir Garfield (Garry), 20-21, 36, 48, 55-56, 59-61, 63-66, 68, 70-73, 79, 81-83, 87, 89-90, 92, 107, 110, 145, 148-150, 153-154, 169, 200, 218, 220, 223, 226, 228, 236
Solomon, Joseph, 5, 8, 25, 53, 58, 72, 77-87, 89, 101, 103, 119, 198, 201, 212, 239, 241
Son of Guyana, 15-16
South Africa, 20, 57, 89, 99-100, 125-127, 148, 153, 159-160, 177, 189, 234
apartheid, 20, 57, 89, 99-100, 102, 189, 223, 229, 231, 233

cricket, 99-100
cricket team, 123-126, 129-131, 154,
    159-160, 164, 169, 174-175,
    177-178, 208, 230-231, 233,
    237
D'Oliveira Affair, 100, 229-231, 234
rebel West Indian tour, 100-102
Sri Lanka, 124-125, 131, 155, 164, 175
cricket team, 97, 131, 133, 136, 155,
    160, 164, 175-176, 179
St Hill, Wilton, 67-68
St John's (Antigua), 145, 154, 163
St Kitts-Nevis, 137, 156, 164, 178, 191
St Lucia, 125, 176, 182, 191, 194
St Vincent, 191, 195
Statham, Brian, 42, 55, 58, 62
Stollmeyer, Jeffrey, 21, 27-29, 41-42, 45,
    49, 54, 214-216, 220, 222, 224, 236
Strauss, Andrew, 140
Swanton, E.W., 42, 58-59, 236

Tafari, Ikael, 107, 108, 116, 227
Tale of Two Tests, A, 81, 235
Tebbit, Norman, 41
Teelucksingh, Yvonne, 41, 214, 236
Tendulkar, Sachin, 167, 169, 234
Tennyson, Alfred, Lord, 171
Thistlewood, Thomas, 16, 205
Thomson, [Jeff], 94, 111, 113
Trent Bridge cricket ground (England),
    96, 115, 121, 167
Trim, John, 53, 85-86
Trinidad/Trinidad and Tobago, 9, 12-15,
    18-19, 21-25, 27-28, 36, 41-42, 44,
    53, 58-59, 63-64, 67-68, 74, 83, 87,
    89-90, 92, 95-97, 101, 103, 105,
    107-108, 110, 113, 116, 119-121, 123,
    125, 127, 129, 131, 133, 136-137,
    140, 145, 151, 154, 160, 163-165,
    176-179, 190-191, 194, 199, 203,
    210, 214, 216, 223-224, 235
    cricket team, 28-29, 106, 109, 125,
        194, 197, 206
Trinidad and Tobago Review, 22, 236
Trueman, Fred, 42, 55, 58-59, 62, 104
Trumper, [Victor], 67, 75

United States of America, 19, 21-22, 74,
    100, 173, 197, 202-205

Valentine, Alfred, 27, 29-31, 34-36,
    38-39, 42-45, 61, 65, 192, 217,
    221-222
Vaughan, Michael, 158
Veerasawmy, J.A., 212
Venkataraghavan, S, 101-111
Verity, Hedley, 116
Victor, D., 103, 237
Voce, Bill (William), 112, 116

Walcott, [Sir] Clyde, 20, 27, 30, 34, 40,
    42, 45, 49, 54-55, 65-66, 71, 201,
    213, 221, 236
Walcott, Derek, 23
Walsh, Courtney, 109, 112, 116, 123, 207
Wardle, Johnny, 32, 220-221
Warne, Shane, 117, 129, 147
Warner, Sir Pelham (Plum), 194
Warwickshire County Cricket Club, 100
Washbrook, Cyril, 30, 32, 34, 37, 218,
    221-222
Waugh, Steve, 129
Webster, Dr Rudi, 174
Weekes, [Sir] Everton, 27, 30, 34, 40, 43, 46,
    54, 65, 86, 159, 215, 220, 225, 232
Wellington cricket ground (New
    Zealand), 121, 134, 146, 148
West Indian Players' Association
    (WIPA), 124, 156
West Indies Cricket Board (WICB), 19-20,
    54, 58, 72, 124, 154, 156, 190,
    199, 224
West, Peter, 29
Whitlam, Gough, 71
Whitman, [Walt], 53, 65
Williams, Alvadon, 97
Williams, Dr Eric, 14, 16, 23-24, 194, 236
Williams, Owen, 229
Wisden Cricketer's Almanac, 146, 171,
    188, 233, 237
Woolloongabba ('The Gabba') cricket
    ground (Australia), 37, 77, 87
Woolridge, Ian, 62-63, 236
World Series Cricket (WSC), 74, 96, 110,
    115, 154, 156
Worrell, [Sir] Frank, 27, 30, 38, 40-41,
    45, 49, 55-56, 59-61, 63-66, 68,
    79, 81, 83-84, 87, 117, 148, 207,
    218-222, 225-226, 228, 232, 236

Wright, Edgar, 197
Wright, Edward, 200, 203

Youssuf, Mohammad, 179

Zimbabwe, 148, 175-176
   cricket team, 119, 125, 148, 159,
      175-176